South Dakota

South Dakota Tourism

South Dakota

Marion L. Head

with photographs by the author

The Countryman Press ✳ Woodstock, Vermont

FIRST EDITION

ISBN 978-0-88150-838-3

Cover photo courtesy of South Dakota Tourism
All interior photos by the author unless otherwise noted.
Book design by Bodenweber Design
Page composition by PerfecType, Nashville, TN
Maps by Mapping Specialists Ltd., Madison, WI © 2009 The Countryman Press

Published by The Countryman Press, P.O. Box 748, Woodstock, Vermont 05091

Distributed by W. W. Norton & Company, Inc., 500 Fifth Avenue, New York, NY
10110

Printed in the United States of America

10 9 8 7 6 5 4 3 2 1

EXPLORE WITH US!

Welcome to *An Explorer's Guide: South Dakota*. If you've never been to South Dakota and are contemplating a visit, you are in for a treat. If you are a long time visitor, this guide will help you find new places to go and things to see. South Dakota is a diverse state full of history and natural beauty waiting to be explored, as well as great towns and cities with fun attractions for the whole family. All listings in this guide have been included based on interest and merit; no payment was accepted for inclusion.

WHAT'S WHERE

This alphabetical section includes important information for quick reference and particular highlights. Since South Dakota is made up of many small towns there is a section at the end of each city called *Nearby*. This highlights some of the activities and events in nearby small towns.

LODGING

South Dakota has a variety of motels, B&Bs, cabins, ranches, campgrounds, and RV parks. Some are part of the state park system, which is a great choice as South Dakota state parks offer great camping and other activities like swimming, hiking, and boating. Some camping choices are on federal land, mostly in the Black Hills National Forest. I have not reviewed chain motels and hotels but often they are the best choice in small towns or along the interstates. In those cases I have included the phone number. Rates for reviewed lodging are based on double occupancy and are for the summer season. Tax is not included but varies widely as most every town has its own bed and booze tax, on top of the state tax. Innkeepers and owners were not charged for inclusion in this guide.

RESTAURANTS

Please note the distinction between *Eating Out* and *Dining Out*. *Eating Out* is more the norm in South Dakota and implies the restaurant is less expensive and less formal. There is *Dining Out*, or more formal dining, in South Dakota's larger cities, but even then casual attire is perfectly acceptable.

KEY TO SYMBOLS

🏅 The blue ribbon appears next to attractions, restaurants, or lodgings that are a special value.

✍ The crayon appears next to attractions, restaurants, or lodgings that are particularly kid and family friendly.

☂ In South Dakota when it rains in the summer, it often pours. Fortunately it seldom lasts long. The umbrella signifies good rainy day activities.

♿ The wheelchair symbol means the restaurant or lodging is wheelchair accessible.

❄ The summer is the South Dakota tourist season but there are many fall and winter activities, especially for hunters, skiers, and snowmobilers. The snowflake indicates activities outside of the traditional Memorial Day to Labor Day season.

We welcome any comments or corrections on this guide.

Please address correspondence to Explorer Guide Editor, The Countryman Press, P.O. Box 748, Woodstock, VT 05091, or email countrymanpress@wwnorton.com.

ACKNOWLEDGMENTS

First and foremost I would like to thank the South Dakota Office of Tourism for their ongoing support of this project, in particular Wanda Goodman. Also, thanks to the various chambers of commerce and visitors bureaus I was in touch with—true professionals all, and people who really appreciate what South Dakota has to offer.

Many friends helped me with research and I couldn't have done it without them. Thanks go to: Pat Briesmeister, Shauna Hayes, Jill Heintzman, Michela Meredith, Jackie Newell, Sue Skovran, Melinda Sterling, Val Todd, and Mike, Nancy, and David Williams.

Love to my big sister, Ellen Sloyer, who has always believed in her little sister; and mostly I want to thank my partner, Denise Roth, for her unabashed enthusiasm for everything I attempt. Everyone should be so lucky.

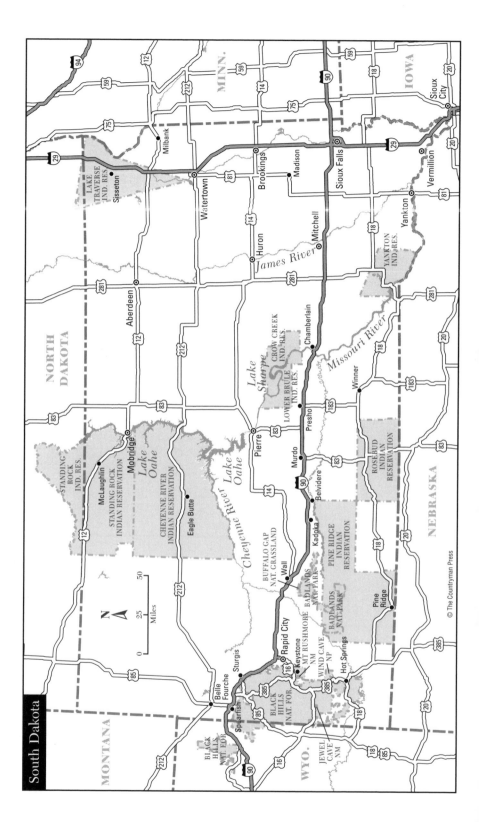

South Dakota

CONTENTS

INTRODUCTION

South Dakota is really two states. The residents refer to it as "East River" and "West River," which simply means the two sides of the state, divided by the Missouri River. It is not just a geographical distinction, however, eastern and western South Dakota really are quite different.

In the east, you'll find the prairie, where farming is a way of life. In the west, you'll find the Badlands and Black Hills, known for mining, ranching, and tourism. The differences are as clear as John Deere ball caps versus cowboy hats and bib overalls versus Wrangler jeans.

Historically speaking, when South and North Dakota were still united as the Dakota Territory and trying to become states, many thought the Missouri River made a natural divider and the territory should become East and West Dakota. It was only when the Dakota Territory capital of Yankton was changed to Bismarck, farther north, that the South decided they had endured enough and asked Congress to declare them a separate state. In 1889 the South got their wish, and became the 40th state in the Union.

THROUGHOUT SOUTH DAKOTA LOOK FOR HISTORIC MARKERS THAT GIVE MORE INFORMATION ABOUT THE STATE'S HISTORY.

Variety is part of what makes South Dakota such an interesting place to visit. If you have never experienced a horizon that seems to stretch to infinity, then you have not experienced the American plains. It's easy to see what attracted farmers to this treeless grassland and just as easy to see why it drove some of them to madness: so much space, so few people.

Travel over the Missouri and you experience one of America's great rivers. The longest tributary of the Mississippi River, the "Big Muddy" travels from its source in Southwest Montana to where it enters the Mississippi near St. Louis, Missouri. It was the main waterway for Lewis and Clark on their Voyage of Discovery two hundred years ago as they followed it from St. Louis

INTERSTATE HIGHWAYS HAVE WELL MAINTAINED REST STOPS, MANY WITH TOURIST INFORMATION.

to the headwaters. The Missouri River is now largely tamed with six dams and man-made channels, but it is still a spectacular waterway and home to 160 species of wildlife and 150 species of fish.

Then there are the bizarre spires, buttes, and mesas of the Badlands. Once prairie, the Badlands are 244,000 acres of ever changing natural sculptures created by wind and water—each year as much as one inch erodes. Watch a thunderstorm move over the Badlands and see how the colors of the buttes change from rust to crimson, how the layers stand out like colored blocks stacked atop one another, and how everything looks completely renewed after a hard rain. It's a bewitching place, a place of ancient land animals, native peoples, and bandits on the run.

From the interstate it is apparent where the Black Hills got their name. Rising thousands of feet above the prairie, the pine forests of the hills make them appear pitch black. Despite the first impression, the Black Hills reward visitors with a diversity of landforms ranging from towering granite cliffs to open grasslands, from emerald mountain meadows to barren, deep cut valleys. It is no surprise that Native Americans hold the Black Hills sacred.

South Dakota calls itself the Mount Rushmore state but it is so much more than one monument. It is a diverse landscape of plains, rivers, buttes, and mountains. It is gold, and brown, and green, and the bright blue of an unpolluted sky goes on forever. It is generations of people who have worked the land and who respect it. It is a place well worth exploring.

This guide is arranged according to the regions within South Dakota; two in the west, the central Missouri River region, and two in the east. Each region is then divided by towns and cities, south to north, each with their distinct appeal to visitors. Things to do and see, lodgings, and places to dine are found within the descriptions of towns and cities.

To get to South Dakota you can fly to Sioux Falls or Rapid City or, like many visitors, drive. I-90 runs east to west through South Dakota and most places are accessible from I-90. The exception is traveling north from Sioux Falls to Aberdeen where a little highway jogging is necessary. It is not a great idea to travel off the beaten path in South Dakota unless you know where you are going, especially in the winter when people can get trapped in their cars for days. It is also important to fill up with gas whenever you can because it can be long drive between gas stations. Take your sense of adventure, a cooler of drinks, a few munchies, and enjoy the journey!

WHAT'S WHERE IN SOUTH DAKOTA

AGRICULTURE South Dakota relies more heavily on agriculture for income than any other state with annual sales of $3 billion. There are over 31,000 farms in South Dakota covering 43.7 million acres, some family farms, some large corporate operations. Corn, soybeans, wheat, hay, and sunflower are some of the major crops and every town, large or small, has a grain elevator where the products are sold and then marketed. There are also 3.7 million cows, 1.27 million hogs and pigs, and 380,000 sheep being raised in South Dakota. Cows and sheep are in the west, pigs and hogs are in the east. The Black Hills are also constantly being logged for ponderosa pine, which is used for sawlogs, posts, and poles.

AIR SERVICE There are two major airports in South Dakota, one in Rapid City and another in Sioux Falls. With a few exceptions, like a quick hop to Las Vegas, there is no such thing as a direct flight to South Dakota. From Rapid City you either change planes in Denver, Salt Lake City, or Minneapolis. In Sioux Falls you'll change planes in Minneapolis, Chicago, or Denver, if you are headed west.

Northwest, Delta, and United Express are the main carriers although Rapid City recently added Frontier. Do not plan on flying within the state, it is much cheaper to drive and doesn't make a lot of sense to fly from Rapid City to Minneapolis to get to Sioux Falls. There are airports for small planes in many of the towns throughout South Dakota, if you happen to own a light plane.

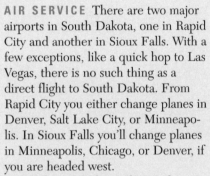

ARCHAEOLOGY Given that people have lived in South Dakota for at least 11,000 years it is no surprise that there are a number of archaeological digs. There is an ongoing dig in Mitchell that you can visit called the **Prehistoric Indian Village**. There have also been digs that traced pioneer settlements, Custer's expedition, and Deadwood's Chinatown.

AREA CODES All of South Dakota is covered by area code 605.

ATTIRE Nowhere in South Dakota is formal attire required; cowboy boots and jeans are even acceptable at weddings and funerals. Do be aware that the weather changes quickly in South Dakota and while it may have been shorts weather in the morning it can become jacket weather by lunchtime. Layers are highly recommended or you, too, can contribute to the busy tourist trade and buy a sweatshirt.

BICYCLING Mountain bikers are in heaven in the Black Hills. There are trails and Forest Service roads everywhere you look. There is also the George S. Michelson Trail, a 110-mile rails to trails project, which includes trestles and tunnels and the Centennial Trail that traverses 111 miles from Bear Butte State Park to Wind Cave National Park. In Rapid City there is a 12-mile paved trail that follows Rapid Creek and is used by walkers, joggers, and bikers. Sioux Falls has a 20-mile trail, which circles through the city parks. But bicyclists are seen everywhere throughout the state as it is an east–west connection for cross-country bikers. Don't be surprised to see them inching up a narrow mountain highway or flying down a hill in the Badlands.

BIRD WATCHING South Dakota is home to over 400 species of birds and is a flyway for a variety of migratory birds including pelicans, herons, and Canada Geese. In the Northeast numerous small lakes provide a breeding area for waterfowl and many landowners are actively involved in managing habitat for the many ducks and geese that are bred in South Dakota. Many also encourage pheasants to nest on their property, ensuring sustainability for hunting. Throughout the state you are likely to see raptors gliding on the thermals, including bald eagles that nest along the Missouri River and lakes in the Black Hills. There are two birding trails in South Dakota, and more information on these can be found South Dakota's Game, Fish, and Parks Web page, www.sdgfp.info/Publications/Parks/BirdingBooklet.pdf.

BOATING There are so many lakes and reservoirs in South Dakota it would be impossible to list them all, and that's without mentioning the Missouri River. In the eastern part of the state there are hundreds of "pothole" lakes created by glaciers coming and going. In the Black Hills the lakes are all man-made and are generally reservoirs. If you like to boat, fish, kayak, canoe, sail, or water ski, there is a place to do it in South Dakota. There are, of course, regulations. The best way to find out what you need to know is to go to the South Dakota Game, Fish, and Parks Web site, www.sdgfp.info/Wildlife/Boating/Index.htm.

CAMPING Camping is popular in South Dakota, primarily due to the great state parks that are located on lakes and rivers and within the Black Hills National Forest. In each section of this book, campgrounds are highlighted, both public and private. If you have never taken your family camping, South Dakota is a great place to try it out since the choices of campgrounds are tremendous and one should fit your needs for a family vacation. For information on state campgrounds go to www.sdgfp.info/Parks. To make campground reservations on federal land go to www.recreation.gov.

CAR RENTALS Except for the larger cities, public transportation is not available in South Dakota. If you fly in you will need to rent a car and the major rental companies are available at the airports, as well as in most cities.

CAVES There are 75 mapped calcite crystal caves in the Black Hills, including two run by the National Park Service: Wind Cave and Jewel Cave. There are also eight privately owned caves with tours. If you are a spelunker contact the park service for information on special tours of Jewel Cave (605-673-2288, ext. 0) or Wind Cave (605-745-4600) a month ahead of time as the spelunking tours sell out.

CITIES The largest city in South Dakota is Sioux Falls with a population of 139,000. Rapid City is next with 62,000, followed by Aberdeen at 24,000. Depending on your definition, Sioux Falls and Rapid City are the only real cities in South Dakota, the rest are towns ranging in size from several thousand to a handful of residents. Because of the population distribution Sioux Falls and Rapid City are the regional centers of the state. People come to these two cities to shop, see a medical specialist, be admitted to the regional hospital, or catch a plane.

CLIMATE The South Dakota climate is extreme. The saying goes, "if you don't like the weather wait fifteen minutes and it will change." The winter can be way below zero, the summer can be above a hundred and in the eastern part of the state, especially around the Missouri River, there is humidity to contend with. This is not to say that the weather can't be wonderful, as it often is, but don't be terribly surprised if it snows in June. May and September are generally gorgeous, early summer is usually mild but August can be very hot. The best advice is to overpack, be careful when outdoors, and be prepared for most anything.

South Dakota Tourism

EMERGENCIES Use 911 for all emergencies in South Dakota. Each chapter lists hospitals and clinics in the immediate area as well.

EVENTS PowWows, rodeos, fairs, car and motorcycle rallys, races, cook-offs, and much more take place every year in South Dakota. Special events are listed at the end of each chapter. For a searchable calendar sponsored by the Department of Tourism go to: www.travelsd.com/about/events.

FISHING With all the lakes, the Missouri River, and miles of streams, fishing is very popular in South Dakota. There are thirty species of fish including walleye, salmon, bluegill,

South Dakota Tourism

trout, bass, and pike. Trout, as well as some river fish, are raised in hatcheries and released yearly into streams and lakes. Fishing is year-round, including lots of ice fishing, which is a fine way to while away the long winter months. Licenses are required and available in every town and a few outlets are mentioned for each town. Further information can be found at the state fish and game site: www.sdgfp.info/Wildlife/fishing/Index.htm.

GAMBLING There are three kinds of gambling in South Dakota: Indian casinos, Deadwood small stakes gambling, and state sponsored video lottery. When you see "casino" signs outside a bar that means they have video lottery machines and you can play poker, blackjack, and keno and make a contribution to the state's tax base.

GEOGRAPHY The geography of South Dakota ranges from mountains, river basin, and glacial lakes to vast prairie. The diversity is one of the many things that make South Dakota so interesting to visit. And it's all within a days drive.

GEOLOGY Beginning 1.5 million years ago glaciers advanced and retreated across the eastern part of South Dakota leaving behind sediments as much as one hundred feet thick and depressions that became lakes. Below the glacial sediment are Cretaceous age shale, limestone, and sandstone full of marine fossils from an inland sea that once covered the area. The Badlands are the eroded remains of fine grained sediments from the mountains to the west. Deposited 2.5 to 65 million years ago, the area was once diverse with flora and fauna that has resulted in amazing fossil beds. During the Cretaceous the Black Hills were thrust up, once towering 15,000

feet. The oldest rocks, 2 billion years old, are in the central dome that includes the granite of Mount Rushmore and Harney Peak. There are lots of great finds for rockhounds, including mica, tourmaline, rose quartz, calcite, agates, feldspar, and fossil bearing rocks.

GOLF Despite the short season, golf is amazingly widespread in South Dakota. Every town seems to have at least a 9-hole course, adding up to 129 courses throughout the state, both public and private. Each chapter includes all courses open to the public with a short description. For a complete listing go to www.golfcourses.com/sd.

HIGHWAYS I-90 runs east to west through South Dakota, I-29 runs north to south in the eastern part of the state. There are many state highways throughout the state.

HISTORICAL MARKERS Historical markers are spread throughout South Dakota highways and are often well worth a stop. In the Black Hills many of these tell the work of the Civilian Conservation Corp, which was responsible for building the Black Hills dams and reservoirs during the Great Depression. And the highway signs with the red X saying "Why Die?" mark the site of a fatal traffic accident. Every marker represents one person killed.

HISTORIC HOMES AND MUSEUMS Throughout South Dakota there are homes, farms, and ranches dating back to the 1870s and there are numerous opportunities to learn more about the pioneer history of the state by visiting any of these. Many of the more notable homes have been restored by local historic groups and now serve as museums. Almost every town in South Dakota has a local museum of the town, the county, or the area's history. Most of them are operated by the town or a historic society and provide visitors another opportunity to learn about the Native Americans and settlers of South Dakota or do research from the archives collected about the local area. Under each chapter you will find listings for these homes and museums.

HISTORY Native people inhabited South Dakota as early as 11,000 years ago. The earliest people were hunters and gatherers, who left behind Clovis points and petroglyphs as evidence of their existence. The first known white men in South Dakota were French brothers, named Verdendrye, who were exploring for a northwest passage in 1743. On their return trip they buried a lead tablet claiming South Dakota for France in the area of Fort Pierre. South Dakota remained a French territory until it became part of the Louisiana Purchase in 1803.

In 1804 Lewis and Clark set out to explore the new lands and to search for a route to the Pacific. As they traversed the Missouri River much of their early journey went through South Dakota. They managed to cross through the native lands without incident, leading others to believe that white people could settle the west without conflicts with the Native Americans.

Most of the white men in South Dakota before 1860 were fur traders and few in number. The Native Americans also participated in the fur trade and made good profits from buffalo skins. In 1823 conflict broke out between the Natives and whites over control of the fur trade, resulting in the first signed treaty between Natives and white men in South Dakota.

Things really changed in South Dakota after the Custer Expedition of 1874. Rumors of gold in the Black Hills had spread to the Yankton area and Colonel Custer was sent to investigate. He found gold in French Creek and set off an influx of miners into lands that had been given to the Lakota Indians by treaty. Initially the army backed the treaty and forced out illegal miners but the task soon became impossible. The government attempted to buy the Black Hills from the Lakota but they refused. The government told the Lakota to leave the hills and return to their reservations but many would not go. In defiance of the order, Lakotas and Cheyennes joined together on the Little Big Horn River in Montana. The Seventh Calvary under George Armstrong Custer was sent to force the Indians back to the reservation but in an ill conceived attack every soldier was killed by the Indians. It was the last great victory for the Native Americans but they had little to celebrate as buffalo herds were decimated and the armies had moved onto the reservations and were confiscating Indian horses and rifles. Crazy Horse took his people to the reservation, Sitting Bull and Great Gall fled to

Canada. The U.S. Congress passed a bill that cut off payment to Native Americans unless they sold the Black Hills. Some leaders agreed because the people were starving but others refused, though it did not matter in the end.

Settlers began moving to South Dakota and wheat was successful in the east as mining continued in the hills. As railroads began arriving and crossing the empty prairie, towns were built to serve as railroad stops. The railways encouraged more settlers, German, Russian, and Scandinavian immigrants hoping to claim 160 acres, in accordance with the Homestead Act of 1862. Wood was scarce so most settlers lived in sod houses and burned twisted wheat stocks for cook stoves and heat. It was a hard existence that many were not up for and many did not stay.

In 1889 South Dakota became a state. Land was often taken from the Indian reservations to be auctioned to newcomers. The available land was in the west and proved poor for farming so landowners turned to ranching and cattle. The needs of World War I were a boon for South Dakota farmers and ranchers, but after the war prices crashed and everyone suffered. Then the weather turned dry and South Dakota was swept by wind, becoming part of the central plains Dust Bowl.

South Dakota modernized in the following decades and electricity and phone service came to the most rural portions of the state. The basic economy did not change, though the increase in paved roads led to increased tourism, particularly in the Black Hills. During the Cold War South Dakota housed numerous Minuteman Missile silos, most of which have been since decommissioned.

South Dakota's population continues to grow, primarily in the cities.

Mining is no longer a major industry, but farming and ranching continue to provide jobs. Some high-tech industry has moved to the state but South Dakota remains, as it has always been, largely rural and agricultural. It is a continuing challenge for South Dakota to keep its young people in the state, because there are not enough high paying jobs for college graduates. The state government is continually trying to entice new businesses to South Dakota to end what is commonly called the "brain drain" and to keep born South Dakotans in South Dakota.

HORSEBACK RIDING South Dakota is full of horses and, especially in the hills, there are trail rides available. Some riding centers are better than others, so use your judgment about the trails and condition of the horses. In each relevant chapter, good value trail rides have been listed.

INDIAN TRIBES There are nine Indian tribes in South Dakota: Cheyenne River, Crow Creek, Lower Brule, Oglala, Rosebud, Sisseton-Wahpeton, Yankton, Standing Rock, and Flandreau Santee. These Indian groups are known collectively as Sioux but are made up of the Lakota, Nakota, and Dakota people. The Indian reservations in South Dakota are rural and do not have the amenities found in more urban areas, but they are open to visitors. To learn more about visiting the reservations and Sioux culture go to www.travelsd.com/ourhistory/sioux/index.asp.

LEWIS AND CLARK South Dakota was one part of the Louisiana Purchase in 1803. President Thomas Jefferson appointed his secretary Meriwether Lewis and William Clark to map the purchase and find a route to the Pacific Ocean.

The Corps of Discovery set out from St. Louis on May 21, 1804. They spent the late summer and early fall of 1804 in South Dakota and journals from the expedition describe herds of buffalo, the prairies, and encounters with various Indian tribes, some peaceful, some not.

There are many opportunities in South Dakota to follow the Lewis and Clark Trail and many interpretive sites and museums devoted to the expedition. The best place to start is at the Lewis and Clark Visitors Center 4 miles west of Yankton, South Dakota, on Highway 52 at the Gavins Point Dam. Other links to Lewis and Clark are mentioned in each chapter as appropriate. Further information can be found at www.travelsd.com/our history/lc/index.asp.

MINING Most of the towns in the Black Hills, past and present, were built on mining and, until it closed in 2001, the Homestake Mine in Lead was the largest gold mine in North America. While few got rich on mining gold or silver, other minerals have become an important part of the state's economy, including pegmatite mining for mica, feldspar, and rose quartz; Sioux quartzite for building materials; sand and gravel for road construction; and limestone and gypsum. There are many sites to explore the Black Hills mining history, including the Homestake Mine, Wade's Gold Mill in Hill City, and the Big Thunder Gold Mine in Keystone.

MOTORCYCLING The Sturgis Rally and Races attract upwards of 500,000 motorcyclists to the Black Hills every year. Bikers come from every state in the country to enjoy the winding roads in the hills and to meet up with friends who share an interest in motorcycles. Despite the short season, motorcycling is also popular in South Dakota because the lack of helmet laws add to the freedom of riding.

MUSEUMS There are many museums in South Dakota that are devoted to paleontology and the history of Native Americans and the west. Some are operated by the National Park Service, the state, or a city, and others are privately owned and operated. Every town has a historical society that has put together the town or county's history and many of these museums are free. Check each chapter of this guide for further information about museums in the area you are visiting.

NATIONAL FORESTS The Black Hills National Forest was established in 1897 and encompasses 1.2 million acres in South Dakota and Wyoming. The Black Hills National Forest includes 11 reservoirs, 30 campgrounds, 32 picnic areas, 1,300 miles of streams, 353 miles of trails, and 13,000 acres of wilderness. The forest is 95 percent ponderosa pine, with a small percentage of white spruce and other trees, such as aspen. Details about recreational opportunities in the forest can be found throughout chapter 1.

NATIONAL PARKS There are two National Parks in South Dakota, Wind Cave (Hot Springs) and Badlands (Interior). There are also Jewel Cave National Monument (Custer), Mt. Rushmore National Monument (Keystone), Minuteman Missile National Historic Site (Wall), and the Missouri National Recreational River (Yankton). Details about each can be found in the relevant chapters.

NEWSPAPERS The two major South Dakota newspapers are the *Rapid City Journal* and *Sioux Falls Argus Leader*.

Most communities have at least a weekly paper.

PALEONTOLOGY Some of the best-preserved and most complete dinosaurs, including Sue, the T-Rex, have been dug up in South Dakota. Part of the Hell Creek Formation, an Upper Cretaceous deposit, runs through South Dakota and is where the dinosaurs were found. There are also paleontology sites in the Badlands where more modern but equally amazing animals are found, such as an ancient cousin of the pig. In Hot Springs you will find the Mammoth Site, a former sinkhole, which is the largest dig for North American Mammoths. There are a number of great fossil museums to visit and each is listed, including museums in Hill City, Rapid City, and Hot Springs.

POPULATION The population of South Dakota is 781,000. More interestingly, the population density is 9.9 people per square mile. The national average is 79.6.

RECOMMENDED READING To understand the experience of those intrepid pioneers in the Dakota Territory, many of whom were new immi-

South Dakota Tourism

grants from Europe, read *Giants of the Earth* by O. E. Rolvaag. This fictional tale tells of a group of Norwegians who settled in the territory in 1873 and the many hardships they endured. It is a book that will stay with you long after you have finished it.

For the story of Lewis and Clark there is no better choice than Stephen Ambrose's *Undaunted Courage: Merriweather Lewis, Thomas Jefferson and the Opening of the American West*. Ambrose puts the Corps of Discovery's journey into historical perspective and quotes liberally from the journals of Lewis and Clark.

Finding a book that tells both sides of the conflicts between Native Americans and settlers in the West is difficult, but from the perspective of South Dakota one of the best is *Bury My Heart at Wounded Knee* by Dee Brown. You may end up feeling less than proud of the treatment of Native Americans but it is a history lesson we all need to learn.

No doubt one of the most central and controversial figures in the American West was George Armstrong Custer. A hero during his lifetime, history has not been kind to Custer. He played a pivotal role in South Dakota and a great book about him is *Son of the Morning Star* by Evan S. Connell. This book will help you understand Custer's motivations and actions and how they affected South Dakota and American history.

For rock hounds and geology lovers pick up *Roadside Geology of South Dakota* by John Paul Gries—he'll even tell you where the dinosaurs are. And for information about the early mining history of the Black Hills try *Black Hills Ghost Towns* by Hugh K. Lambert and Watson Parker. This book may even inspire you to go in search of some of the ghost towns while you are in the hills.

REST AREAS There are rest areas and information centers located along the two interstate highways in South Dakota. Most feature racks of brochures for tourists. If you are not on the interstate do not wait to find a gas station or restroom because they are few and far between. When adventuring farther out in the hills or prairie, take along a roll of toilet paper.

RESTAURANTS In the larger cities and towns in South Dakota you will find the same variety of restaurants as in any other town, including ethnic cuisine. In smaller towns do not expect anything other than traditional American café fare. Beef is the king of cuisine in South Dakota so you can't go wrong ordering it. The closer you are to the Missouri the more likely you are to find fresh walleye or other fish.

ROAD REPORTS Keeping up on the South Dakota road reports is a state obsession, especially in the winter when it can mean canceling a planned trip. Call 511 and you will get updated road reports for the interstates and major highways or go to hp.state.sd.us/road.htm.

SCENIC BYWAYS The following scenic byways are absolute must-sees while visiting South Dakota. Don't forget to bring your camera.

Peter Norbeck National Scenic Byway, US 16A and SD 87. This byway twists through the Black Hills, up a hill, down a hill, through tunnels, and over pigtail bridges. It also includes awesome views of Mt. Rushmore and the Needles, which are very odd rock formations popular with rock climbers.

Spearfish Canyon State and National Forest Service Scenic Byway, US 14A. This route takes you 20 miles through Spearfish Canyon to Deadwood following Spearfish Creek and featuring an awesome waterfall. Locals take this route to enjoy the fall colors.

Badlands Loop National Scenic Byway, SD 240. The best way to see the Badlands is to find all the interpretive sites and scenic overlooks by following this 30-mile loop through the park.

Wildlife Loop State Scenic Byway, SD 87 and US 16A. Running 18 miles through Custer State Park, this byway offers the best opportunity to see the buffalo herds, antelope, wild mules, prairie dog villages, and too many birds to mention. When you enter the park ask the ranger where the buffalo are and they will tell you exactly where they can be found.

SMOKING Smoking is allowed indoors in South Dakota. Virtually any place that sells liquor, from bars to bowling alleys, will allow smoking. Most restaurants have smoking sections but more and more are becoming nonsmoking. Hotels and motels also have smoking and nonsmoking rooms, with a few being completely nonsmoking. The best advice is to check before you commit to a restaurant, motel, or entertainment venue if smoking is an issue for you.

STATE PARKS One of South Dakota's best-kept secrets is the dozens of great state parks, many offering camping, hiking, fishing, and boating. Parks of particular interest are included in the chapters of this guide. If you want a complete list of the parks go to www.sdgfp.com. To reserve campsites go to www.CampSD.com or call 1-800-710-CAMP.

STATE TRIVIA Fun facts to know and quiz the kids on about South Dakota:

The state bird is the ring-necked pheasant. The state mineral is rose quartz. The state mammal is the coyote. The state tree is the Black Hills spruce. The state flower is the pasqueflower. South Dakota has the lowest per capita state tax in the United States. Only 8.8 percent of South Dakotans are Native American, while 88.5 percent are Caucasian. Belle Fourche, in the northern hills, is the geographical center of the United States. Harney Peak is the highest point in the United States, east of the Rockies. The best-preserved T-Rex was found near Faith, South Dakota.

TAXES South Dakota's state sales tax is 4 percent but each town adds on to that so it varies widely. There is no state income tax or inheritance tax in South Dakota.

TIME ZONES There are two time zones in South Dakota, divided down the middle of the state through Pierre. Those east of the river are on central daylight time (CDT) and those west of the river are on mountain standard time (MST).

TRAVEL INFORMATION The State Office of Tourism has a great Web site (www.travelsd.com). You can also link to local chambers of commerce from there, as well as order or download travel guides. Stop at any visitors center along the interstates and talk to the nice people who are there to help tourists find activities they would enjoy. Local visitors centers are listed in each chapter under the particular town you are visiting.

WATER SPORTS Despite being 1,500 miles from an ocean South Dakota is passionate about water sports. With the many lakes, large and small, and numerous rivers, including the Missouri, there are opportunities to swim, boat, fish, Jet Ski, water ski, canoe, kayak, and even wind surf. If you visit South Dakota in the summer, plan on a bringing a swimsuit and whatever gear you need to enjoy your favorite water sport and remember there are boats and other watercraft for rent if you don't have your own. In the winter the water turns to ice but that doesn't stop South Dakotans from enjoying the water. Locals can be found ice fishing in shacks on virtually every lake, and snowmobile racing on the larger lakes.

WEATHER The weather can be extreme in South Dakota. During the summer beware of severe thunderstorms or tornadoes. In the winter the concern is blizzards. To check the latest weather and advisories, go to the National Weather Service site at weather.noaa.gov. If the weather looks threatening while traveling in South Dakota, tune your radio to any local station and they will have up to the minute watches and warnings issued by the National Weather Service.

WILDERNESS AREAS There are two designated wilderness areas in South Dakota. Black Elk is part of the Black Hills National Forest and encompasses 13,426 acres and 25 percent of the Badlands are designated as the Sage Creek Wilderness Area.

WILDLIFE South Dakota has abundant wildlife, including mule and white tail deer, antelope, elk, bighorn sheep, mountain goats, coyotes, bobcats, and too many birds and fish to mention. There is only one poisonous snake, the prairie rattler, and the only predator a hiker would need to be concerned about is the mountain lion. All the bears were killed in the Black Hills in the 1800s.

WILDLIFE AREAS There are a number of wildlife areas or refuges in South Dakota.

Karl E. Mundt National Wildlife Refuge near Pickstown provides habitat for bald eagles. **Lacreek National Wildlife Refuge** near Martin covers 16,000 acres and is used by migrating and nesting waterfowl. **Maga Ta-Hohpi Waterfowl Production Area** is west of Huron. **Lake Andes National Wildlife Refuge** near Wagner has waterfowl, pheasant, shorebirds, and deer. **Sand Lake National Wildlife Refuge** is northeast of Aberdeen and is for migrating and nesting waterfowl. **Waubay National Wildlife Refuge** is near Waubay. There is also the nonprofit **Black Hills Wild Horse Sanctuary** near Hot Springs that covers 11,000 acres and is home to wild mustangs.

WINERIES Making wine is a pretty new addition to South Dakota agriculture and the vintners are making a name for themselves with flavors unique to the area like chokecherry and dandelion wines. All of the winer-

South Dakota Tourism

ies that have tasting rooms or otherwise welcome visitors are listed in the relevant chapters.

WINTER SPORTS One advantage to living in snow country is great winter sports. South Dakotans are avid snowmobilers, cross-country and downhill skiers, and ice fishermen. There are two ski areas in the Black Hills, Terry Peak and Deer Mountain, and one in the Sioux Falls area, Great Bear. There are 350 miles of groomed snowmobile trails throughout the state. To find maps go to www.sdgfp.info/Parks/Recreation/Snowmobiling/index.htm.

Black Hills

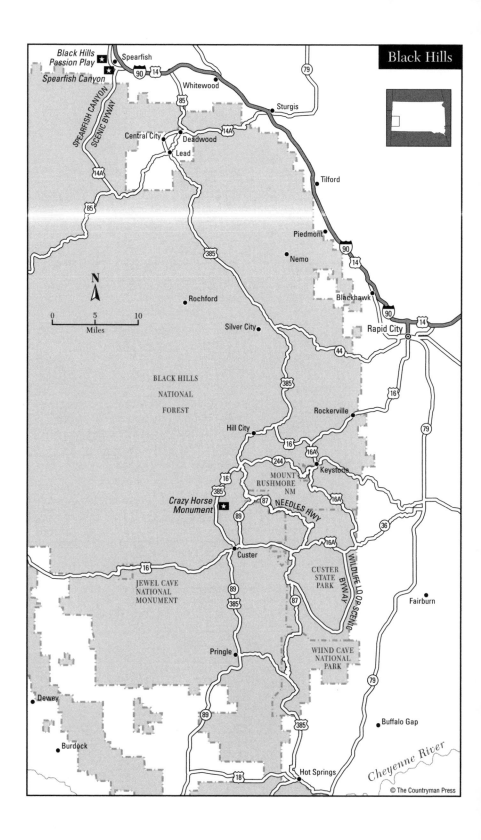

Black Hills

THE BLACK HILLS

The Black Hills of South Dakota are one of the hidden treasures of the United States. Most everyone who has ever been to the Black Hills leave wanting to return for future vacations, others leave wanting to live there. Most who have not come to the Black Hills hold the misconception that South Dakota is made up of plains and farmland.

The Black Hills are the oldest mountains in the United States, estimated to have been uplifted 60 million years ago, about the same time as the end of the age of the dinosaurs. At one time the hills rose 15,000 feet but have since eroded to where the highest point, Harney Peak, stands at 7,242 feet. The Black Hills cover an area of over 100 miles from Spearfish in the north to Edgemont in the south, and over 40 miles east to west, from Rapid City to the Wyoming border.

Named *Paha Sapa*, or "hills that are black," by Native Americans, the hills were once the sacred hunting ground of the Lakota. Due to their isolated location and Indian treaties, the Hills were one of the last areas in the United States to be explored by white men. It wasn't until rumors of gold circulated that an expedition

THE BLACK HILLS WERE NAMED PAHA SAPA, OR HILLS THAT ARE BLACK, BY NATIVE AMERICANS.

lead by George Armstrong Custer was sent to the hills. He did indeed find gold in the streams of the Black Hills and in a short time the Native Americans were forced out as miners poured in.

The Black Hills National Forest encompasses 1.2 million acres and 13,000 acres of wilderness. Thanks to the national forest, the Black Hills have never been overgrown with development. Dotted with small towns and long established homesteads, the Black Hills are fundamentally rural and the main sources of income for those fortunate enough to live here are tourism and logging. This makes the Black Hills an amazing place for those who want to experience nature up close and personal. It is still possible to spend a day driving and hiking the Black Hills without encountering another car or another person—a rare experience for outdoor enthusiasts in most of our country.

Today the Black Hills offer visitors a wealth of choices. There is hunting, fishing, boating, rock climbing, camping, and hiking for the outdoor lover. There are two National Parks, Wind Cave and Jewel Cave, and one very famous National Monument, Mount Rushmore. There is history to be found at Crazy Horse Memorial and the restored 1880 Train, and paleontology at the Black Hills Institute of Geological Research and the Mammoth Site. For families there are the Black Hills Wild Horse Sanctuary, Bear Country, and Evans Plunge. For adults there are gambling in Deadwood and, surprisingly, wineries to tour. And every August, motorcycle lovers return to ride the miles of twisting highways through the Black Hills and join their friends and fellow motorcycle enthusiasts at the Sturgis Rally.

Clearly, you can't help but find something to do in the Black Hills and likely far more than you had imagined. Like most, you'll be back, if not as a permanent resident, then surely to visit.

HOT SPRINGS

Hot Springs is at the southern end of the Black Hills and known for its mineral water hot springs and the spring-fed river that winds through town. Originally known by the Native American name, *Minnekahata,* "warm waters," Hot Springs was settled as a ranching town. In 1890 a group of local businessmen, including Fred Evans, decided to turn the town into a health spa to make the most of the natural hot springs. Evans enclosed one giant thermal spout of warm mineral water and a group of smaller springs, creating Evans Plunge. The railroad delivered tourists and River Street became built up with sandstone hotels and restaurants to cater to the visitors.

Over 100 years later, Evans Plunge is still operating and the springs are still pouring out 5,000 gallons a minute of 87-degree water. An outdoor pool, water slides, and other entertainment for families have been added and tourists and locals still flock to the site year-round to enjoy the warm waters.

But there are other things to do in the Hot Springs area, including Wind Cave National Park, the Mammoth Site, and the Wild Horse Sanctuary. The Hot Springs Historic District features the early sandstone buildings, some that are newly refurbished hotels and spas, some with long-standing businesses that serve the local population year-round and tourists in the summer.

GUIDANCE **Hot Springs Chamber of Commerce** (605-745-4140; www.hot springs-sd.com), 801 S. Sixth St., Hot Springs 57747.

GETTING THERE *By car:* Hot Springs is 55 miles from Rapid City on SD 79. From Custer, take US 385 south.

GETTING AROUND There is no public transportation in Hot Springs so a car is essential.

MEDICAL EMERGENCIES **Fall River Health Services** (605-745-3157), 209 N. 16th St., Hot Springs.

✳ To See

CULTURAL SITES ✐ ⊤ **Mammoth Site** (605-745-6017; www.mammothsite .com), 1800 US 18 Bypass. Open 8–8, May through August; 9–5 in winter. Some 26,000 years ago a sinkhole formed outside of Hot Springs. Warm artesian water

THE MAMMOTH SITE IN HOT SPRINGS IS THE WORLD'S LARGEST MAMMOTH RESEARCH FACILITY.

filled the sinkhole and, enticed by the water and vegetation, mammoths climbed into the sinkhole but were unable to escape. For 350–700 years the watering hole was active and then began filling with silt and sediment, burying the animals who had died there. In 1974 the first bones were found in what is known today as the Mammoth Site, which presently is an ongoing dig for North American Columbian Mammoths and other animals, including woolly mammoths, the giant short-faced bear, and wolves. It is the world's largest mammoth research facility and open to visitors year-round with 30-minute guided tours. Visitors view the ongoing work on raised sidewalks above the dig as the bones are so fragile most are uncovered but left in the ground. There is also a working paleontology lab, an Ice Age Exhibit Hall, and short films about geology and paleontology. The Mammoth Site is must-see when you are in the Hot Springs area. Free for children under 4, $5.50 for children ages 5–12, $7.50 for ages 13–59, $7 for ages 60 and older.

MUSEUMS & **Pioneer Museum of Hot Springs** (605-745-5147), 300 N. River St. Open 9–5, mid-May through mid-October. Built in 1893 as a school, this sandstone building is one of the finest examples of the early buildings in Hot Springs made from locally quarried stone. It now houses the Pioneer Museum, giving visitors a glimpse into daily life of the earliest settlers in the Black Hills area. The museum's collection includes a wide variety of pioneer and ranching items such as old tools, washing machines, woodstoves, and kerosene lamps. They also have complete collections grouped together, such as a replica of a pioneer classroom, a doctor's office, and a country store. If you enjoy antiques and local history this place is a good deal and offers a lot to see. $5 for ages 12 and older, $15 for an entire family.

MANY OF THE ORIGINAL HOT SPRINGS BUILDINGS WERE CRAFTED FROM NATIVE SANDSTONE.

✳ To Do

BIKING/HIKING **Angostura Recreation Area,** see listing under *Boating and Fishing.* If you want a break from the water there are two trails at Angostura:

Angostura Breaks Nature Trail, 1.2 miles. The trailhead is above the cabin area. This is a hilly trail made up of grass and dirt.

Reservoir View Bike Trail, 1.2 miles. The trailhead is at the ski beach. This trail is moderately strenuous and is covered by dirt and grass.

Wind Cave National Park (605-745-4600; www.nps.gov/archive/wica/Hiking .htm), US 385. Wind Cave offers 30 miles of hiking trails through the prairie, several with interpretive signs along the way. Ask for a map at the visitors center.

BOATING AND FISHING Angostura Recreation Area (605-745-6996; www .sdgfp.info/Parks/Regions/SouthernHills/Angostura.htm), 13157 Angostura Rd. Open year-round. By damming the Cheyenne River for irrigation in 1949, Angostura Reservoir was created. Today it is immensely popular for recreation and is used for skiing, fishing, boating, and swimming from the miles of sandy shoreline. Angostura is well known for its walleye catches, crappie, and small mouth bass. Fishing licenses are available at **Ace Hardware**, 207 Chicago Street, and **Common Cents**, 28075 Recreation Road, among others. Locals come for the day or the weekend but you can stay much longer and enjoy the four campgrounds, six rental lodges, a marina, a boat launch, a beach house, canoe and kayak rentals, and concessions. Angostura is definitely one of the nicest places to play in the Black Hills and worth more than a quick visit if you enjoy the water. Entrance fee is $5 per vehicle.

CAVES ✔ ☂ **Wind Cave National Park**, see listing under *Biking and Hiking*. For hundreds of years Lakota Indian traditions talked of a "hole that breathes cool air" near Buffalo Gap. While riding their horses in 1891, Tom and Jesse Bingham heard a sound like that of wind blowing. When they investigated, Jesse followed the sound to a hole in the ground that blew his hat off. In 1902 the first formal survey of the cave was conducted and today new portions of the cave are still being explored. Wind Cave National Park was established in 1902, the first national park created to protect a cave. The cave is over 300 million years old and covers over 120 miles, under just 1 square mile of land. The park also includes camping, trails, prairie dog villages, a bison herd, and a visitors center. There are interpretative ranger programs including a two-hour prairie hike and campfire presentations in the evening. There are four tours of the cave ranging in length from one to two hours. Most involve stairs, but call ahead for limited tours available for those in wheelchairs. Also remember caves are chilly so bring a jacket. Cave tours range in price from $4.50 to $9, tickets are first come, first served, so call ahead and reserve tickets to avoid disappointment.

FAMILY FRIENDLY ✔ ☂ **Evans Plunge** (605-745-5165; www.evansplunge .com), 1145 N. River St. Open 5:30 AM–10 PM weekdays, 8 AM–10 PM Saturday and Sunday during the summer; 5:30 AM–8 PM weekdays, 10 AM–8 PM Saturday and Sunday in the off-season. Fred Evans was one of the first to see the potential of the warm water coming from the ground of Hot Springs and in 1890 he put a building over an 87-degree spring and promoted it as a cure for numerous ills including gout, rheumatism, and chronic diseases of the liver and gastrointestinal tract. Evans Plunge may not be a cure-all but it's still a fun place to spend the day with your family enjoying the indoor and outdoor swimming and playing in the spring fed waters. Besides swimming and floating around there are rings and slides, as well as a kid's pool. There ar also a snack bar and health club. Do be aware that it can get pretty crowded during the summer, especially on weekends. Free for ages 2 and under, $8 for ages 3–12, $10 for ages 13 and older.

⚓ **Putt 4 Fun** (605-745-PUTT (7888); www.putt4fun.us), 604 S. Sixth St. This is a nicely designed mini golf course with 18 holes, including waterfalls, fountains, and sand traps. It's a nice stop for a little friendly competition. $5 for ages 3–11, $7 for ages older than 11.

GOLF Southern Hills Municipal Golf Course (605-745-6400), 303 River St. With really beautiful scenery of the hills, this 18-hole course has fast greens and enough trees to make you alter your shot. Green fees $30 on weekdays, $34.50 on weekends; carts are $26.

SWIMMING Angostura Recreation Area, (605-745-6996; www.sdgfp.info/ Parks/Regions/SouthernHills/Angostura.htm), 13157 Angostura Rd. Open year-round. Angostura has lots of sandy beaches for swimming and sunbathing.

UNIQUE ADVENTURES Black Hills Wild Horse Sanctuary (1-800-252-6652; www.wildmustangs.com) Off SD 71 South, look for a road sign on the right side of road. Open May 1 through October 31. Wild mustangs have no natural predators and as a result compete with cattle for available rangeland in the West. The Bureau of Land Management instituted a program of birth control measures and adoptions but there were still too many horses that were not adoptable and ended up in feed lots with no hope for the future. In 1988 writer and environmentalist Dayton Hyde convinced the bureau to let him care for the horses no one would take and established this nonprofit, which is home to over 500 wild horses living in

GOING STRONG SINCE 1890, EVANS PLUNGE IS GREAT FUN FOR THE ENTIRE FAMILY.

complete freedom on the South Dakota prairie. Take a two-hour bus tour and see the horses, Indian petroglyphs, movie sites, and Native American ceremonial sites at the sanctuary. Pricey but if you can afford it, this could be the high point of your vacation and your visit will help support the horses. $50 for adults, $45 for seniors, and $15 for children under 16.

Wild Cave Tour, Wind Cave National Park, see listing under *Caves*. If you are claustrophobic forget it, but for the

SEE OVER 500 WILD MUSTANGS LIVING FREE AT THE WILD HORSE SANCTUARY.

truly adventurous Wind Cave offers four-hour tours of parts of the cave that are not included in the normal tour schedule. You must be at least 16 years old and bring your own grubby clothes since there's lots of crawling through dirt and mud. The park provides kneepads, lights, and hard hats. Reservations must be made a month in advance by calling 605-745-4600.

✳ Green Spaces

Angostura Recreation Area, see listing under *Boating and Fishing*.

ALONG THE RIVER FRONT IN HOT SPRINGS WATERFALLS CAN BE FOUND.

NATURE PRESERVES The Wind Cave National Game Preserve, see listing under *Caves*. This preserve was established on August 10, 1912, with the primary goal of restoring the environment to what it was prior to European entry into the area. By the turn of the century many of the wild animals of the Black Hills, including bison and Eastern Elk, had been wiped out and had to be reintroduced into the park. Today there are herds of bison, elk, and thriving prairie dog colonies for visitors to enjoy. Management of the wildlife has been a constant learning experience for the park and includes both ups and downs. Trying to establish a natural balance among the animals and the environment continues to be a challenge as the park struggles with an overpopulation of prairie dogs and diseases affecting the elk. Studies continue in an effort to restore balance in this ecosystem that had been neglected for hundreds of years.

✳ Lodging

BED & BREAKFAST INNS Anise's BnB4Pets (1-800-794-4142; www
.bnb4pets.com), 1 Canyon View Circle.
Open year-round. At the base of Battle
Mountain this 15-acre property is
home to a unique bed-and-breakfast
that specializes in pets: dogs, cats,
horses, or even llamas at no extra cost.
With a fenced yard for pups to play in
and nearby hiking trails, as well horse
stabling, your pets will be treated as
well as you are. There are two suites,
one with a full kitchen and fireplace,
one with a kitchenette and a Jacuzzi
tub. While you dine on Caramel Apple
French Toast on the deck your canine
pal gets homemade dog biscuits to
munch on. They also provide doggie
daycare or boarding should you need to
leave your four-footed companion for
awhile. Rate range from $120–$165.

**CABINS/CAMPING Angostura
Recreation Area,** see listing under
Boating and Fishing. Open year-round.
Angostura has 162 sites in four campgrounds and is very popular because of
the lake and some campsites adjacent to
the water. There are showers, water,
and two dump stations. $12–$16 a
night.

Elk Mountain Campground, Wind
Cave National Park (605-745-4600),
US 385. Open year-round. Camping in
the middle of Wind Cave is a great way
to get up close and personal with the
park wildlife, just remember the animals are wild. There are no dump stations, showers, or electrical hookups.
There is running water and toilets are
available. First come, first served for
campsites and RV pull-through sites.
There is a campground host onsite.
$12 per night during summer, $6 per
night when the water is turned off.

Hot Springs KOA (605-745-6449;
www.koa.com/where/sd/41114), 27585

US 79. Open April 19 through October
12. With campsites and camping cabins, this campground has lots of trees
and ample shade. Clean and well
maintained, there are also a pool, mini
golf, camp store, and a playground.
Rates vary for campsites, RVs, and
cabins, starting at $25 a night.

**GUEST SUITES The Flat Iron
Guest Suites** (605-745-5301; www
.flatiron.bz), 745 N. River St. Located
in a historic, sandstone building there
are four guest suites with kitchenettes,
ranging in size from two bedrooms and
one bath to a studio with a sunporch.
All of the suites are nicely decorated
with amenities like ceiling fans and have
unique floor plans that were developed
around the buildings structure. This is a
great location for everything Hot
Springs has to offer and right downstairs is the Flat Iron Grill. $110–$150.

RESORTS Red Rock River Resort
(1-888-306-8921; www.redrockriver
resort.com), 603 North River St. Take a
little time to pamper yourself while in
Hot Springs. This is a clean, nicely decorated spa and hotel offering massage,
sauna, hot tub, and reflexology. Prices
vary depending on what you want but a
60-minute massage runs $65. The five
guest rooms are spacious and attractive
and they also offer overnight packages
for one or more nights that include spa
services. New to the resort is the **Blue
Vervain Restaurant,** so you never
have to leave to have a great vacation
experience. $95–$125.

SPAS Red Rock River Resort, see
listing under *Resorts.*

Springs Bath House (605-745-4424;
www.springsbathhouse.com), 146 N.
Garden St. This clean, spacious spa
pumps in the warm waters of the mineral springs for soaking in hot tubs of
different temperatures. If you would

like some skin treatment, they offer body wraps including seaweed or clay and face treatments with cucumber or honey almond. They also offer massage therapy, including Watsu, which is done while you are floating in the warm waters. Sounds mighty relaxing! Rates vary by service. A day pass for the mineral spring pools is $12.

✴ Where to Eat

DINING OUT **Blue Vervain** at the Red Rock River Resort (605-745-7642), 603 N. River St. Open for dinner Tuesday through Saturday 5–9. Originally opened in Hot Springs in 2002, then moved to Colorado Springs, the Blue Vervain is back in Hot Springs and run by a young graduate of the Culinary Institute of America. Rebecca Christensen won "Best Fine Dining" among other awards with her restaurant in Colorado Springs, with a wide-ranging seasonal menu of diverse culinary influences including Southwest and Asian. This is not your average South Dakota steak house and the menu includes contemporary items like Thai-Style Chicken and Herbed Chicken Piccata. They also offer a vegan menu, beer and wine, and a scrumptious dessert menu with selections like the Rhubarb Lavender Tart. Entrées between $18 and $42.

EATING OUT **Blue Bison Café** (605-745-4226), 509 N. River St. Open 9–9. You can't miss this place because there is a life-size blue bison on the roof. In one of the historic buildings along River Street, this café has plenty of seating either at tables or at the counter. They serve all manner of coffees, teas, and ice cream treats, as well as a variety of sandwiches, soups, and their award-winning bison chili. $3–$8.

Fall River Bakery (605-745-6190), 407 N. River St. Open 7 AM. This honest-to-goodness small-town bakery

has all the standard baked goods like bread, muffins, and rolls. They also serve a limited lunch menu including stromboli. There is a small area for eating in, if you don't want to get your food to go. $2–$3.

Flat Iron Coffee Bar (605-745-6439; www.flatiron.bz), 745 N. River St. Open 7–3 Tuesday through Thursday, 7–10 Saturday. With hardwood floors and sandstone walls, this attractive coffee bar has all the varieties of coffee drinks and baked goods to start your day off right. They also have breakfast sandwiches, lunch sandwiches, homemade soups, quiche, salads, and a nice wine list. If you're being diet conscious try their yogurt, fruit, and granola bowl, which is filling and lighter on the calories, for breakfast or lunch. There is a very comfy outside patio with padded wicker furniture for dining and they have live music on the weekends. $2–$10.

Mi Cocina (605-745-4666), 445 N. River St. Open for lunch and dinner. This family restaurant features good American-style Mexican food like burritos and enchiladas served with beans and rice. They also have sandwiches, if you don't care for Mexican. Entrées $6–$14.

✴ Selective Shopping

Black Hills Books and Treasures (605-745-5545; www.blackhills-books .com), 112 S. Chicago St. Open 10–6 Monday through Friday, 10–3 Saturday. Specializing in Black Hills books and regional history this shop has everything you would want to know about the hills or the West. They also have a large selection of first editions and rare books to browse through. If you are looking for a gift, they have Native American arts and crafts. The owner is extremely knowledgeable about the area and books so stop in for a chat.

CUSTER

Custer has the distinction of being named for Lieutenant Colonel George Armstrong Custer, who led a massive expedition into the Black Hills that found gold in French Creek in the vicinity of today's downtown Custer. The discovery of gold drew miners into the Black Hills, which broke a treaty with the Native Americans that granted them the Black Hills. The broken treaty led to the last great Indian battle, which took place two years later at Little Big Horn in Montana and resulted in the death of Custer and the defeat of the Seventh Cavalry.

Ironically, one of the major attractions in the town named for the fallen colonel is a mountain carving (incomplete to date) honoring Crazy Horse, the Lakota Sioux warrior who led the Indians into battle at Little Big Horn. Custer has his town, Crazy Horse has his mountain—such is the nature of American history.

Custer never lived up to expectations for gold mining, although at one time as many as 10,000 people were in the area. But then, word spread of a gold strike in a little town to the north called Deadwood and Custer emptied overnight leaving a population of just 14.

Today there are 1,800 residents in Custer and it is the seat of Custer County. Primarily a tourist destination due to its location at the entrance to Custer State Park and its historical name, Custer is a friendly town that is largely self-sufficient because of its distance from Rapid City.

GUIDANCE **Custer Chamber of Commerce** (1-800-992-9818; www.custersd .com), P.O. Box 5018, Custer 57730.

GETTING THERE *By car:* from Rapid City take US 16/385. It takes about 50 minutes but is a really pretty drive on good roads.

GETTING AROUND There is no public transportation in Custer.

MEDICAL EMERGENCIES **Custer Regional Hospital** (605-673-2229), 1039 Montgomery St., Custer.

✷ To See

CULTURAL SITES **Crazy Horse Memorial** (605-673-4681; www.crazyhorse .org), US 16/385, 11 miles north of Custer. Open 7 AM until after the laser light

A MEMORIAL TO THE LAKOTA PEOPLE AND THE WARRIOR CRAZY HORSE CAN BE FOUND JUST OUTSIDE CUSTER.

show, May 23 through October 13. Winter hours are from 8–5. "My fellow chiefs and I would like the white man to know the red man has great heroes, too." Those were the words Chief Henry Standing Bear wrote to sculptor Korczak Ziolkowski in 1939 inviting him to come to the Black Hills to carve a mountain sculpture honoring Native Americans. Ziolkowski began the project in 1948 in honor of the Lakota leader Crazy Horse and it continues today under the direction of his family. It is the largest mountain carving attempted to date and when finished Crazy Horse will stand 641 feet long and 563 feet high. When you visit the mountain you will see Crazy Horse's head and what will someday be his arm. Models of the sculpture show the eventual final product, the Lakota warrior riding his horse. While at the memorial, also visit the very informative Native American Education and Cultural Center, a museum, and many buildings open to tour, such as the sculptor's home. There are a number of special events every year, including night blasts, which are a spectacular show to witness. Crazy Horse Memorial also has the distinction of holding the most popular Volksmarchs in the nation, drawing as many as 15,000 walkers. *Volksmarch* simply means "people's march" and is a non-competitive walk. At the memorial the walk is 6.2 miles and goes from the base of the mountain and turns around on Crazy Horse's outstretched arm. It is the only time the public is allowed to the top of the sculpture. Check the Web site for dates of the Volksmarch and other special events at the memorial. $10 per adult or $27 per car load.

HISTORIC SITES Custer State Park (1-888-875-0001; www.sdgfp.info/Parks/Regions/Custer), 7 miles east of Custer on County Road 344. Open year-round.

Custer State Park is the crown jewel of the South Dakota parks and situated in one of the prettiest parts of the Black Hills, including pine covered hills, rocky outcrops, and grassy prairie. There are well-kept campgrounds, four Western-style lodges, spectacular scenic drives, wildlife viewing, hiking trails, Jeep tours, and an annual buffalo roundup. A million and a half visitors come to the park every year but you never feel crowded. Entrance fee: $5 per person or $12 per vehicle.

Badger Hole, located in Custer State Park. The home of Charles "Badger" Clark, the first poet laureate of South Dakota, has a trail that includes his poetry. The cabin was built in the 1930s by Clark and is a South Dakota Historic Landmark.

Gordon Stockade, located on the western edge of Custer State Park, was built 1874–75 by the John Gordon Party, one of the first mining parties in the Black Hills. The party was made up of 26 men, one woman, and one small boy. They stayed the winter and were then removed by the army. The one woman was Annie Tallent, who later returned to the hills and became a teacher and the superintendent of the Pennington County Schools. At one time she was highly regarded for her pioneer roots and contributions to public education. Tallent has since been relegated to a footnote in history due to her racist attitudes toward Native Americans, which she expressed in a book she wrote. The stockade has been restored and includes interpretive signs that tell more about the early prospectors in the hills.

State Game Lodge, in Custer State Park. Built in 1920 and adjacent to Grace Coolidge Creek, the game lodge was considered the Summer White House for President Calvin Coolidge in 1927. A beautiful building of wood and stone, the game lodge is worth visiting for its history, even if you don't plan on staying there.

THE NEEDLES GET THEIR NAME FROM THE BIZARRE GRANITE SPIRES RISING ABOVE THE BLACK HILLS.

SCENIC DRIVES The **Peter Norbeck Scenic Highway**, made up of the three routes listed below, is considered one of the best scenic drives in America. Senator Norbeck himself hiked and rode the area on horseback in 1933 to design the routes. If you want to drive the entire route, plan on spending 4 hours as you will want to stop at lots of scenic overlooks for pictures.

Needles Highway, located in Custer State Park, is 4 miles in length on SD 87. Needles Highway is probably the most popular drive in the hills and features spectacular Black Hills scenery including granite spires, the Needles Eye, narrow tunnels, and hairpin curves. Traveling on this road, you will also pass beautiful Sylvan Lake in the park. Start early to avoid getting stuck behind a slow moving RV or not being able to find somewhere to park at a pull off.

Iron Mountain Road, 17 miles in length on US 16A and SD 36 from Keystone into Custer State Park. Along the highway are pigtail bridges, which are exactly what the name implies, bridges that go in tight cork screws, and three tunnels, which frame Mount Rushmore in the distance. The map may say Iron Mountain Road is only 17 miles but since you go up and down the mountains and in circles around the bridges it seems much longer. Not recommended at night, if you don't know the road.

Wildlife Loop Road, located in Custer State Park. This 18-mile loop goes from forests to prairie grasslands. Be on the look out for bison, pronghorn, deer, elk, prairie dog villages, and the world's friendliest burros that will eat anything you offer them including your car upholstery, if you aren't paying attention. When you enter the park ask the attendants where the buffalo are and they will be able to tell you exactly where they were last seen, as they keep up-to-date information. Follow the information in the park pamphlet about safety. You will be astonished at the number of people who ignore the warnings and get out of their cars to take pictures of the buffalo or crawl around in the prairie dog villages. While they may be cute as can be, remember that the animals are wild. Bison run really fast and are protective of their young, prairie dogs have the same fleas that cause the plague, and rattlesnakes like hanging out in prairie dog tunnels waiting for lunch to stop by. Fortunately, very few people ever get hurt.

✳ To Do

BICYCLING There are numerous trails for mountain biking in Custer State Park (www.sdgfp.info/Parks/Regions/Custer/mtbikeguide.htm). Some of them include the following:

Centennial Trail, this 111-mile trail spans the length of the Black Hills from Bear Butte State Park in the north to Wind Cave National Park in the south. Approximately 22 miles of the trail are located within Custer State Park. The trail is marked with a combination of brown fiberglass posts and gray diamonds fastened to trees.

Iron Creek to Badger Hole is 7.3 miles one way. The trail begins at the Iron Creek Trailhead, north of SD 87 (Needles Highway), on gravel road CSP 345. There are several small stream crossings and, around the 6-mile mark, the trail crosses US 16A near Legion Lake Resort and Campground. The trail continues to the Badger Hole and the Centennial Trail's Badger Hole Trailhead.

Badger Hole to French Creek is 3.5 miles one way. The trail begins at the Centennial Trail's Badger Hole Trailhead, 1 mile off US 16A on CSP 9, then west to the Badger Hole Cabin. This is the most strenuous section of the Centennial Trail within Custer State Park.

French Creek to the Wind Cave Border is 10.3 miles one way. From the Centennial Trail's French Creek Trailhead located 3 miles from the Blue Bell Stables on CSP 4, follow the trail markers west through the Horse Camp and across French Creek. The trail intersects with the Wildlife Loop Road and continues across the road to the south. This section of trail enters the open grasslands and is home to large herds of bison. The trail passes through a gate and continues south

South Dakota Tourism

WIND CAVE IS A SPELUNKERS DELIGHT
WITH NUMEROUS ROOMS AND FORMA-
TIONS TO VISIT.

to the border of Wind Cave National Park. Wind Cave National Park regulations prohibit bicycles on hiking trails.

Big Tree Robbers Roost Draw is a 15.5-mile loop. This trail is shared by horse trail #2 and is marked with brown fiberglass posts. From the Centennial Trail's French Creek Trailhead, located 3 miles from the Blue Bell Stables on CSP 4, follow the trail markers through the Horse Camp and across French Creek. The trail follows this draw to the south and meets with gravel road CSP 3. The trail turns left on CSP 3 and follows the road to CSP 4 where the trail turns left again. The trail follows CSP 4 back to the Centennial Trail's French Creek Trailhead.

Grace Coolidge Walk-in Fishing Area is 3 miles one way. This trail may be started at either the north end, located adjacent to the swimming beach at Center Lake, or the south end, on the north side of US 16A across from the Grace Coolidge Campground. The trail follows the creek for its entire length, crossing it many times. Several of the creek crossings can be challenging even when the water is low. Watch for poison ivy along this trail, especially near the stream banks.

*J***CAVES** **Jewel Cave National Monument** (605-673-2288; www.nps.gov/jeca), 13 miles west of Custer on US 16. Open year-round. Jewel Cave is the second longest cave in the world and no one has yet found the end of it. Jewel Cave was originally a 1900 mining claim but Frank and Albert Michaud soon discovered the calcite deposits were of no commercial value and began to develop the cave as a tourist attraction. In time they developed a trail to the cave and built a lodge nearby but due to the difficulty of traveling in the area, the idea went bust. Locals began campaigning for the cave to be protected and the Michaud brothers sold their claim to the government for $750. The National Park Service began administrating the site in 1933, with a park ranger sent over from Wind Cave for the summer. By 1959 only two miles of the cave had been discovered and the government was wondering whether it was worth protecting, but a pair of cave explorers, Herb and Jan Conn, came in and found an additional 15 miles of passages. Today 143 miles of the cave have been explored and there is no end in sight.

For visitors there is one cave talk available that is handicap accessible, and there are two other tours ranging from one hour to an hour and a half that require walking stairs, bending, and stooping. There are also two self-guided trails in the 1279-acre park of particular interest because the entire area was part of the August 2000 Jasper Fire. These trails give visitors a chance to discover how the forest heals itself. There are a number of ranger-guided talks on various subjects, including fire ecology. Call ahead for cave tour reservations. $8 for adults, $4 for youth for the Scenic Tour or Lantern Tour.

FAMILY FRIENDLY Blue Bell Hayride and Chuckwagon Cookout (1-800-658-3530; www.sdgfp.info/Parks/Regions/Custer/bluebellinfo.htm), Blue Bell Lodge at Custer State Park. Departure 5:30, return 8. Open mid-May through October. You don't have to be staying at Blue Bell to enjoy this event. Take an old-fashioned hayride down back roads to a mountain meadow for a chuckwagon dinner of steak or hamburger, Cowboy beans, potato salad, coleslaw, watermelon, and cookies. There is country music and sing-a-longs throughout the evening and everyone gets a souvenir bandana and cowboy hat. $40 for adults, $30 for children. Call ahead for reservations.

FISHING There are four lakes in Custer State Park (see listing under *Historic Sites*): **Legion, Stockade, Sylvan,** and **Center,** as well as **French Creek** running through the park. All are well stocked and offer great fishing, especially in the spring or early summer. Fly-fishing is very popular in the creek, but you can be just as successful with a rod and reel and a few worms. Trout is the primary game fish but there are other species, such as crappies, perch, and bass. South Dakota fishing licenses are required and are available at the general stores at Sylvan and Legion Lakes.

GOLF Rocky Knolls Golf Course (605-673-4481), US 16, Custer. This nine-hole executive course has beautiful views of the Black Hills and a nice club house for relaxing afterward. Green fees, $41 with a cart.

HIKING The following hiking trails are in Custer State Park. A map can be found at www.sdgfp.info/Parks/Regions/Custer.

Badger Clark Historic Trail is 1 mile, 0.5 mile south of US 16A on CSP 8. This trail is located behind the historic Badger Hole. The trail winds through a mixed pine, hardwood forest, and along rocky hillsides. A portion of the rock-lined trail was built by the poet himself.

Prairie Trail is a 3-mile loop along the Wildlife Loop Road, 13 miles from the State Game Lodge or 5 miles from the Blue Bell Entrance Station. This trail explores a portion of the park's rolling prairie grasslands. The trail is marked with brown fiberglass posts and rock cairns.

Sunday Gulch Trail (closed during the winter) is a 2.8-mile loop. The trailhead is reached by following the Sylvan Lake Trail behind the dam to the top of Sunday Gulch. Descending into Sunday Gulch the trail crosses the stream several times while passing over large boulders and beneath granite walls.

Sylvan Lake Shore Trail is a 1-mile loop. The trail may be started at various points along the lakeshore. This trail makes a complete loop around Sylvan Lake and is one of the easiest trails in Custer State Park.

MANY FASCINATING ROCK FORMATIONS ARE FOUND ALL OVER THE BLACK HILLS.

Lovers Leap Trail is a 3-mile loop located behind the schoolhouse (across the highway from the Peter Norbeck Visitors Center). At the highest point on this trail there is a rocky outcrop named Lover's Leap where legend has it that two Native American lovers leaped to their deaths.

Stockade Lake Trail is a 1.5-mile loop, 0.3 mile south of US 16A on Stockade Lake Drive. Beginning at the trailhead located on the southeast side of Stockade Lake the trail ascends through a ponderosa pine forest to a ridgeline.

&. **Creekside Trail** is 2 miles long, parallel to US 16A, running from the Game Lodge Campground to Grace Coolidge Campground. The trail passes by the State Game Lodge, the Peter Norbeck Visitors Center, Coolidge General Store, and the park office. You may park at any of these locations to access the trail.

French Creek Natural Area is 12 miles long, one way. Access the west end, 3 miles from Blue Bell Lodge on CSP 4; the east end, 4 miles south of the State Game Lodge on the Wildlife Loop Road. French Creek gently meanders through Custer State Park and into the French Creek gorge. Because of the uniqueness and diversity of this area, 2,200 acres surrounding the gorge has been set aside as the French Creek Natural Area. There are no marked trails through the natural area, hikers make their own way along the creek or follow paths of previous hikers. Overnight camping is only allowed within the canyon bottom. Campsites must be at least 50 feet from the stream and everything must be carried in and carried out.

Grace Coolidge Walk-In Fishing Area is 3 miles long, one way. From the south end, enter at the parking area along US 16A, opposite from Grace Coolidge Campground. From the north end, enter adjacent to swimming beach at Center Lake. This trail is nearly level and follows Grace Coolidge Creek, crossing it many times as it meanders through the valley. Crossings may be difficult any time of the year and wet feet are almost assured. The ponds and creek sides offer excellent trout fishing. In the spring and summer, wildflowers abound.

Centennial Trail This 111-mile trail spans the length of the Black Hills from Bear Butte State Park in the north to Wind Cave National Park in the South. Approximately 22 miles of the trail are located within Custer State Park. Three trailheads provide access points to Custer State Park's portion of the trail. The trail is marked with a combination of brown fiberglass posts and gray diamonds fastened to trees. This trail is also used for horseback riding and mountain biking. Ask for a brochure at the park entrance.

Harney Peak At 7,242 feet, Harney Peak is the highest point east of the Rocky Mountains and a popular hike for those in good condition. The main trailhead is in Custer State Park near the Sylvan Lake Beach, in the northwest corner of the parking lot. The hike is 7 miles, climbs 1,000 feet, and

HARNEY PEAK IS THE HIGHEST MOUNTAIN EAST OF THE ROCKIES.

takes over 5 hours. There is an old fire tower at the top and the grave of Valentine McGillycuddy, the physician who tended Crazy Horse in 1877 before he died. On a clear day the view is incredible, overlooking the entire region from mountains to plains. Remember this is in a wilderness area, no one is going to guide you, and there are no facilities so you are on your own and need to be prepared with the proper shoes, snacks, and plenty of water. Also bring along a jacket as it will be much colder or could even be snowing at the top when you get there.

NATURE PRESERVES **Black Elk Wilderness and Norbeck Wildlife Preserve** (www.fs.fed.us/r2/blackhills/maps/recguide5x.shtml). North of Custer State Park is the 13,605-acre Black Elk Wilderness Area. It is the only wilderness area in the Black Hills and home to deer, mountain goats, turkeys, coyotes, and mountain lions. Only foot and horse travel are allowed and visitors are required to self-register at the trailheads just to be on the safe side. Camping is allowed but no fires and you must bring in everything you need and walk out with everything. Pick up complete information at any ranger station before venturing into wilderness areas.

SWIMMING There are a number of great swim beaches at Custer State Park, including **Sylvan Lake, Center Lake,** and **Legion Lake**. Center Lake is probably the least frequented, so if you want to get away from the crowds on a hot day give it a try.

TRAIL RIDES ✐ **Blue Bell Stables and Trail Rides** in Custer State Park (1-888-875-0001). If you want to try horseback riding, Blue Bell is very popular and great for families. One-hour trail rides are $28 for adults, $22 for children under 12 years. Two-hour trail rides are $40 for adults, $32 for children under 12 years.

EVERY FALL THOUSANDS OF BUFFALO ARE ROUNDED UP AND SORTED IN CUSTER STATE PARK. VISITORS ARE INVITED TO JOIN IN THE FUN OF THE ROUNDUP.
South Dakota Tourism

UNIQUE ADVENTURES **Buffalo Roundup and Arts Festival** (www.sdgfp.info/Parks/Regions/Custer/round.htm). Every year some 1,500 of the Custer State Park buffalo are rounded up and driven into corrals for sorting, immunizations, and branding. Some of the buffalo are released back into the park, others are held up for auction the third Saturday in November to help control the size of the herd. Before the roundup there is an arts festival and a chili cook-off in the park. If you are in the area, in late September or early October when the roundup takes place, it is truly awe inspiring to see and feel more than 1,000 buffalo thundering across the prairie just as they did 150 years ago.

Spelunking at Jewel Cave (see listing under *Caves*) (605-673-2288, ext. 1352). This 0.67-mile, 4-hour tour involves using a hand line to climb a vertical wall and belly crawling through small passages, so you must be fit and unafraid of tight places. The park provides hard hats and lights but you must bring old clothes, a pair of boots that go above your ankle, knee pads, and a change of clothing and shoes. No one under 16 is allowed, but if you have a sense of adventure and want to see parts of the cave others don't, call for reservations at least a month in advance.

✳ Lodging

BED & BREAKFAST INNS Custer Mansion (605-673-3333; www.custer mansionbb.com), 35 Centennial Dr. This Victorian Gothic-style home was built beginning in 1890 by one Newton Tubbs, a successful potato farmer and sheep rancher. The "house that potatoes built" later served as an old folks home, a church, a preschool, and a rental home until it was converted into the first bed-and-breakfast in the Black Hills in 1988. Listed on the National Register of Historic Places, it features five nicely decorated guest rooms with private baths, each named for a song. The Shenadoah is referred to as the anniversary suite with romantic pastels and a Jacuzzi tub for soaking. The Evening Star and Mexicali are adjoining for families and feature a claw-foot tub. Breakfast includes cooked fruit and their signature Overnight French Toast, along with an assortment of coffee, tea, and juices. $80–$130 per night, with a two-night minimum stay from June 15 through August 15.

CABINS/LODGES Custer State Park: Blue Bell Lodge, State Game Lodge, Sylvan Lake Lodge, Legion Lake Lodge (1-888-875-0001; www .custerresorts.com/reservations.php). Open May 1 through October. You can spend your entire vacation in Custer State Park and there are great lodges and cabins to accommodate a couple or families. Each lodge has a restaurant and different activities available, such a trail rides, Jeep tours, and boat

or bike rentals. Rates vary from $100 per night for a room to $525 for a cabin that sleeps 14. Call ahead for reservations.

Blue Bell Lodge is the most casual of the three and with an Old West theme you'll feel completely comfortable here in a pair of jeans. These log cabins may look rustic but have all the amenities, including modern bathrooms, TV, and some have kitchenettes. The cabins accommodate three to six people so it's great for families.

The State Game Lodge has several lodging options including rooms in the historic lodge and a new motel and cabins that house three to six people. If you are planning on staying awhile, get one of the new housekeeping cabins, the larger ones include kitchens, while the smaller ones have kitchenettes.

Sylvan Lake Lodge is next to the very popular Sylvan Lake where you can fish, swim, and rent boats. Overnight options include rooms in the lodge with queen- or king-size beds, as well as one or two bedroom cabins.

Legion Lake Lodge is right on the lake and another great spot for fishing and water sports. There are a variety of cabins available to accommodate a family or a couple and some include kitchens.

CAMPING/CABINS Custer State Park (see listing in *Historic Sites*). ✐ **Flintstones Bedrock City** (605-673-4664; www.flintstonesbedrock

city.com). Open May 17 through September 1. Established in 1966 this is a very popular spot for the kids as it includes all the Flintstones characters and a Bedrock City with various stops to visit, including Fred and Wilma's house. There is also a pool, mini golf, and a drive-in restaurant where you can order a Brontoburger. Campsites begin at $21 with no hookups or $43 for cabins. If you don't want to stay over, you can visit the park and let the kids play for $9 per person.

✳ Where to Eat

EATING OUT **Custer State Park** has restaurants at all of the lodges, from casual to more formal.

Blue Bell Lodge features complete menus for all three meals. Breakfast includes Wrangler Iron Skillets such as corned-beef hash or biscuits and gravy that come with hash browns and toast. The dinner menu features steaks, buffalo, and fresh trout. There is a complete bar. $9–$25.

The State Game Lodge serves three meals a day but is more upscale with breakfast choices such as buffalo benedict and dinners including grilled elk chops and Asian duck breast. They have an extensive wine menu and offer wine pairing for each entrée. $19–$30.

Sylvan Lake Lodge serves a breakfast buffet daily, which includes eggs, Belgian waffles, potatoes, and sides. You can also order breakfast off the menu. Dinner selections include steaks, trout, pasta, and chicken Wellington. All dinners include their Harvest Salad Bar. $10–$32.

Legion Lake Lodge serves all the traditional breakfast fare including a variety of omelets. For lunch or dinner there are burgers, hot dogs, sandwiches, and salads with the all-important sides of fries and onion rings. There is also a deck menu so you can dine in your

swimsuit with burgers and hot dogs or, if you want to go back to your cabin, order a take-out pizza. $7–$14.

Baker's Bakery and Café (605-673-2253), 541 Mt. Rushmore Rd. Open for breakfast and lunch 6:30 AM–4 PM Monday through Sunday. You can pick up something at the delectable bakery case as you walk in or take a seat and order a full meal. Complete breakfasts, or homemade soups, sandwiches, and salads for lunch. $7–$9.

Elk Canyon Sports Pub & Grill (605-673-4477), 511 Mt. Rushmore Rd. Opens at 11 AM. This family restaurant features salads, sandwiches, pasta, chicken, and steak. You can also build your own burger with a beef, buffalo, or elk patty—you pick what goes on it. $6–$24.

Sage Creek Grille (605-673-2424). 611 Mt. Rushmore Rd. Open 11 AM–2 PM and 5–9 PM Monday through Saturday. Sage Creek serves fresh food from the Black Hills with a varying menu of daily specials that are a little beyond the normal café offerings. They also have a nice selection of beer and wine. $8–$19.

Purple Pie Place (605-673-4070; www.purplepieplace.com), 19 Mt. Rushmore Rd. Open 11 AM–10 PM May 1 through October 15. When it comes to homemade pie and gourmet ice cream, everyone in Custer goes to the Purple Pie Place, which is not really the name but a description of a very purple building.

✳ Selective Shopping

There are a number of tourist shops with the all-important T-shirts and postcards but downtown Custer also has some unique shops worth a visit.

A Walk in the Woods (605-673-6400; www.walkwoods.com), 506 Mt. Rushmore Rd. Open 9–9 every day. This is a lovely little shop that carries a wide variety of home decorating items. Check out the colorful tableware and glassware, as well as fun bar items like colored beer bands, so no one mixes up their bottles. They also have lighting, furniture, kitchen items, and candles as well as books, music, and lawn and garden décor. This is a great place to buy your house a present.

Claw, Antler, Hide (605-673-4345), 735 Mt. Rushmore Rd. Open 8–7 every day. This small store carries exactly what the name suggests and more: beads, furs, leathers, shells, feathers, skulls, bones, mounts, knives, sheepskins, elk and deerskin gloves, crafts, and rustic home decorations. If you are into crafts, you can pick up some fun items to work with that you may not find elsewhere.

Frontier Photos (605-673-2269; www.frontierphotos.com), 512 Mt. Rushmore Rd. Open 9–7 every day. Come in and dress up in Old West clothing for a family portrait to take

---

The Black Hills National Forest is much more than the small towns dotting it. To truly appreciate the many sights and adventures that await you, stop at the first ranger station you see (there is a large, new station on US 16 between Rapid City and Keystone) and purchase a Forest Service map of the Black Hills.

In the mid-1990s the Forest Service completed surveying and signing all the roads in the forest, so it is pretty tough to get lost, if you have a map. You may find yourself somewhere you didn't quite expect, but that's half the fun. Just use common sense and beware of water on roads, don't mess around with wild animals, don't trespass on private land, and bring along supplies like toilet paper and a cooler.

A few places that are well worth the drive include:

Flag Mountain has an old rock fire tower that provides incredible views of Reynolds Prairie, which is a large plain at the top of the hills. Take Deerfield Road toward the lake and follow County Road 308 around the lake, take a right on FSR 189, and watch for the signs.

Mystic is a Black Hills ghost town that has been preserved and has interpretive signs to explain what was what back in the day. Look up on the hills and you will also see a number of abandoned mines. Take Deerfield Road out of Hill City, then take the gravel road C138 to Mystic. The site is off C138, across from the church.

Rochford is a tiny wide spot in the road but has the coolest bar and grill in the hills, as commemorated by Jon Crane in one of his watercolors. The Moonshine Gulch is visited by hunters, bikers, and locals in the know. Make sure you leave behind a business card, hat, or some other sign of your visit, like everyone else has. There's also great fishing in the creeks along the way, but don't tell anyone. Take Deerfield Road out of Hill City, then take the gravel road C138 and pick up FSR 231 to Rochford.

home or drive your motorcycle in and dress like a cowboy on it. Frontier Photos provides the costumes and the props, you provide the people. The owner is also a fine wildlife photographer and has her work for sale at the store.

High Pine Log Furniture (605-673-2295; www.highpinelogfurniture.com), 12455 E. Hwy 16A. Open 8–5:30 Monday through Saturday, 12–5 on Sunday. These folks build furniture for every room of the house as well as cabinets from beautiful lodgepole pine. If you don't have room in the car to take something home, place an order.

Reader's Retreat (605-673-2525; www.custerbookstore.com), 607 Mt. Rushmore Rd. Open 10–8 Monday through Saturday, 11–7 Sunday. With over 100,000 titles, 70 percent from private estates, this is the bookstore for rare editions or collector's editions. If you are interested in learning more about the West and Native Americans, they have a fine selection of books to choose from. They also offer rare book searches in case you are looking for something special.

✳ Entertainment

THEATER **Black Hills Playhouse** (605-255-4141; www.blackhillsplay house.com). Since 1946 this professional theater company has produced plays and musicals in the middle of Custer State Park during the summer months. Actors and crews apply or audition to become part of the company and live in dorms onsite. Enjoy a really special experience in a historic theater in the middle of the park. Call for the performance schedule.

✳ Special Events

JUNE PRCA/GPIRA Crazy Horse Rodeo at Crazy Horse Memorial

HILL CITY

Like most of the Black Hills, Hill City began as a mining town. Tin mining was Hill City's contribution to the industry and when the mining died out, logging and tourism became the economic base.

Until 1995 Hill City rolled up the sidewalks in the winter when the tourists were no longer in town. All of that changed when noted watercolorist Jon Crane opened his gallery in Hill City. With Jon Crane came a surge of interest in the arts and numerous artists joined together to open a member-owned gallery called Artforms. From the rise of Artforms, another half dozen other galleries opened, public art went on display, and a bronze foundry moved in. Hill City is now known as the place to go for art in the Black Hills and the historic downtown buildings have been restored. It is also home to the 1880 Train, a restored steam engine that draws thousands of visitors.

Hill City calls itself the Heart of the Hills due to its central location and from Hill City it is an easy drive to Mount Rushmore, Deerfield, Pactola and Sheridan Lakes, and Keystone. Hill City is no longer just a sleepy little logging town but has become a major tourist draw and a bedroom community for Rapid City.

GUIDANCE **Hill City Chamber of Commerce** (1-800-888-1798; www.hillcitysd .com), 555 E. Main St., Hill City, SD 57745.

HILL CITY OFFERS TOURISTS MANY SHOPPING OPTIONS, INCLUDING NUMEROUS ART GALLERIES.

GETTING THERE *By car:* Hill City is 26 miles west from Rapid City on US 16.

49

HILL CITY

GETTING AROUND There is no public transportation in Hill City. Cars are essential, horses and bikes are acceptable.

MEDICAL EMERGENCY Hill City Clinic (605-574-4470), 114 E. Main St., Hill City.

MUSEUMS ✍ **Black Hills Museum of Natural History** (605-574-4505; www
.bhmnh.org), 117 Main St. Open Monday through Saturday 9–6, Sunday 10–6.
Owned by the Black Hills Institute of Geological Research, the museum has an
amazing collection of complete dinosaur skeletons and skulls, minerals, and
enough information about paleontology to make any dinosaur fan happy. You may
very well run into the founders, Neil and Pete Larson, who are infamous for their
run-in with the feds over "Sue" the T-Rex and losing her to the Chicago Field
Museum (see sidebar Who is Sue?). Not to worry, "Stan," a more complete T-Rex
that has been studied throughout the world, is on display. The museum also
includes a gift store that will complete your Christmas shopping, selling beautiful
jewelry, books, kid's toys, T-shirts, and one of the finest collections of minerals you
will find for sale anywhere. $5 for adults, $3 for juniors, and children are free.

✍ **Wade's Gold Mill** (605-574-2680), Deerfield Rd. Open 9–6 Memorial Day
through Labor Day. Turn up Deerfield Road at the Exxon Station and Wade's is on
the right. With a large assortment of
antique mining equipment and a one-
stamp gold mill, Wade's is a great place
to learn about mining and how it
affected the settlement of the hills.
The tour includes demonstrations of
gold mining and the chance to try your
hand at gold panning. Guided tours
with panning lessons: $12.50 for
adults, $9 for children.

SHERIDAN LAKE ROAD CONNECTS HILL
CITY TO PACTOLA RESERVOIR AND RUNS
ALL THE WAY TO LEAD AND DEADWOOD.
IT'S A BEAUTIFUL DRIVE.

✳ To Do

**BICYCLING George S. Mickelson
Trail**, 114 miles of rails-to-trails going
from Edgemont to Deadwood. The
trail goes through Hill City and maps
are available at most retail stores. Bike
rentals are available at **Rabbit Bicycle
Repair, Rentals and Sales** 175 Walnut St. (605-574-4302; www.rabbitbike
.com). They provide shuttle service to
various drop-off points on the trail.

**BOATING AND FISHING Sheri-
dan Lake** is located on US 385, 6
miles east of Hill City. The marina is

WHO IS SUE?

In August of 1990 the Black Hills Institute of Geological Research from Hill City was finishing up a monthlong dig near Faith, South Dakota. One of the workers, Sue Hendrickson, had been eyeing an outcropping in the distance for some time and decided to hike to it and see what was there. What was there turned out to be one of the largest, most complete T-Rex skeletons ever found and in Hendrickson's honor, it was named Sue.

The sandstone cliff where Sue was found was land held in trust for Maurice Williams, a one-quarter Native American who ranched on the Cheyenne Sioux Reservation. Pete Larson, the president of the institute told Williams that they had found something and offered him $5,000 for the remains. Williams agreed and accepted a check from Larson.

The excavation took 17 days and on September 1, 1990, the institute left the site with a 9,000-pound block containing Sue's skull and hip bones and three other trucks carrying 5 tons of rock, bones, and dirt to sift through back in Hill City.

Pete Larson and the institute announced their find to the world and Larson presented initial research on Sue to his fellow paleontologists at a meeting in October 1991. He invited other scientists to come to Hill City to research Sue and dozens eagerly signed up to do so.

In the spring of 1992, word spread that the government was looking into whether Sue had been illegally taken from federal land. On May 14, 1992 teams of FBI agents descended on tiny Hill City and had the National Guard

open May through September (605-574-2169). **Pactola Reservoir** is located on US 385 about 15 miles north of Sheridan Lake and has a marina and boat rentals. **Deerfield Lake** is located 16 miles west of Hill City on Deerfield Road. Several boat ramps are available to access the lake. These lakes are stocked and contain bass, brown, rainbow, and brook trout, perch, and crappies. Fishing is from boats or anywhere along the banks. The lakes are also busy during the winter for ice fishing. South Dakota fishing licenses are required and are available at many retail stores in the area, such as the **Heart of Hills Convenience Store** on the corner of Main Street and Deerfield Road.

There are also smaller lakes that are stocked around Hill City. **Major Lake** is in town near the football stadium and popular with families. **Newton Lake** is about 3 miles up Deerfield Road and has a nice picnic area. There are trout streams all over the area. **Spring Creek**, west of Sheridan Lake, wanders all the way to Rapid City and has many pull offs for fishing. Spring Creek also runs through Hill City and you can fish from the city park. **Castle Creek**, just north of Deerfield Lake, is also popular and a great place to catch a rainbow trout or two.

load up Sue's bones onto flatbed trucks. The town turned out in mass to protest the seizure but their pleas to "Save Sue" fell on deaf ears. In three days Sue was gone and in storage at the South Dakota School of Mines and Technology in Rapid City. Thus began the legal battle over ownership of Sue.

For three years the argument over Sue went on in federal court and in the end it was decided that Maurice Williams was the legal owner, despite his selling the fossil to the institute. He was to return the $5,000 paid to him by the institute and was free to sell the fossil to whomever he wished. Meanwhile, the Larsons faced criminal charges from all the records the government had seized and gone over with a fine-tooth comb. There were 154 charges in total and of these they were convicted of eight felonies and five misdemeanors. Pete Larson got the worst of it and ended up spending 18 months in federal prison for charges, having nothing to do with Sue, for failing to declare cash he had taken on two business trips overseas.

In October 1997, Maurice Williams became a multimillionaire when Sue sold at auction for $8.36 million. The winning bidder was the Chicago Field Museum with backing from McDonald's and Disney. Sue is on display there today.

The Black Hills Institute of Geological Research has rebounded from the loss of Sue and has since found two more T-Rexs, Stan and Duffy, as well as many other fossils. They still dream of building a world class paleontology museum in Hill City where they will have the room to display all the amazing fossils they have found over their many years of searching.

FAMILY FRIENDLY ✐ **1880 Train**
(605-574-2222; www.1880train.com), Truck Bypass. Open mid-May through mid-September. One of Hill City's biggest tourist attractions, the 1880 Train is a vintage steam engine that pulls train cars from Hill City to Keystone. The original standard gauge track was built between Hill City and Keystone in the 1890s, during the mining boom but was eventually replaced to accommodate diesel-powered engines. (Technically, the name 1880 Train is not correct but it's been called that for so long it's stuck.) The 1880 train gives riders a chance to experience what early Black Hills trains were

FAMILIES WILL ENJOY A TRIP FROM HILL CITY TO KEYSTONE ON THE 1880 TRAIN.

like and the Black Hills Central Railroad continues their work to restore old engines and cars for the world to enjoy, with a number of them on display. The views of the Black Hills are less than spectacular but the train experience is worth the ride. Round-trip tickets are $21 for adults, $12 for children.

HIKING
Deerfield Lake Loop Trail, 10 miles suitable for nonmotorized travel. Four trailheads are located around the lake. This trail takes you through Reynolds Prairie, a rather strange bare spot at the top of the hills that has been ranched by the Reynolds family for generations, with an amazing view of the lake and Harney Peak.

Deerfield to Mystic, this 6-mile trail is accessible from Kinney Canyon, which is a walk-in fishing area on Rochford Road, north of Deerfield Road. The trail connects with the Mickelson Trail to Castleton, a former mine dredging site. Check out the slag piles by Castleton Creek for garnets on slate. Nonmotorized travel only.

Flume Trail, 11 miles of trail accessible from Sheridan Lake Campground, off US 385. The trail follows much of the Rockerville Flume, which carried water 20 miles from Spring Creek west of present day Sheridan Lake, east to the placer diggings near Rockerville. The flume operated until 1885 and enabled miners to take over $20 million in gold. This trail goes through several tunnels and ends in Rockerville. This trail is moderately difficult and is for hiking only. Take a flashlight for the tunnels and adequate water.

George S. Mickelson Trail (see listing under *Bicycling*).

HUNTING During November, Hill City is full of men and women dressed in blaze orange, hunting the illusive buck. If you are not a hunter, be aware that there are many of them in the woods, especially at dawn and dusk, so dress in clothing that will make it easier for them to see you. Turkey season runs from October to December and other seasons are open for antelope, elk, and some smaller game. Licenses are required and more information is available through the State Game, Fish, and Parks Department at www.sdgfp.info/Index.htm. You can also get licenses and hunting supplies at **Hiway Hardware** (605-574-2035; www.hillcitysd .com/hiwayhardhome), on Main Street at the east end of town.

SWIM BEACHES Sheridan Lake has two swimming beaches with lifeguards. **Pactola** has one swimming beach. When the summer temperature reaches the 90s or 100s these beaches are packed with locals trying to beat the heat.

TRAIL RIDES High Country Guest Ranch (605-574-9003; www.highcountry ranch.com), 12172 Deerfield Rd. This company operates under a special use permit with the Forest Service so rides go through public land, providing a nice view of the hills, and follow along the creek where you may see the beavers at work on one of their dams. Rides range from one to three hours; the three-hour ride includes a visit to an old gold mine. $25–$50.

UNIQUE ADVENTURES Black Hills Bronze (605-574-3200; blackhillsbronze .net), 23942 Thompson Dr. Open 8–4. Ever wonder how bronze sculptures are fabricated? A wonderful new addition to the Hill City art scene, this place takes the artist's clay model and casts it in wax. The wax mold goes to Colorado for pouring the bronze, then returns to Hill City for all the finishing work on the piece. Stop in for a tour and they will be happy to show you around and explain the process in detail.

Sylvan Rocks Climbing School and Guide Service (605-484-7585; www.sylvanrocks.com). Learn to rock climb and rappel in Custer State Park and even climb Devil's Tour in Wyoming. These folks are avid climbers and provide private classes, group classes, or guided climbing. $68.50–$170 per person for beginner classes, all ages.

WINTER SPORTS ❋ Hill City is a popular snowmobile area and snowmobile rentals are available at **Deerfield Lake Resort** (605-574-2636; www.deerfieldlakeresort.com), at the west end of the lake. This is a great starting point for 350 miles of groomed and marked trails that go all the way to Spearfish or Lead and Deadwood. Snowmobilers also enjoy racing on Deerfield Lake where they can easily reach speeds approaching 100 m.p.h. Cross-country skiing is popular throughout the hills and takes place on any trail or Forest Service Road.

South Dakota Tourism

BE ON THE LOOKOUT FOR ROCK CLIMBERS IN THE BLACK HILLS, PARTICULARLY IN THE NEEDLES.

❋ Lodging

There are a number of chain motels in Hill City, including **Best Western Golden Spike** (605-574-2577), **Comfort Inn** (605-574-2100), and **Holiday Inn Express** (605-574-4040).

BED & BREAKFAST INNS **Coyote Blues Village** (1-888-253-4477; www.coyotebluesvillage.com), 23165 Horseman Ranch Rd. With six theme rooms of various sizes and three motel-size rooms, there is something for everyone at this bed-and-breakfast. Four of the rooms have private patios with hot tubs and one, the Lakota, has a whirlpool bath. Located in 30 acres

surrounded by Forest Service lands there is also plenty of privacy and quiet. There is a recreation room with a Ping-Pong table as well as a tanning bed available. $105–$150 per night.

CABINS ✄ **Creekside Country Resort** (605-574-2380; www.creeksidecountryresort.com), 12650 S. US 16. With 5 acres along Spring Creek you can pretty much fish from the front door of your cabin. All of the cabins are nicely decorated and have a kitchen, living room, dining area, bedrooms, and bathrooms. This is a great spot for families, with amenities such as mini golf, a playground, and an adjacent hamburger stand where you can have dinner or just an ice cream cone or shake. $135–$190 per night, with a three-night minimum stay.

✿ **High Country Guest Ranch** (605-574-9003; www.highcountryranch .com), 12172 Deerfield Rd. With one to seven bedrooms and cabins that will sleep up to 18, as well as camping cabins, there are accommodations to fit any family vacation at High Country. All the cabins are fully furnished, have kitchens, color TV, deck, and some have fireplaces and/or Jacuzzis. This family-owned and -operated ranch offers a full-service vacation experience including cowboy breakfasts and suppers with entertainment, trail rides, outdoor movies, hot tubs, and a heated pool. It's a large operation but seems secluded due to the location. $89–$250 per night depending on the size of the cabin.

Heart of the Hills Vacation Rentals (1-800-937-7977; www.blackhills.com/ vacation). This company brokers vacation rentals for private owners and has a variety of cabins available that sleep up to 10. Check the Web site to see what they have.

CAMPING Camping is available throughout the **Black Hills National Forest**. Fees range from $6 to $21 a night. Call 1-877-444-6777 or go to www .recreation.gov for reservations. Most campgrounds are situated near creeks, lakes, and trails, providing for recreational opportunities. On the south shore of Deerfield Lake there is **Dutchman,** which has a boat ramp and great fishing access. On the south shore of Sheridan Lake is **Sheridan Lake South**, which is good for boating and fishing. **Pactola Reservoir** also has a campground near the lake for

boating and fishing. All national forest campgrounds are managed by concessionaires and reservations are suggested during peak summer season. Dispersed camping, which is camping outside of an organized campground, is allowed in the forest as long as fires are not used. If you are going to hike into the forest to camp, remember to take what you need in, and bring everything out.

✿ **Crooked Creek Resort** (605-574-2418; www.crookedcreeksd.com), 24184 US16/385. With 11 acres directly on the main road from Hill City to Custer, with Mount Rushmore in between, you can't be more centrally located to enjoy the hills. Crooked Creek has pull-through RV sites, tent sites with shade, as well as a motel and cabins. There is a pool, playground, and arcade for the kids to enjoy, as well as a laundromat and camp store. The resort is also adjacent to the Michelson Trail so hop on for a hike. $25–$44.

✿ **Rater J Bar Ranch Campground** (605-574-2527; www.rafterj.com), 12325 Rafter J Rd. Divided into five camping areas for privacy, this large, well-maintained operation has RV and tent sites as well as cabins to choose from. With 170 acres you can choose a secluded site or one right next to the activity center. There is fishing along the creek, access to the Michelson Trail, a pool, hot tub, camp store, arcade room, horseback riding, and pancake breakfasts offered every morning. The campground is away from the main highway so it feels secluded. $29–$148.

✴ **Where to Eat**

DINING OUT The Alpine Inn (605-574-2749; www.alpineinnhillcity.com), 225 Main St. Open 11 AM–2:30 PM and 5–10 PM. This is as close to fine dining as Hill City gets and it is immensely popular throughout the region. The dinner menu is the choice of "a big steak or a little steak," or two different sizes of filet mignon, served with a half wedge of lettuce, a baked potato, and Texas toast. But save room for dessert since this is what sets the Alpine Inn apart, with 30 different choices including killer tiramisu and cheesecakes. Beer and wine are available and in the summer you can eat on the porch or come by for a traditional German lunch menu, including brats and German potato salad. Even if you get there early plan on waiting because the Alpine is that popular. Entrées $9–$11.

EATING OUT **Bumpin' Buffalo Bar and Grill** (605-574-4100), 245 Main St. Open for lunch and dinner. Housed in one of Hill City's historic downtown buildings this restaurant has a beautiful wood interior with a loft for seating and an antique bar. Steaks, burgers, and sandwiches make up this menu and they offer a good selection of beer and wine. Entrées $7–$18.

Slate Creek Grille (605-574-9422), 198 Main St. Open for breakfast, lunch, and dinner. This place has changed hands a few times, burned down and was rebuilt once, and still manages to maintain itself as a very respectable diner. Nothing fancy, but good, solid diner food with complete menus for three meals everyday. Breakfast is a sure winner with eggs, omelets, hash browns, and all the sides. There is a bar downstairs and an open mike on Saturday nights. Entrées $5–$15.

Route 16 Diner and Pizzeria (605-574-3905), 417 Main St. Open for lunch and dinner. With a 1950s theme in the décor and waitresses' outfits, this diner serves good pizza, good hamburgers, and sandwiches, and

superthick shakes. Nothing spectacular but you will get your money's worth. Entrées $5–$15.

✳ Selective Shopping

Artforms (605-574-4894; artforms .smugmug.com), 280 Main St. Open 9–8:30 daily. A member-owned gallery, Artforms shows and sells the work of 30 local artists. As a cooperative, the members not only show their work but work at the gallery so there is always someone on hand that knows the artists and can talk to you about what they do. You will find sculpture, pottery, painting, jewelry, and various crafts including wood and glass. Prices are very reasonable as there is no "middle man," making this a great place to buy original art.

Granite Sports (605-574-2121), 201 Main St. Open 10–7. Granite Sports is owned and operated by people who love the outdoors and are all experienced rock climbers and hikers. They sell high-end outdoor apparel, hiking and climbing shoes, and equipment with an emphasis on rock climbing. With name brands like Patagonia, Montrail, and Black Diamond you will find only the best gear available. They also carry maps and guidebooks for

A HILL CITY FAVORITE, THE ALPINE INN OFFERS LUNCH AND DINNER WITH A GERMAN FLAIR.

ROCKHOUNDING IN THE BLACK HILLS

The Black Hills are considered one of five "best places" in the United States for its variety of minerals. The state mineral is rose quartz. There is also mica, feldspar, and tourmaline, and all are included in the pegmatites that surround the Harney Peak granite. There are 24,000 pegmatite intrusions in the Black Hills as old as 1,700 million years. As the Black Hills have eroded, and exposed the granite dome, these intrusions have also been exposed.

At the base of the hills there is gypsum and agate. The state gemstone is Fairburn Agate found in the grasslands around Kadoka, Interior, and Fairburn. Teepee Canyon agate is found in Teepee Canyon near the Wyoming border.

While hiking and exploring the Black Hills pay special attention to any outcroppings, or exposed road cuts, and you will find quartz, pegmatites, or conglomerates with numerous minerals melded together. Rock collecting in small amounts for personal use is allowed in the Black Hills National Forest but not digging or excavating. Recreational gold panning is allowed in some locations, so contact the local Forest Service office for more information on locations and rules. Metal detectors are allowed, as long as you don't dig holes. Federal law prohibits the collection of fossils. Make sure you are on federal land or ask the landowner for permission to collect.

There are numerous old mines throughout the Black Hills and the vast majority are on private land. Most are unsafe so landowners will not grant permission to explore them.

There are rock shops in most communities so stop in and talk to the experts.

Ken's Minerals (605-673-4935), 12372 US 16A, Custer
Scott's Rock Shop (605-673-4859), 1020 Mt. Rushmore Rd., Custer
Dakota Stone (605-574-2760), 23863 Palmer Gulch, Hill City
The Rock Shed (605-666-4813), 515 First St., Keystone
Earth Treasures (605-666-5222), 409 First St., Keystone

hiking and climbing. Check the back of the store where sale racks can often be found.

Jon Crane Gallery (1-888-948-1948; www.joncranewatercolors.com), 256 Main St. Open 9–7 Monday through Thursday and Friday, 9–8 Saturday, and 11–4 Sunday. Jon Crane is one of the best-known and most beloved artists in the Midwest and virtually everyone in the Black Hills has at least one Jon Crane print in their home. Crane's work is transparent watercolor on paper and is a realistic representation of Midwest and Black Hills scenes including landscapes, farms, cabins, old mines, and trout streams. His originals sell for thousands of dollars but, being a shrewd businessman, Crane reproduces his work in prints of various sizes. At his Hill City gallery just about everyone can afford a print with a mat and frame.

Mistletoe Ranch (605-574-4197), 23835 US 16. All things Christmas, all year-round! These folks have been so successful with the Christmas theme that they have added on to the original historic home a number of times. They have ornaments, trees, stockings, and collectibles, like Department 56—anything you could possibly want for Christmas.

Prairie Berry Winery (605-574-3898; prairieberry.com), 23837 US 385. Open 10–7 Monday through Saturday, 12–5 Sunday. This family has been in South Dakota since the 1870s when great-great-grandma first made wine from the "prairie berries" she found growing nearby. The winery moved to Rapid City in 1998, then Hill City in 2004 for more space and a larger tasting area and retail area. Their 15 wine varieties include chokecherry, buffalo berry, rhubarb, and currants. They offer a tasting room as well as a patio with a light menu of cheeses, meats, and sandwiches, such the vegetarian panini with herbed goat cheese, olive tapinade, red peppers, and red onions, to enjoy with their wine.

Scribes Hut and d'Italiano Coffee Garden (605-574-3288; www.scribes hut.com), 205 Main St. Open 9–6:30 daily. This is a great place for fine coffee and there is generally a line out the door. Two businesses in one small space, they also have a nice line of books about the Black Hills and the West and magazines and offer business services like copying and office supplies.

Warrior's Work and Ben West Gallery (605-574-4954; www.leather framegallery.com), 277 Main St. Open Monday through Saturday 9–6, Sunday 11–4. If you like Western or Native American art, this is the place to visit. This gallery represents the work of well-known contemporary artists and sells originals as well as giclée prints. The owner also makes custom leather frames that are very unique and beautiful. Some are on display or you can order a frame to match the artwork you buy or already have.

KEYSTONE AND
MOUNT RUSHMORE

In the 1880s Keystone sprung up as a gold-mining town along the banks of Battle Creek. The Holy Terror Gold Mine and the Big Thunder Gold Mine were some of the many mines that came and went during Keystone's heydays. Portions of old Keystone still remain and can be visited, such as Halley's General Store, which was established in 1885, or the old Keystone schoolhouse, now a museum that houses displays from the early days. When gold mining ended, Keystone turned to mining pegmatites for minerals such as mica, feldspar, spodumene, and quartz. Some of the Keystone mines are known for producing amazing specimens of these minerals.

Then along came sculptor Gutzon Borglum with the notion of carving a massive monument for America in the Black Hills. The carving began in 1927 and continued until Borglum's death in 1941, employing Keystone miners through the Depression. Every year 3 million visitors come to Mount Rushmore to marvel at their accomplishment.

THE OLD KEYSTONE SCHOOL IS NOW A LOCAL HISTORY MUSEUM, INCLUDING THE MEMORABILIA OF CARRIE INGALLS.

Today Keystone has a permanent population of around 250 people that swells dramatically in the summer months as seasonal workers and tourists come to town. Stores, motels, and restaurants that are closed eight months during the year, stock up with new supplies for another season of greeting visitors. Everyone comes through Keystone on the way to Mount Rushmore, a good place to stop to eat and buy some souvenirs. But there is more to do and see in Keystone than just Mount Rushmore. There are outdoor activities like hiking, biking, and fishing. There are historic sites, caves, the 1880 Train, and a tramway with incredible views. Drive through on the way to Mount Rushmore, but stop for awhile and enjoy the hospitality and history of Keystone.

GUIDANCE **Keystone Chamber of Commerce** (1-800-456-3345; www.keystone chamber.com), 110 Swanzey St., Keystone, SD 57751.

GETTING THERE *By car:* Keystone is 22 miles southwest of Rapid City on US 16.

GETTING AROUND There is no public transportation in Keystone or to Mount Rushmore.

MEDICAL EMERGENCIES **Rapid City Regional Hospital** (605-719-1000), 333 Fairmont Blvd., Rapid City, SD 57702.

❋ To See

HISTORIC SITES **Mt. Rushmore National Monument** (605-574-2515; www .nps.gov/moru), On SD 244, follow the signs from Keystone. Open all year, 7 days a week. Summer hours 8–10; winter hours 8–5. Yes, Mount Rushmore is as spectacular and awe inspiring as you may have heard and well worth the visit. Plan on spending enough time to not just see the carving but to visit the various exhibits that explain how the sculpture was created, as it is an astonishing story. Every night in the months of May through September the National Park Service presents a lighting program. The program begins at 9 PM, lasts about 20 minutes, and includes a film, a short talk, and the lighting of the monument. There is a restaurant at the park and a nice gift shop, so take your time and enjoy the experience. $10 parking fee good for one year.

MUSEUMS ❀ ✿ **Old Town Keystone Walking Tour** (605-255-5280; www.key stonechamber.com), Keystone Historical Society, 410 Third St. There are 19 stops on this very interesting tour that includes buildings from the 1880s, several mines,

STILL OPERATING AS A GENERAL STORE, HALLEY'S IS IN ONE OF KEYSTONE'S OLDEST BUILDINGS.

and the Historical Society's Museum in the old schoolhouse. The museum includes memorabilia of Carrie Ingalls (Laura Ingalls Wilder's sister), who lived in Keystone for many years. There is also the James Langer's Gem and Mineral Collection. The people who operate and work at this museum are very knowledgeable about the history of the area and can provide you with lots of interesting information. There are also extensive archives should you want to research your own connection to the area. Free.

✦ ♿ **Big Thunder Gold Mine Mining Museum** (1-800-341-3917; www.big thundermine.com), Swanzey St. Open 9–6 May 1 through October 15. One of the few old mines that have been kept in good enough condition to serve as a tourist site, the Big Thunder began operation in 1882 but it never really panned out. Today there is renewed interest in the mine and rights have been sold to explore below the 300-foot level for possible gold mining exploration. The museum contains a large collection of mining equipment dating back to the mine's beginnings, as well as a display of an original assay office where miners sold their gold. Tours of the mine and gold panning are also available, giving visitors a look at the mining industry of the past. The tour and gold panning cost $21 per adult and $18 for children; the museum is free.

✦ **National Presidential Wax Museum** (605-666-4455; www.presidentialwax museum.com), SD 16A. Open April 1 through October 31. Forty-one of the past presidents are immortalized in wax and placed in a historical setting in this museum. There is information about each president, providing an educational experience for the entire family. There is an 18-hole mini golf course, snack bar, and gift shop adjacent to the museum. $10 for adults, $8 seniors, $7 for children.

♿ **Rushmore Borglum Center** (605-666-448; www.rushmoreborglum.com), Winter St. Open May 1 through October 1. Gutzon Borglum was a renowned sculptor before he took on the carving of Mount Rushmore at the age of 60. This museum has an extensive collection of his work as well as insight into the creation of Mount Rushmore, including a life-size replica of one of the eyes so you can really appreciate the scale of the carving. There is also a movie about the carving of Mount Rushmore, which truly rounds out a visit to the memorial. $7 for adults, $3 for children.

SCENIC DRIVES **Peter Norbeck Scenic Byway**. From Keystone take SD 244. This scenic drive covers 68 miles and takes over 4 hours to complete but it is not necessary to drive the entire length as many people get on and off it when traveling from Keystone to Custer, or to Custer State

LOOK FOR MOUNTAIN GOATS HANGING OFF THE EDGE OF HILLS, ESPECIALLY AROUND MOUNT RUSHMORE.

South Dakota Tourism

Park. The byway encompasses the Needles Highway, Iron Mountain Road, the Wildlife Loop in Custer State Park, and other areas that can be driven in parts. For more details see the Custer chapter, under *Scenic Drives*.

✳ To Do

CAVES **Beautiful Rushmore Cave** (1-800-400-6194; www.beautifulrushmore cave.com), 5 miles east of Keystone on SD 40. Open June through August 8–8 and May, September, and October 9–5. Discovered in the 1870s tours in this cave began in 1952 by kerosene lantern. Still family-owned and -operated they now have all the modern conveniences and offer one-hour tours on maintained walkways. Photography is encouraged. $9 for adults, $5 for children.

FAMILY FRIENDLY ♨ **Rushmore Tramway and President's Alpine Slide** (605-666-4478; www.rushmorealpineslide.com), 203 Cemetery Rd., Keystone. Open Memorial Day weekend through the summer. Ride a chair lift to the top of a hill overlooking Keystone and Mount Rushmore for the views but the fun really begins on the way down when you then hop on a wheeled sled and ride down the hill on a special track. Two tracks run side by side so you can race your friends and family. It's fast and fun for all ages. $15 for adults, $4 for children.

✳ Lodging

There are numerous chain and locally owned motels in Keystone. It is wise to book ahead as Keystone is a popular visitor location. The Keystone Chamber maintains a list of their members at www.keystonechamber.com/hotel motel.html

CAMPING/CABINS **Kemps Kamp** (1-888-466-6282; www.kempskamp .com), 1.5 miles west of Keystone, on County Road 323. Open mid-May through Labor Day. This is a family-owned, well-maintained campground that is adjacent to a creek and has cabins, tents, and RV sites. There is also a pool, showers, coin laundry, and satellite TV. They are always busy so book ahead. Cabins range from $69–$99, camping from $20–$33.

RESORTS/LODGES **K Bar S Lodge** (1-866-522-7724; kbarslodge.com), 434 Old Hill City Rd. New in 2006, this lodge has 64 rooms, some with private decks. While mostly catering to bus tours, it is also open to individuals and

families. They are located on 45 beautiful, private acres and offer a free breakfast. $99–$149.

Mt. Rushmore President's View Resort (1-800-504-3210; www.mtrush moreresorts.com), 160 Hwy. 16A. This place describes itself as fine economy lodging for the family and features an indoor heated pool for some family fun. Some rooms have balconies with views of Mount Rushmore. $110–$169.

Mt. Rushmore White House Resort (1-866-996-6835; www.mtrushmore resorts.com), 115 Swanzey St. This hotel has been rebuilt since a fire in 2003 destroyed several downtown businesses, including the White House. Nice benefits here include the indoor pool and a very convenient location next to the downtown boardwalk. $119–$169.

✳ Where to Eat

DINING OUT **Powder House Lodge** (1-800-321-0692; www.powder houselodge.com/restaurant.htm) On

US 16A as you enter Keystone. Open 7 AM–9 PM. A modern log building, the Powder House is appropriate for families or couples. Known for their prime rib, the menu also includes fish, pasta, steaks, buffalo, and sandwiches, serves cocktails, and has a good selection of wine. Entrées $9–$21.

Ruby House (605-666-4274; www .historicrubyhouse.com) 126 Winter St. Open daily 11–9. The Ruby House is styled as an Old West Saloon and restaurant, with lots of antiques on the walls with a great collection of antique guns. The food is very good, as is the service, and there is dining on the front deck overlooking the main street. The menu is heavy on beef and buffalo but also includes dinner salads, pasta, and chicken entrées. It can be very crowded during the summer and impossible to get a seat during the Sturgis Rally. There is also a great bar, the Red Garter Saloon, complete with waitresses in period costumes. Dinner entrées range from $12–$26.

EATING OUT There are a number of fast-food restaurants and small diners in Keystone. Just a walk downtown may peak your appetite.

Ariba Mexican Grill (605-666-4733; www.blackhillsarriba.com), 221 Swanzey St. Open for lunch and dinner 11:30–9:30. The menu features burritos, tacos, fajitas, and chimichangas, but there are also burgers, vegetarian selections, and a nice kids, menu. If you need a break from South Dakota beef, this is the place. Beer, wine, and margaritas are also available. Entrées $7–$15.

✳ Selective Shopping

Keystone has tourist shops from one end of town to the other. If you want souvenirs, this is the place to get them. In Keystone many stores have Black Hills Gold jewelry, making it a good place to comparison shop.

Black Hills Glassblowers (605-666-4542), 901 Old Hill City Rd. Open Monday through Saturday 9–5, Sunday 11–5. Blown glass creations are made onsite by the owners and they sell what they make, including vases, bowls, and decorative pieces. Get there at the right time and you can watch them in action.

Iron Creek Leather and Glass (605-666-4732; www.ironcreekleather.com), 126 Winter St. Open 9–9 daily. For

THE RUBY HOUSE IS A POPULAR RESTAURANT AND LOUNGE WITH AN OLD WEST THEME.

INTERESTING FACTS ABOUT MOUNT RUSHMORE

The name "Mount Rushmore" actually refers to the mountain the carving is on. The name of the monument is "Shrine of Democracy."

Mount Rushmore was named for a New York attorney, Charles E. Rushmore.

The mountain is 5,500 feet above sea level.

The four presidents on Mount Rushmore were chosen because they "commemorate the founding, growth, preservation, and development to the United States."

The presidents were originally intended to be full figures.

The carving of Jefferson was originally begun to the left of Washington. Due to bad rock it had to be blown off and recarved.

Each president's head is 6 stories high.

The president's eyes are 11 feet across, their noses are 20 feet long, and their mouths are 18 feet wide.

Over 800 million pounds of rock were removed in the carving of the mountain.

Workers climbed 506 steps to the top of the mountain every day.

Blasting was done, when the weather permitted, each day at noon and 4 PM.

Not a single person died while working on the mountain.

Work on the mountain took place over 14 years, of which only 6 were devoted to carving. It took so long because of constantly seeking funding for the project.

There is a 50-foot tunnel behind Mount Rushmore that was envisioned as a Hall of Records where copies of important U.S. documents would be stored. The hall was never completed. In 1998, at the urging of Borglum's family, a repository of records was placed at the front of the Hall of Records. A titanium vault was placed inside the granite floor, which contains a teakwood box that stores 16 porcelain panels.

fine leather goods this is the place. They have Western and Southwestern-style shirts and jackets, as well as all things biker, including leather jackets and chaps from the Jack Daniels Rider Collection. With a nice assortment of Native American-made silver jewelry you can pick up a little "bling" or find a gift from their selection of hand-blown glass.

The Rock Shed (605-666-4813; www.therockshed.com), 515 First St. Open Monday through Saturday 9–6, Sunday 1–6. A rock and mineral shop featuring rough-cut rock, landscaping rock, finished jewelry, books, and lapidary supplies for the rock hound. If you are an experienced rock hound or just getting started, the folks here will be able to answer your questions about where to find the best stuff in the hills.

Rushmore Mountain Taffy Shop
(605-666-4430; www.rushmore
mountaintaffy.com), 203 Winter St.
Open 8 AM–9 PM daily. If you like taffy
you will love this place because they
make it fresh and you can watch the
pulling machine right through the front
windows. They use no preservatives
and have over 30 flavors to choose
from, including some fairly unique
ones like Buttered Popcorn and Margarita. They also have sugar-free varieties of taffy and other confections,
such as brittles, fudges, and caramels.

✳ Special Events

JULY **Fourth of July Fireworks at
Mount Rushmore.** One of the top
three fireworks displays in the country,
this spectacular show takes place on
July 3. If you plan on going, start very
early as traffic and parking can be a
nightmare, or find a place a little further away with an unobstructed view
toward the mountain. Some years the
fireworks have been canceled or
rescheduled due to weather or fire
danger so check before you go.

RAPID CITY

Located on the eastern edge of the Black Hills, Rapid City is the second largest city in South Dakota. Named for Rapid Creek that runs through town, Rapid City was founded in 1876 by a group of prospectors that had come to the hills in search of gold. Today Rapid City is the center of commerce, education, and transportation for the region and people travel here from the entire eastern part of South Dakota, Nebraska, North Dakota, and western Wyoming to shop, visit the hospital, or catch an airplane. Rapid City is also home to Ellsworth Air Force Base, one of two bases housing B-1 bombers, planes that have had major roles in Afghanistan and the Iraq War.

Tourism is Rapid City's economic base as hundreds of thousands of visitors stay in or pass through on the way to the Black Hills and Mount Rushmore. The downtown area is full of beautiful historic buildings and a collection of life-size, bronze statues of American presidents.

THE AMERICAN PRESIDENTS ARE REPRE-SENTED IN LIFE SIZE-BRONZE STATUES THROUGHOUT DOWNTOWN RAPID CITY.

A system of parks runs through the middle of Rapid City, following the course of the creek. These green spaces were developed after a 1972 flash flood of Rapid Creek ripped through town and cost 200 lives. Building is not allowed along the creek to avoid the same kind of disaster.

Rapid City is a friendly town with solid Midwestern values and fairly representative of South Dakota as a whole. It's a great base of operations for exploring the hills and there is a lot to do. Rapid City is definitely worth a few days of individual attention.

GUIDANCE **Rapid City Convention Visitors and Visitors Bureau** (1-800-427-3223; www.visitrapidcity.com).

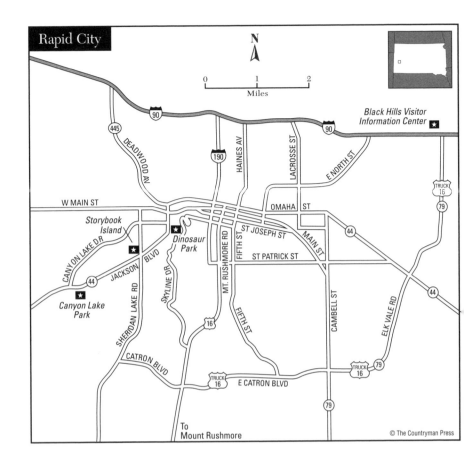

Rapid City

Black Hills Visitor Information Center

Storybook Island
Dinosaur Park
Canyon Lake Park

To Mount Rushmore

© The Countryman Press

Black Hills Visitor Information Center (605-355-3700; www.black hillsbadlands.com), 1851 Discovery Circle or I-90, exit 61. Well staffed by folks who know the area and can offer you personal assistance.

RIDE THE RAPID CITY TROLLEY TO GET TO ALL THE SIGHTS IN DOWNTOWN.

GETTING THERE *By air:* Rapid City Regional Airport has service from United Express, Northwest, Delta, Allegiant, and Frontier airlines. *By car:* via I-90 east to west, SD 79 intersects Rapid City north to south.

GETTING AROUND There are rental car agencies at Rapid City Regional Airport. Rapid City also has city buses and schedules are available at www .rapidride.org/rapid-ride. During the summer a trolley runs through downtown Rapid City offering free rides. Information on the schedule can be found at the Rapid Ride Web site above or look for trolley stops along the main downtown streets.

MEDICAL EMERGENCIES Rapid City Regional Hospital (605-719-1000), 333 Fairmont Blvd., Rapid City.

✷ To See

CULTURAL SITES ✿ **Dahl Arts Center** (605-394-4101; www.thedahl.org); 713 Seventh St. Open 9–5 Monday through Saturday. The Dahl is the center of art in Rapid City and sponsors events and classes for the community. There are two galleries with changing exhibits, as well as a theater with a variety of performances. Drop in and see what's showing, check their Web site, or call for performance schedules. Free.

FOR FAMILIES ✔ **Bear Country U.S.A.** (605-343-2290; www.bearcountry usa.com); 13820 US 16. Open 8–6 June through August. With bears, wolves, elk, and buffalo along the 3-mile road there is a lot of wildlife to see at Bear Country. Some of the animals are in enclosures and some will be wandering the road and you'll have to wait for them to move before you drive through. If you have never seen these animals up close, it is a fun experience. But the best part of the park is after you leave your car and go to Babyland where the bear cubs and other park offspring are kept. Baby bears are beyond cute and you'll end up spending a lot of time watching and taking pictures of them wrestling, climbing trees, and running about. Bear Country also has a great gift shop with all sorts of wildlife gifts, T-shirts, and stuffed animals, as well as a snack bar. During the motorcycle rally, cars are available for use by bikers because no matter how tough you are it's never a good idea to ride up to a bear on a motorcycle. $13 for adults, $11 for seniors, $7 for children, or $50 maximum per vehicle.

✿ ✔ **Cleghorn Springs Fish Hatchery** (605-394-2391; www.sdgfp.info/ Wildlife), SD 44, west of the Rapid City limit. Open Memorial Day through Labor Day. Newly renovated to better raise trout for stocking area streams and lakes, the hatchery offers the public opportunities to learn about the harmful and beneficial human actions on streams and the watershed at their interpretive center. You can also wander around and check out concrete raceways full of trout that will someday be released into the wild. It's a very informative stop and a popular school field-trip site. Free.

✔ **Cosmos Mystery Area** (605-343-9802; www.cosmosmysteryarea.com) 17 miles south of Rapid City on SD

BEAR COUNTRY U.S.A. IS A DRIVE-THROUGH WILDLIFE PARK AND HOME TO MANY ANIMALS, INCLUDING BEARS, ELK, WOLVES, COYOTES, AND DEER.

Bear Country USA

16. Open 7–dusk June through August. Cosmos offers a 30-minute tour with demonstrations designed to show the power of the Cosmos "force." People seem to change heights on level platforms and water flows uphill, which is good for lots of laughs. There is also a snack bar and gift shop on site. $9 for ages 12 and older, under age 12 is free with an adult.

Dinosaur Park (605-343-8687) Skyline Dr. Open year-round, concessions available in the summer. You can't help but notice a bright green brontosaurus on a ridge overlooking the Baken Park area of Rapid City. Actually there are seven life-size concrete dinosaurs up there and they have been there since their creation in 1936. Not exactly a paleontology exhibit but they are cute and very popular with kids for climbing. For adults the view of the city is really terrific from Skyline Drive. Free.

Flying T Chuckwagon Supper and Show (605-342-1905; www.flyingt.com) 8971 US 16. Open at 3 for tickets, dinner at 6:30. Put on your jeans and cowboy boots and get ready for some foot-stomping fun! The Flying T puts on a complete chuckwagon supper of beans, BBQ, biscuits, spice cake, and drinks followed by a show of old-time country western and bluegrass. Very big with bus tours, they will have you singing and clapping along so there are certainly worse ways to spend an evening. $18 for adults, $17 for seniors, $9 for ages 5–12, $4.50 for ages under 5.

Old MacDonald's Farm (605-737-4815; www.oldmacsfarm.blackhills.com) 23691 Busted Five Ct., off US 16 south of Rapid City. Open 9–6 May 3 through Labor Day. A large petting zoo with a farm theme, the kids can feed the animals, take a train or pony ride, watch pig races, and play on the playground. Good family entertainment, the kids will especially have a great time. There is a snack barn and gift shop as well. $8 for adults, $7 for seniors, $5 for ages 2–12, free for ages under 2.

Reptile Gardens (605-342-5873; www.reptile-gardens.com) US 16, 5 miles south of Rapid City. Open 8–7 April through December. Reptile Gardens has been open and run by the same family since 1937. They started out with a few snakes, including one rattlesnake the originator liked to keep under his hat and today they do wildlife rehabilitation, shows with birds, alligators, and snakes, and have a tropical garden under a dome where the animals slither and fly freely with you. They also have a famous Galapagos turtle, Methuselah, that was born in 1881 and every year they have a birthday celebration for him. If you don't have a snake phobia, Reptile Gardens is a lot of entertainment for the money. Check out their massive gift shop, and concessions are available. $12 for adults, $7 for ages 5–12, and free for ages 4 and under.

Storybook Island (605-342-6357; www.storybookisland.com) 1301 Sheridan Lake Rd. Open 9–7 Memorial Day through Labor Day. This 4-acre park was created by the Rapid City Rotary Club in 1959 and, with support from the city and the Rotary, it remains a free attraction that kids love. With a nursery-rhyme theme throughout there is playground equipment and a train, offering a great place for parents to relax while the kids run off some excess energy. There is also a children's theater that does shows in the summer, so call for the schedule. Located adjacent to one of the city parks on Rapid Creek, bring along a picnic and spend a day. Free.

HISTORIC SITES **City of Presidents Information Center** (605-484-2162) Corner of Main and Seventh St. Throughout the downtown area of Rapid City

STORYBOOK ISLAND IS A WONDERFUL PLACE FOR THE KIDS TO RIDE AND PLAY.

there are very impressive life-size bronze statues of the U.S. presidents. The intent of the project was to foster tourism and it has been a nice addition to downtown Rapid City. Take plenty of pictures of you and the family with your favorites. This is also popular with the locals who are known to do the same on special occasions, like proms. To get complete information on this project and the various locations, stop by the information center.

MUSEUMS ⋔ **The Journey Museum** (605-394-6923; www.journeymuseum .org), 222 New York St. Open 9–5 Memorial Day through Labor Day; off-season 1–5 Monday through Saturday. This city sponsored museum begins your journey with the formation of the Black Hills through a large screen movie presentation. As you move through the exhibits you learn about the fossils of the area, the history of the Native Americans, and the settlement of the Black Hills through displays and artifacts. They also have galleries that feature rotating art exhibits. $7 for adults, $6 for seniors, $5 for ages 11–17, free for ages under 10.

Museum of Geology (1-800-544-8162; www.sdsmt.edu/services/museum), 501 Joseph St., on the campus of the South Dakota School of Mines and Technology. Open in the summer 8–6 Monday through Saturday and 12–6 Sunday; in winter 8–5 Monday through Friday, 9–4 Saturday, and 1–4 Sunday. This is one of the best deals in town if you or the kids love dinosaurs, fossils, or minerals. Part of the paleontology and geology departments in the School of Mines, the museum offers displays of complete fossil skeletons and skulls, many collected by students and professors from the school. The museum also has an awesome mineral collection, including many that are fluorescent. Free.

❦ **South Dakota Air and Space Museum** (605-385-5189; www.sdairandspace museum.com), at Ellsworth Air Force Base, 7 miles east of Rapid City off I-90. Open year-round. This museum has a nice collection of Air Force planes and plenty of history about the evolution of air and space travel. Displays include 25 aircraft, including a B-1 Lancer, and four missiles, including a Minuteman II, with a mock up of the control center for one of the missiles. There are also numerous displays of aviation history and a great gift shop for air and space fans. Free.

✳ To Do

BICYCLING **Storm Mountain** This trail offers 10 miles of single track mountain biking with steep climbs and descents. Take US 16 south of Rapid City 11.3 miles. Turn right on Silver Mountain Road and go 0.15 miles to the Flume Trail parking lot on the right.

Loop 15 This is a 15.5-mile mountain bike ride through fairly flat terrain. Travel south on Sheridan Lake Road to mile marker 8. Turn right onto Victoria Lake Road. and go 0.5 miles. Park at the "No Motorized Vehicles" gate and walk down into the meadow and pick up the access trail that runs along the right edge. Take this just over 0.1 miles to the start.

Rapid City Parks There are 13.5 miles of paved walking and biking paths that follow along Rapid Creek. Stop at any park area, unload your bike, and start riding.

CAVES ☂ **Crystal Cave Park** (605-342-8008; www.southdakotacaves.com/ crystal_cave.htm), 7700 Nameless Cave Rd. Open 9–7 May through September. This cave is 80 percent covered with formations and, while it is privately owned, 40-minute tours are offered. Discovered in the 1880s by early American settlers, it was known to Native Americans for hundreds of years, and though the cave has been explored, no one has found the end. $8 per person.

☂ **Sitting Bull Crystal Caverns** (605-342-2777; www.sittingbullcrystalcave.com), 13745 Mt. Rushmore Rd. Open 8–8 June through August; 8–6 May and September. This cave is owned by one of Rapid City's founding families, the Duhamel family, who is still very active in the city. They began developing the cave and running tours shortly after it was discovered in 1929. The tours run around 45 minutes long, don't forget a jacket since it's only 45 degrees inside. $9 for adults, $5 for children ages 7–12.

FAMILY FRIENDLY ⚘ **Black Hills Maze** (605-343-5439; www.blackhillsmaze .com), US 16 south of Rapid City. Open 8:30 AM–9 PM May 1 through September 30. Tell your family or friends to get lost at this attraction featuring a mile-long maze. If you would prefer, they also have bank shot basketball, batting cages, a climbing mountain, and water wars, otherwise known as shooting your friends with water cannons. It's great fun for the family, especially competitive siblings. $8 for the maze, packages range from $15–$18.

☂ ⚘ **Flags and Wheels Indoor Racing** (605-341-2186; www.flagsandwheels .com), 405 12th St. Open 4–10 Tuesday through Friday, 12–10 Saturday, 6–10 Sunday. Great for a rainy day, this indoor center has go-kart racing, paintball, lazar tag, slot cars, and bumper cars. Prices vary depending on activity.

⚘ **Pirates Cove Adventure Golf** (605-343-8540; www.piratescove.net), 500 LaCrosse St. Open 9–10 May through mid-October. A pirate-theme mini golf course featuring waterfalls, shipwrecks, and a lagoon. Fun for families or kids' parties. $6–$7 per person.

↑ ♂ **Putz and Glo** (605-716-1230; www.putznglo.com), US 16. The latest entry in the mini golf arena, this place does mini golf indoors and under black lights. All the rage for birthday parties and, since it's indoors, it's fun even on a rainy day. $8.50 for adults, $7.50 for kids.

♂ **Ranch Amusement Park** (1-877-302-3321; ranchamusementpark.com), 6303 US 16. Open 10–8 Memorial Day through Labor Day. The ranch has been open for a long time and is continually popular with kids and families. The ranch features go-karts, bumper boats, mini golf, rock climbing, and an arcade. There is a snack bar available. Family Fun Packages range from $25–$85 for a variety of rides and games.

♂ **Rushmore Waterslide Park** (605-343-8962; www.rushmorewaterslide.com) 1715 Catron Blvd. Open 10–7 Memorial Day through Labor Day, weather permitting. When the weather is hot this place is packed with families enjoying 10 slides, a River Run, and a kiddie pool. There is a video arcade, free mini golf, snack bar, hot tub, and picnic area, so bring some food and stay all day. $8–$14 per person.

♂ ↑ **Watiki Indoor Waterpark Resort** (605-718-9600; www.watikiwaterpark .com) 1314 North Elk Vale Rd., right off the interstate at exit 61. Open 9–9 year-round. This new indoor waterpark has 30,000 square feet and six slides, an inner tube ride, numerous play areas, and a snack bar. It is adjoined to two motels, La Quinta and Fairfield Inn. $15 per person.

FISHING **Canyon Lake Park** (605-394-4175), Canyon Lake Dr. and Jackson Blvd. Open year-round, free. One of the many parks in Rapid City but, arguably, one of the nicest for trout fishing at **Canyon Lake**. A South Dakota fishing license is required. **Rapid Creek** runs through town and heads west out of town along SD 44. The creek is stocked with trout and can be fished anywhere it is accessible. There are restrictions on the creek east of **Pactola Reservoir** for catch and release so be sure and consult the South Dakota fishing guide you will receive when buying a fishing license. Licenses are available at **Hardware Hank**, 770 Mt. View Road, **Wal-Mart**, 1200 La Crosse Street, **Ace Hardware**, 1724 West Main, and other hardware and sporting goods stores.

GOLF There are lots of good golf courses in Rapid City, some with 18 holes and some with 9 holes. You will have no trouble finding one to fit your skill level and interest.

Meadowbrook (605-394-4191; www.golfatmeadowbrook.com), 3625 Jackson Blvd. This city-owned course is very popular for its layout and price. At over 7,100 yards in total length, the course is a challenge for even the best of players. The 18 holes are located along Rapid Creek, which comes into play at five of the holes. Green fees are $37.

Hart Ranch (605-341-5703), 23645 Clubhouse Dr. This award-winning 18-hole course provides a challenge for a scratch golfer but allows the novice to have a memorable golfing experience. Set in a beautiful Black Hills valley just outside of Rapid City. Green fees range from $39–$50.

Golf Club at Red Rock (605-718-4710; www.golfclubatredrock.com), 6520 Birkdale Dr. Eighteen holes. Red Rocks is a new development in Rapid City and the

18-hole golf course is described as "embedded in the Black Hills terrain, the course features lush fairways, surrounded by native fescue grasses and tall ponderosa pine trees." Green fees are $49.

Executive (605-394-4124; www.rcgov.org/parks_recreation/golf), 200 12th St. This 9-hole course is a bargain and has flat terrain that makes it an easy course to walk. Mature trees line the fairways, and there are water hazards that come into play on some holes. Green fees are $11.

Fountain Springs (605-342-4653), 1750 Fountain Plaza Dr. This 9-hole, 3,000-yard, par-35 course has a variety of water features, trees, and landscapes. Green fees range from $41–$45, with cart.

La Croix (605-718-9953; www.rcymca.org/golf.htm), 830 East Minnesota St. With 9 holes that are an easy walk, this course is good for beginners and seniors. Green fees are $8.

HIKING **Rapid City Parks**. There are 13.5 miles of paved walking and biking paths that follow Rapid Creek. It's a really pretty way to get some exercise and to see the city. Your walk can begin at any park along the creek.

SWIMMING ✿ **The Rapid City Parks Department** has four pools; three outdoors, one indoors. They are available to visitors for the small fee of $5 for adults and $4 for children.

☂ **Rapid City Swim Center** (605-394-5223), 125 Waterloo St. This indoor swim center features a leisure pool, a lap pool, a hot tub, and water slides.

Horace Mann Pool (605-394-1891), 818 Anamosa

Jimmy Hilton Municipal Pool (605-394-1894), 940 Sheridan Lake Rd.

Parkview Pool (605-394-1892), 4221 Parkview Dr.

UNIQUE ADVENTURES **Dakota Angler and Outfitter** (605-342-2450; www.blackhillsflyfishing.com), 513 Seventh St. Open 9–5:30 Monday through Friday, 9–4 Saturday. Want to learn to fly fish? This place will set you up with all the equipment and take you on a guided tour. They also sell rods, flies, clothing, and custom-built rods. The tours are $250 for a half day (two people) and $375 for a full day.

❦ **Landstrom's Black Hills Gold Factory Tour** (605-343-0157; www.landstroms.com), 405 Canal St. Arguably the best Black Hills gold manufacturer, Landstrom's offers free factory tours from 10–1 Monday through Friday. See how the jewelry is made and pick yourself up a little something.

✳ Green Spaces

PARKS After the 1972 Rapid City flood, all of the area adjacent to Rapid Creek became off-limits to buildings and much of it became parkland. Rapid City boasts 1,650 acres of municipal parks with hiking, biking, Frisbee courses, picnic shelters, playgrounds, formal gardens, tennis, and baseball fields. There are also five off-leash dog parks. All parks are open to the public during daylight hours and are free. For further information and locations go to www.rcgov.com/parks.

✴ Lodging

Every chain motel is represented in Rapid City, many along the I-90 exits. Some of the more popular choices are: the **Radisson** (605-348-8300), **Rushmore Plaza Holiday Inn** (1-877-786-9480), **Fairfield Inn** (605-718-9600), and **Holiday Inn Express** (1-877-786-9480).

HOTELS **Alex Johnson Hotel** (605-342-1210; www.alexjohnson.com), 523 Sixth St. Open year-round, rates vary by season. This hotel was built in 1927 and is listed on the National Register of Historic Places. The interior is very beautiful with wood rafters, brick floors, and a chandelier made of war spears. With 143 modern rooms and suites on six floors, they offer all the amenities of a first-class hotel including the Landmark Restaurant and a lounge on site. $99–$139, $20 additional for a family room or a suite.

Grand Gateway Hotel (1-866-742-1300; www.grandgatewayhotel.com), 1721 N. LaCrosse. One of the few independently owned hotels in Rapid City, the Gateway is located right off I-90 for added convenience. This hotel features an indoor pool with slides, and a hot tub, and nicely decorated rooms with upscale amenities. $159.

Hisega Lodge (605-342-8444; www.hisegalodge.net), 23101 Triangle Trail. This lodge is 7 miles outside of Rapid City off SD 44 and hidden back in the trees for privacy. Often used for business retreats or reunions, the lodge has eight guest rooms, a large dining room for gatherings, three fireplaces, a great room, and a library. Each room has a private bath and breakfast is included. Dinner can be ordered for larger groups. $99–$129.

✴ Where to Eat

DINING OUT **Botticelli Ristorante Italiano** (605-348-0089), 523 Main St. Open 11–2:30 and 5–10 Monday through Friday, 11:30–10 Saturday, and 5–9 Sunday. You know it's authentic Italian food when they start the meal with bread and olive oil. The menu includes a variety of pasta, shellfish, and salads. They also have Rapid City's best wine selection. Come on Tuesday for half-price wine. Entrées from $6–$20.

The Corn Exchange Restaurant Bistro (605-343-5070; www.cornexchange.com), 727 Main St. Open 5–9 Tuesday through Saturday. The Corn Exchange's menu varies seasonally but is always made up of fresh, mostly organic ingredients and the imagination of chef/owner, M. J. Adams. With small and large plates, look for dishes like pan roasted quail and pheasant dumplings with Japanese dipping sauce. This restaurant has been featured in numerous national magazines, including *Gourmet*. Beer and wine are available. Entrées $14–$30.

Fireside Inn (605-342-3900; www.hillcitysd.com/firesidehome.html), 2301 Hisega Rd. Open 5–9 daily. This is where Rapid City residents go for special occasions. The menu features prime rib, steaks, seafood, and pasta in a cozy setting around a massive rock fireplace. There is a full bar. Entrées $12–$25.

Minervas Restaurant (605-394-9505; www.minervas.net/restaurants.php), 2111 LaCrosse St. Open 6:30 AM–10 PM daily. Minervas is a Midwestern chain but doesn't feel like one. The menu includes stir-fry, pastas, filet mignon, steaks, and chops. Minervas is very popular for their Sunday brunch.

There is also a full bar. Entrées range from $7–$25.

Pirate's Table (605-341-4842), 3550 Sturgis Rd. Open 5–8:30 PM Monday through Saturday. This is another place Rapid City folks go for special occasions and features seafood, prime rib, steaks, and pasta. The tables are in private alcoves and the service is great. There is also a full bar. Entrées $8–$28.

Wine Cellar Restaurant (605-718-CORK; www.winecellarrestaurant .com), 513 Sixth St. Open 3:30–9 Tuesday through Friday, 5–9 Saturday. A newer restaurant in Rapid City and earning rave reviews, the Wine Cellar offers fine dining in a casual atmosphere with a menu that includes pasta, calzones, and risotto. They have a very extensive wine list, with 40 varieties available by the glass. Entrées $12–$20.

EATING OUT Colonial House (605-342-4640), 2501 Mt. Rushmore Rd. Open 7 AM–9:30 PM daily. This place gives a whole new meaning to the term "family restaurant." The Beshara family owns and operates the restaurant and they are open for breakfast, lunch, and dinner. The food is a huge step up from what you find at a chain restaurant. Try their fresh veggie omelets or one of their sandwiches, stacked high enough with goodies that you will be saving half of it for the next day. For a quick lunch they have a soup, salad, and sandwich bar. There are also incredible baked goods, including caramel rolls, and a complete bar. Entrées $5–$20.

Fire House Brewing Company (605-348-1915; www.firehousebrewing .com), 610 Main St. Open 11–10 daily. The Firehouse is indeed in a former firehouse and has been brewing draft beer since 1991, as well as cooking up

some good food. There is a little bit of everything on the menu, including steaks, burgers, fish, and pasta, but don't miss the gooey cheesy artichoke dip to start off your meal. Entrées $7–$20.

Sanford's Grub and Pub (605-721-1463), 306 Seventh St. Open 11–10 daily. Located in an old warehouse covered with antiques and signs, Sanford's has great burgers, salads, steaks, pasta, and creative sandwich combinations. They also have an amazing selection of beer on tap and a complete bar. Entrées $7–$20.

Tally's (605-342-7621), 530 Sixth St. Winter hours are 7–2:30 Monday through Saturday; summer hours are 7–7:30 Monday through Friday, 7–2:30 Saturday. Tally's doesn't have a Web site, but they don't need one since it's been open for over 50 years and everybody in Rapid City knows about it. They have basic, solid diner food, which is a real value, with good people serving you. Even Hillary Clinton and Rachel Ray ate here. $5–$15.

Fjord's Ice Cream Factory (605-343-6912), 3825 Canyon Lake Dr. Open at 6:45 AM Monday through Friday and at 8 AM Saturday and Sunday. Fjord's makes their own ice cream and it is to die for. With flavors like honey sunflower vanilla and Black Hills gold you won't be happy with just one scoop. They also do breakfast, soups, sandwiches, quiche, wraps, and an espresso bar. But really, it's all about the ice cream!

Alternative Fuel Coffee House (605-341-2202; www.alternativefuel coffeehouse.com), 620 Main St. Open 8–9 Monday through Thursday, 7:30 AM–10 PM Friday and Saturday This coffee house is big enough to have live music but decorated with comfortable chairs and tables that make it feel intimate. They have a complete selection of coffees and teas as well as sandwiches, soups, salads, and to die for desserts, like triple chocolate brownies. $4–$8.

Black Hills Bagels (605-399-1277; www.blackhillsbagels.com), 913 Mt. Rushmore Rd. Open 6–3 Monday through Friday, 7–3 Saturday and Sunday. With a couple dozen bagel varieties like Chocolate Chunk and Cranberry and another couple dozen cream cheese varieties, this place knows their bagels and turned Rapid City into a bagel loving town. Serving breakfast and lunch, the bagels are made fresh daily. They also have all the coffee combos you might want.

B&L Bagels (605-399-777), 512 Main St. Open 6:30–6 daily. Another entry in the bagel wars, B&L may be small but they have a loyal following. They have a wide variety of bagel flavors and you can get just about anything on them from flavored cream cheese to veggies. A variety of drinks are available as well.

Curry Masala (605-716-7788; www.currymasalainc.com), 2050 W. Main St. Open 11–2 and 5–8 Monday through Saturday, 11–2 Sunday. Located in a strip mall, it's not much to look at but the locals are thrilled to have Indian cuisine. This place offers authentic Indian food with all your favorite curries like tandoori chicken or beef vindaloo. There is also a small assortment of Indian grocery items. $3–$6.

Golden Phoenix (605-348-4195), 2421 W. Main St. Open 11–9:30 daily. There are a lot of Asian restaurants in Rapid City but for good Chinese at very reasonable prices you can't beat the Golden Phoenix. Their lunch specials, which include soup and an egg roll, are an incredible value and you will have leftovers. $6–$15.

Little Jewels (605-341-2343), 1315 Haines Ave. Open 11–3 Monday through Friday, 5–8 Thursday and Friday, and 11–8 Saturday. This is a unique little eatery that prides itself on all natural Native American and vegetarian food. They have a wide variety of bison dishes such as burgers, brats, and hot dogs, as well as the good old Indian Taco—seasoned meat, cheese, and lettuce on Indian fry bread, which you really should try sometime. $6–$8.

Piesano's Pacchio (605-341-6941; www.piesanospacchia.com), 3618 Canyon Lake Dr. Piesano's is a small restaurant with some of the best pizza in town, including interesting combinations like sweet and sour cashew chicken but also all the traditional favorites. They have sandwiches, pastas, dinner-size salads, and daily specials. Eat in or call for carryout. $6–$22.

✴ Entertainment

Black Hills Symphony Orchestra (www.bhsymphony.org). For 72 seasons this all-volunteer orchestra has entertained and educated the Black Hills area. The symphony performs December through April. Check their Web site for dates.

Rushmore Plaza Civic Center (www.gotmine.com/events), 444 Mt. Rushmore Rd. The civic center plays host to big-name concerts, Broadway plays, and a variety of events. Check their Web site for schedules.

✴ Selective Shopping

Folks come from all over the region to shop in Rapid City, so the malls and chains along I-90 keep busy. But downtown Rapid City is also alive and well and has some of the best stores in town, as well as galleries, bookstores, restaurants, and lots of nice antique shops. Most of the shopping is located between Eighth and Fourth Streets and St. Joseph and Main Streets, so the area is very walkable. Here are a few shops to be sure to visit:

Prairie Edge Trading Company and Galleries (605-342-3086; www.prairieedge.com), 606 Main St. Open 9–7 Monday through Saturday, 10–5 Sunday. Located in a restored historic building with original tin ceilings, Prairie Edge has a terrific selection of Native American art, crafts, jewelry, books, and music. For beaders there is a vast selection of trade beads. Artists have studios on site and you can watch them work as well as talk to them about their artwork.

Dakota Drum Company (605-348-2421; www.daktoadrum.com), 603 Main St. Open 9–5 daily. The craftsmen at the Dakota Drum Company make traditional Lakota drums with hand-scraped buffalo hide. The drums are perfectly playable or make beautiful home accents or, when covered with glass, coffee tables. They also sell

PRAIRIE EDGE IS A GALLERY AND STUDIO FOR LOCAL NATIVE AMERICAN ARTISTS.

other Native American craft items like painted buffalo skulls and dream catchers, all made by local Native Americans.

Paws (605-388-3925), 607 St. Joseph. Missing your critters while vacationing? Want to bring them home a little something? Paws started out as an in-home pet bakery and got so popular they had to open a store. Besides the baked goodies, they have great gifts for pets and their people, including funny T-shirts, leashes, collars, and the all-important clothing for pooches.

Reflections of South Dakota (605-341-3234; www.jlowephotography.com), 507 Sixth St. Open 10–6 Monday through Saturday. This gallery features the work of photographer Joe Lowe. Lowe specializes in color landscapes with amazing definition. Stop in and enjoy how truly beautiful the Black Hills can be when seen through the camera's lens.

Roam N Around (605-716-1660), 616 Main St. Open 10–6 Monday through Saturday. This cool travel shop has clothing for travel that won't wrinkle, luggage, and other travel accessories. They also carry an assortment of maps and travel guides for destinations around the world.

James Van Nuys Gallery (343-2449; www.jamesvannuys.com), 524 Seventh St. Open Monday through Saturday 10–6. Van Nuys is a well-known Black Hills landscape artist who works in oils, watercolor, and acrylics. He has also done some of the president sculptures downtown and performs music in his "free" time. This gallery is a great resource for what's happening downtown and in the art scene, so stop in and visit with James and friends.

Vino 100 (605-341-8466), 520 Seventh St. Open 10–9 Monday through Saturday, 12–5 Sunday. Know what you like in wine but really don't know what to buy? This shop has a rating system that

BLACK HILLS GOLD

The story goes that a young Frenchman searching for gold in the Black Hills fell asleep and dreamed of grapes growing beside a babbling brook. Inspired by his dream, he created the tricolored gold, grape leaf designs that are known as Black Hills Gold.

The widely accepted creator of Black Hills Gold was S. T. Butler. In 1919 Butler was a goldsmith working in Deadwood and came up with the grape leaf design that has become the standard for Black Hills Gold. Butler's grandson, F. L. Thorpe expanded on his grandfather's designs and the F. L. Thorpe Company is manufacturing jewelry today.

In 1944 Ivan Landstrom bought Black Hills Manufacturing and moved it to Rapid City where it continues today. Tours of the manufacturing process are available at the Landstrom plant.

In the 1980s a federal judge ruled that to be called Black Hills Gold, jewelry had to be made in the Black Hills. With that ruling several new companies began including South Dakota Gold, Mount Rushmore Gold, and Coleman. With each new company, new designs and styles entered the market place, branching off from the original grape leaf design.

In 1995 Landstrom bought F. L. Thorpe, bringing together two of the original companies. Landstrom still makes the original Thorpe designs as well as expanding on them.

How do you choose Black Hills Gold? Some people feel very strongly that one manufacturer is superior to another, and prices might suggest that as they vary widely. The best bet is to go to a number of shops in any large tourist area like Keystone and find what you like. Generally you will find very similar designs by more than one company so compare prices. Then do what the locals do, walk across the street or next door and tell the shop owner the price you were just offered. Nine times out of ten they will match or beat it. Walk back to the original store, quote the new price, and continue until you get what you want for what you want to pay. This can go on for some time but enjoy it, the mark up on Black Hills Gold is high and all this negotiating could be the highlight of your vacation.

helps take the guesswork out of a wine selection. They carry mostly Washington and California wines and also have hookahs and a walk-in humidor with 400 different cigars.

✳ Special Events

JUNE Festival of Presidents Weekend (www.festivalofpresidents.com).

With concerts, craft and food vendors, and a parade.

Black Hills Bluegrass Festival (605-394-4101, ext. 200; www.thedahl.org/bluegrass_festival), at Mystery Mountain Resort, US 16. Held at a campground, you can stay the entire weekend and not miss a moment of some great bluegrass and gospel.

Black Hills Heritage Festival (605-209-4339; www.bhheritagefest.com), Memorial Park, late June or early July. Featuring crafts booths, concessions, and concerts in the evenings. There are also fireworks one night.

AUGUST Central States Fair (605-355-3861; www.centralstatesfair.com/index2.php), Central States Fairgrounds, Rapid City. This is your standard fair with rides, animal judging, a rodeo, and nightly entertainment from nationally known performers.

JANUARY Black Hills Stockshow and Rodeo (605-355-3861; www.blackhillsstockshow.com), Rushmore Plaza Civic Center. All the ranchers come to town for this winter extravaganza. There is a rodeo, stock sales, booths, entertainment, and workshops.

LEAD

Duxring the Black Hills gold rush of 1876, two brothers, Fred and Moses Manuel, and their partners left the raucous town of Deadwood to search for gold a little farther south. One of the Manuel brothers called the vein of ore they found "a lead" (as in, it will lead to gold) and they established a claim calling it the Homestake Mine. More prospectors soon followed and the town of Lead was created. By 1877 there were four hotels, a grocery store, a saloon, bakery, and butcher shop.

The Homestake Mine was soon recognized as one of the richest gold mines in the area. George Hearst, father of William Randolph, bought the mine for $70,000 and the town of Lead became a company town where the economy was based on the success of the mine. Victorian houses sprang up on the hills around Lead, and businesses flourished, providing goods to the miners. George's wife, Phoebe Hearst, was responsible for starting the first kindergarten and built the Homestake Opera House and Recreation Building where miners could see shows, swim in the pool, and bowl.

The Homestake Mine operated continuously for 125 years, producing 40 million ounces of gold. The mine is 1.5 miles deep and has over 500 miles of tunnels. In the deepest shafts the temperature is over 130 degrees and special air conditioners had to be developed to stabilize the temperature at 85 degrees and 75 percent humidity.

When the Homestake Mine closed in 2002, due to low gold prices, much of Lead closed with it. Homes were abandoned as miners left in search of jobs and businesses closed for lack of customers. But Lead will be making a comeback: it was announced in 2007 that the former Homestake Mine will become the site for a multipurpose deep underground science and engineering laboratory. A number of scientific investigations require an underground environment—the deeper the better. For example, there are questions important to the fields of astrophysics and physics that cannot be answered unless experiments are shielded from cosmic rays and other background radiation by thousands of feet of rock.

Today, visitors can explore the mining history of the Black Hills at the Homestake Visitors Center and the Black Hills Mining Museum and learn more of things to come for the mine.

GUIDANCE **Lead Chamber of Commerce** (605-584-1100; www.leadmethere .org), 160 West Main St., Lead.

GETTING THERE *By car:* from the south, take US 385 between Rapid City and Hill City. From the north, take US14A from Sturgis or US 85 from I-90. Lead is about 40 miles north of Rapid City.

GETTING AROUND There is no public transportation in Lead.

MEDICAL EMERGENCIES **Lead-Deadwood Regional Medical Clinic** (605-717-6431), 71 Charles St., Deadwood, SD 57732.

✳ To See

FOR FAMILIES **Presidents Park** (presidentspark.com/index.php), off US 85, 1 mile south of Deer Mountain Rd. Open year-round, 9–6. Artist David Adickes has created 20-foot tall busts of all 42 presidents and they are shown on a walk through the Black Hills woods. Each statue includes information on the president for a little history lesson. There is a café and gift shop at the site. $8 for adults, $6 for children.

HISTORIC SITES **Homestake Visitors Center** (605-584-3110; homestake tour.com), 160 West Main St. Open May through September. This one-hour tour takes visitors through the town of Lead and up to the Homestake surface operation and follows the complete mining process. Stop by, even if you are not interested in the tour, just to see the Open Cut, a massive hole in the ground where much of the gold mining was once done. Tours are $6 for adults, $5 for students.

MUSEUMS **Black Hills Mining Museum** (605-584-1605; www.mining-museum .blackhills.com), 323 West Main St. Open 8–5 May 15 through September. 3. The 45-minute tour takes you through a simulated mining tunnel, created by former miners, which gives you an inside look at the mining experience. There are also exhibits, old mining equipment, and gold panning. $6 for adults, $5 for students.

STAND HIGH ABOVE AND MARVEL AT THE AMOUNT OF ROCK AND DIRT THAT WAS REMOVED IN SEARCH OF GOLD AT THE OPEN CUT IN LEAD.

SCENIC DRIVES **Spearfish Canyon**, accessible just south of Lead on US 14A. This is a dedicated Forest Service Scenic Byway that goes through a canyon carved 30–60 million years ago, now known as Spearfish Creek. There are several incredible waterfalls along the route as well as wildlife and spectacular rock formations. The canyon walls are covered with pine and spruce while the creek sides support aspen, birch, and oak trees making this a popular drive to see the fall colors. Give yourself a couple hours to stop and take pictures.

THE HISTORY OF GOLD MINING IN LEAD CAN BE FOUND AT THE MINING MUSEUM.

✳ To Do

BICYCLING The 114-mile long **Mickelson Trail** is accessible from Lead at Trailhead 2A. A map is available at www.sdgfp.info/parks/regions/northernhills/mickel sontrail/trailheads.htm.

FISHING There are ample trout in **Spearfish Canyon Creek**. Stop at any of the pullouts and find a promising spot. Fishing licenses are required and are available at the **Spearfish Canyon Lodge** and the **Cheyenne Crossing Store**.

GOLF
Lead Country Club (605-584-1852), on Rochford Rd. off US 385. A nine-hole course that is located at 6,000 feet so you can watch your shots soar. Green fees are $33.

HIKING Spearfish Falls Trail, 0.75 mile. Enter at Latchstring Restaurant in Spearfish Canyon. This trail goes to the top of Spearfish Falls.

& **Roughrock Falls**, 1 mile. Enter at the Spearfish Canyon Lodge parking lot. This easy trail goes through deep forest to Roughrock Falls, one of the larger falls in the canyon.

76 Trail-Canyon Vista, 0.75 mile. Enter at Savoy on Forest Service Road 222. This trail ascends 1,000 feet to Buzzards Roost atop the canyon wall overlooking the canyon below.

& **Botanical Gardens**, 1 mile. This trail goes through 11 planting areas that feature native South Dakota plants for your enjoyment.

Little Spearfish and Rimrock Trails, 6-mile loop. Enter at Savoy and go west on Forest Service Road 222, 4.7 miles to the trailhead. Look for the foundation of an old ranger station between the Timon Campground and the Rod and Gun Club.

❋ Winter Sports

SKIING ❋ **Deer Mountain** (1-888-410-DEER; www.skideermountain.com), located 3 miles south of Lead on US 85. Open 9–4 daily. There are 44 trails at Deer Mountain, as well as a tubing park. The season depends on the snow but generally begins in November and runs into April. Full day: $27 for adults, $23 for juniors.

❋ **Terry Peak** (605-722-SNOW; www.terrypeak.com), 21120 Stewart Slope Rd. Chairlifts are open 9–4 during the snow season. Terry Peak's season depends on the snow but generally begins Thanksgiving weekend. There are a number of trails for different experience levels of skiers and snowboarders. Full day: $39 for adults, $30 for children.

SNOWMOBILING ❋ There are 350 miles of groomed snowmobile trails in the Black Hills and the area is considered one of the best in the country. Snowmobiles must be licensed in South Dakota or their home state. For complete maps go to www.sdgfp.info/Parks/Recreation/Snowmobiling/TrailMaps.htm.

❋ Resorts/Lodges

Spearfish Canyon Lodge (605-584-3435; spfcanyon.com), 10619 Roughrock Falls Rd. Open year-round. Located in the heart of Spearfish Canyon, this lodge is popular with skiers, snowmobilers, and for family reunions. Attractively built of log and river rock, the lodge captures the spirit of the Old West but with modern amenities. A standard room with two queen beds is $89–$109 during the winter, $149–$169 June to October. They also have suites with king beds, fireplaces, Jacuzzi tubs, and kitchen for $245 a night in winter, $275 June to October. **The Latchstring Restaurant** is adjacent and is open for breakfast, lunch, and dinner with entrées as simple as a buffalo burger and as extravagant as Trout Amandine. There is also a complete lounge on site.

❋ Where to Eat

EATING OUT Cheyenne Crossing (605-584-3510; www.cheyenne crossing.org/cafe), at the junction of US 14A and US 385. People drive from all over the Black Hills to have breakfast at this café and then drive through Spearfish Canyon. They also serve lunch and dinner, with entrées like steak and fried halibut.

Stamp Mill Restaurant and Saloon (605-584-1984), 305 W. Main. The menu here includes steak, burgers, and salads with a complete bar that locals hanging out at it. $8–$18.

❋ Selective Shopping

Blue Dog Gallery and Framers (606-717-0003), 309 W. Main St. This gallery features fine art, jewelry, and pottery by Black Hills artists, including James Van Nuys, in one of the old downtown brick buildings. There really is a blue dog who likes her tummy rubbed.

DEADWOOD

Deadwood was another town created by the 1876 gold rush in the Black Hills. Stories vary as to who founded Deadwood, but it is agreed that the name came from the dead trees that grew on the canyon walls where Deadwood began.

Deadwood was wild, with hardworking, hard-drinking gamblers in its early history and home to the likes of Wild Bill Hickok, Calamity Jane, and Seth Bullock. Many of these Old West legends found their final resting place in Deadwood at the Mount Moriah Cemetery.

Deadwood was also home to a large Chinese population, workers who built the railroad but came to Deadwood following the gold. The Chinese had a city within the city of Deadwood and elected their own mayor and had their own police and fire department. In the summer of 2001 during a construction project, remains of the old Chinatown were found and subsequently excavated by the Archaeological Research Center. Among items found were traces of boarding houses with artifacts like opium smoking paraphernalia, dishes, toiletries, and a multitude of whiskey bottles.

There was also an active Jewish population in Deadwood. It is said that as many as a third of the business owners were Jewish, including Sol Star who was the business partner of Seth Bullock and served numerous terms as Deadwood's mayor. One section of Mount Moriah Cemetery is known as Hebrew Hill for the many Jewish buried there.

Even though the entire town was listed as a National Historic Landmark in the 1960s, Deadwood fell on hard times and much of the historic area was in disrepair. In an attempt to revive the economy and generate historic restoration funds, the citizens of Deadwood formed Deadwood U Bet in 1986 to advocate small stakes gambling. Finally the legislature agreed and today Deadwood is beautifully restored and home to 80 gaming establishments, 28 hotels, and 41 restaurants. Tourists wander the streets with cups full of change and play the slots and card games, check out the entertainment, and enjoy the Old West feel of the town.

Visit Deadwood and step back into history. There is much to see and do for the entire family, and a little gambling is always fun for the adults.

GUIDANCE City of Deadwood (www.cityofdeadwood.com).

Deadwood Chamber of Commerce and Visitors Bureau (1-800-999-1876; www.deadwood.org).

GETTING THERE *By car:* take I-90 to US 14A (Boulder Canyon), or US 385 north. Deadwood is 41 miles north of Rapid City.

GETTING AROUND Trolleys run to all the hotels and casinos in town and cost $1 per ride.

MEDICAL EMERGENCIES Lead-Deadwood Regional Medical Clinic (605-717-6431), 71 Charles St., Deadwood, SD 57732.

✳ To See

CULTURAL SITES Tatanka: Story of the Bison (605-584-5678; www.story ofthebison.com), 1 mile north of Deadwood on US 385. Open 9–5 May 15 through September 30. This is Kevin Costner's tribute to the bison that once roamed the plains and to the Native Americans that relied on them for food, clothing, and shelter. There are 14 larger than life bronze sculptures of bison pursued by three Native American horseback riders, a hands-on Interpretive Center, Native American gift shop, and snack bar. $8 for adults, $6 for children.

FOR FAMILIES Trial of Jack McCall (605-578-1876), Masonic Hall, Main St. During the summer, 8 PM daily. Every evening there is a shoot-out on Deadwood's Main Street and then a reenactment of the trial of Jack McCall, the man who shot Wild Bill Hickok in the head while he was playing a game of poker. It all starts at the Old Style Saloon No. 10, where Wild Bill was killed playing the famed Dead Man's Hand, a pair of aces and a pair of eights. Exciting for the family, but plug the little ones' ears because it can get loud. $3 per person.

REVENUE FROM SMALL STAKES GAMBLING PAID FOR THE HISTORIC RESTORATION OF DEADWOOD.

Original Deadwood Tours (605-578-2091; www.originaldeadwoodtour.com), departs in front of the Midnight Star Casino. Open May through mid-October. This narrated tour runs four times a day starting at 10:30, covers Deadwood history, and takes you to Mount Moriah Cemetery. This is a great option if you want to learn more about the history of Deadwood and don't want to climb all the hills in Deadwood to see the sites. $8 for adult, $5 for children.

HISTORIC SITES All of **Deadwood** is a National Historic Landmark so look for plaques and signs on buildings that tell the history.

Broken Boot Gold Mine (605-578-1976; www.brokenbootgoldmine.com), upper Main St. Open 8:30–5:30 May through September. This mine was founded in 1878 and was worked off and on until 1907. In 1954 one of the owners' daughters decided to reopen the mine as a tourist attraction and they have been giving tours ever since. One of the few old mines that are in good enough shape for tours, it's a piece of Black Hills history.

Mount Moriah Cemetery (605-578-2600), follow the signs off Main Street. Open year-round. Mount Moriah dates back to the earliest days of Deadwood between 1877 and 1878. Records exist for over 3,500 folks buried there, including 350 children that died in scarlet fever and diphtheria epidemics. There are many notables buried at Mount Moriah, including Wild Bill Hickok and Calamity Jane who are buried side by side. There is also a Jewish section called Hebrew Hill where many of the early settlers of Deadwood are buried, as well as a Chinese section.

MUSEUMS **Deadwood's Adams Museum** (605-578-1714; www.deadwood.org), 54 Sherman St. Summer hours 9–5; winter hours 10–4. The Adams Museum is owned by the city of Deadwood and dedicated to preserving the city's past. This Queen Anne–style home was built in 1892 and is considered the beginning of society in Deadwood, which up until then had been a rough mining town. It has been restored as a museum and includes such relics as Potato Creek Johnny's gold nuggets, the Thoen Stone, Lakota bead and quillwork, and lots of information about Deadwood's colorful Wild West past. $3 donation.

✸ **Days of '76 Museum** (605-578-2872; www.daysof76.com/museum), 17 Crescent St., adjacent to the Rodeo Grounds. Open daily 9–5 April through October. With collections of rodeo memorabilia, carriages, Native American artifacts, and cowboy history, this museum strives to preserve the Old West past of Deadwood and the region. Free, donations accepted.

✷ To Do

FAMILY FRIENDLY **Gulches of Fun** (1-800-961-3096; www.gulchesoffun.com), 225 Cliff St. Open May 23 through August 31. There is not a lot for kids to do in Deadwood, so this place was opened to provide some alternatives for families. Located at the Comfort Inn, Gulches of Fun has go-karts, mini golf, bumper boats, and an arcade to amuse the entire family. All-day wristband prices range from $25–$30.

The Roo Ranch (605-578-1777; www.therooranch.com), 11842 US 14A, 1.5 miles east of Deadwood. Open late10–6 May through September. Kangaroos in Deadwood? Why not? The Roo Ranch started with one wallaby and has grown to six species, and 60 kangaroos, wallaroos, and wallabies. If you can't make it to

Australia, here's your chance to see their most famous residents. $8 for adults, $5 for children.

HIKING The George S. Mickelson Trail (www.sdgfp.info/parks/regions/ northernhills/mickelsontrail/trailheads.htm). The Mickelson Trail begins in Deadwood near the old railroad depot on Sherman Street. This rails-to-trails project continues south for 108.8 miles to the town of Edgemont. Horses, bikes, and hikers welcome.

UNIQUE ADVENTURES Mad Mountain Adventures (605-578-1878; www .madmountainadventures.com), 6 miles south of Deadwood on US 385. Open 8–5 daily. Rent a snowmobile or ATV, depending on the season, and really see the Black Hills. Rentals include helmets and insurance. Must be 18. Rates vary so call for information.

✳ Lodging

The **Deadwood Chamber of Commerce** has a central reservations site (www.deadwood.org/Lodging) for their members. It lists hotels, motels, bed-and-breakfasts, cabins, and lodges with pictures and prices.

HOTELS Bullock Hotel (1-800-336-1876; www.historicbullock.com), 633 Main St. Built in 1895 of native pink and white sandstone by famed Sheriff Seth Bullock, this hotel was once the

THE BULLOCK HOTEL WAS BUILT BY ONE OF DEADWOOD'S ORIGINAL SHERIFFS, SETH BULLOCK.

most highly sought after luxury hotel of its time. Folks claim old Seth haunts the place and seems to be particularly attracted to humming or whistling, so be careful. Modern rooms range from $105–180 for a Jacuzzi suite.

Historic Franklin Hotel (1-800-688-1876; www.silveradofranklin.com), 709 Main St. The Franklin Hotel was built in 1903 and unlike many buildings of that time was ultramodern with telephones, running water, radiant heat, and electricity in every room. It has been completely restored and includes antique furniture and the original back bar and reception desk. The Otis elevator is still hand operated—or you might prefer to stroll down the grand staircase. $89–$209 per night.

✳ Where to Eat

DINING OUT Jake's (1-800-999-6482; www.themidnightstar.com), 677 Main St. at the Midnight Star. The Midnight Star and Jake's are owned by Kevin Costner and his brother, one of the early investors in Deadwood's revitalization. Jake's is the only really high-end restaurant in Deadwood with the service and ambience to match. Enjoy salmon, walleye, and buffalo steaks prepared by top chefs. Entrées $22–$36.

EATING OUT **Cadillac Jack's Restaurant** (1-866-332-3966; www.cadillacjacksgaming.com), 360 Main St. Cadillac Jack's Restaurant is open 24-hours a day and features "Lobster and Prime" nightly for $19.99.

Chinatown Café (605-578-7778), 647 Main St., upstairs at the Bullock Hotel. Open 11:30–2 and 5–9. The Chinatown offers very good, traditional Chinese entrées in a nicely decorated dining room of red and gold. $9–$15.

Diamond Lil's (605-578-3550; www.themidnightstar.com), 677 Main St. at the Midnight Star. This is a bar and grill with movie memorabilia from Kevin Costner's many movies, including *Silverado* and *Dances with Wolves,* decorating the walls. Diamond Lil's is much more casual than Jake's, which is just upstairs, and a great place to have a sandwich and a beer while watching a game on TV. Sandwiches and pizza range from $5–$11.

Like all gambling areas, buffets are big in Deadwood. Here are three of the most popular:

4 Aces (1-800-834-4384; www.fouracesdeadwood.com/restaurant.htm), 531 Main St. The 4 Aces claims to have the best buffets in Deadwood. Breakfast is from 6–10:30 AM for $6.99, lunch is 11 AM–4 PM for $6.99, and dinner is 4–closing for $12.99. On Friday and Saturday night they also have a prime rib and crab leg buffet for $14.99.

Gold Dust Restaurant (1-800-456-0533; www.golddustgaming.com), 688 Main Street. The Gold Dust has buffets for three meals a day and people line up for them. Breakfast is 7–10:20 AM for $5.99. Lunch is 11 AM–3 PM for $7.99. Dinner is 4–11 PM and ranges from $11.99–$13.99. The menu features prime rib, chicken, and a huge soup and salad bar.

Silverado Grand Buffet (800-584-7005; www.silveradofranklin.com), 709

Main St. This buffet is very popular, but if you time it right they also do a lot of free food on Friday and Saturday night. People line up out the door for the free buffet. Friday and Saturday night 4:30–10 PM, Crab Feast Festival $13.95. Sunday through Thursday 4:30–9:00 PM, Grand Buffet $11.95. Lunch Buffet [hours?] $6.95.

✳ Entertainment

The main entertainment in Deadwood is the gambling, from nickel slots to $100 bet limit black jack and poker. There are 80 casinos, including convenience stores with slots, so finding somewhere to gamble is not a problem.

Once you have parked in one of the city lots start wandering up and down Main Street and take in the sights. Stick your head in various casinos and check out the difference in style and, if it's evening or weekends, what kind of entertainment is playing. Some of the casinos are done up to mimic the Old West, like the Saloon #10, which even has sawdust on the floor, others are more upscale like the Silverado and Gold Dust, which are Vegas casinos on a much smaller scale. Pick one you like and go up to the cashier's window to

SLOT MACHINES AND CARD GAMES MAKE UP DEADWOOD'S GAMING INDUSTRY.
South Dakota Tourism

get rolls of quarters or nickels and a cup to hold them. If you play cards, watch the tables to see what they are playing until you find the game you like. They play most every form of poker, including the wildly popular Texas Hold 'Em, and Blackjack. There is also every kind of slot machine, including the old-fashioned kind with spinning wheels and the newest digital models. It is perfectly acceptable, and safe, to take your cup of change from one casino to the next when checking out the various games. Find a place you like, settle in, and before long a server will offer you free drinks, the object being to get you to spend your money in their casino.

When you're done for the day or night, go to the nearest cashier and turn in your winnings, you hope, and they will count your change and give you bills. The great part is that for $20–$100 you can gamble, get free drinks, and enjoy all the free entertainment and sightseeing. It really is a lot of fun and pretty cheap entertainment. And who knows, you might come home with a few extra bucks in your pocket.

✷ Selective Shopping

At one time, every retail spot in Deadwood was a casino but today there are a number of nice shops featuring souvenirs, leather goods, jewelry, and gifts—just wander down Main Street.

✷ Special Events

Deadwood has a special event about once a month. Check out the chamber's Web site for dates. A few notable events include the following:

JUNE Wild Bill Hickok Days kicks off the summer with Wild West re-enactors, a fast draw championship, and free concerts.

Days of '76, which features a PRCA Rodeo and a parade with lots of cowboys and Indians.

AUGUST Kool Deadwood Nites, which features nightly concerts and a car rally.

SEPTEMBER Deadwood Jam has two days of big name concerts in the middle of Main Street.

A REENACTOR PORTRAYS WILD BILL HICKOK IN DEADWOOD.

South Dakota Tourism

STURGIS

When people think Sturgis, they generally think of the Sturgis Motorcycle Rally and Races. It is their premier event and it entirely changes the quiet town of 7,000 into a city of, on average, 500,000. Regular businesses close down and vacate their storefronts to make room for some 800 temporary vendors and the entire hills are filled with the roar of motorcycle engines. If you love crowds, motorcycles, great entertainment, and shopping, then the Sturgis Motorcycle Rally is for you. You don't need to be a biker to attend but you better plan way ahead because finding a place to stay, an empty seat in a restaurant, or a quiet road for sightseeing is virtually impossible during the two weeks of the rally.

For those who are not so enthusiastic about crowds and bikes, there is more to Sturgis than the rally. It is a historical town, dating back to 1876. It was named for Major Samuel D. Sturgis, who was the commander of the Fort Meade Cavalry Post. Fort Meade was established on the Western frontier to protect settlers from Indian attacks and the Seventh Cavalry, reformed after the disaster at Little Big Horn, was the first permanent garrison at the post. Fort Meade became an important post for all U.S. cavalry units, training troops that fought in every war from the Spanish American to World War II. Today Fort Meade is home to a large Veterans Administration Hospital that serves veterans from throughout the region. For visitors Fort Meade is also home to the Black Hills National Cemetery and the Fort Meade Museum, which houses artifacts from the post's long history. In early June, Cavalry Days is celebrated with reenactments, a parade, and exhibits.

Sturgis sits at the foot of Bear Butte, or as the Lakota call it *Mato Paha* or "Bear Mountain." Bear Butte is sacred to many Native American groups who come there to hold religious ceremonies. If you visit, you will see colorful pieces of cloth and small bundles or pouches hanging from the trees. These represent the prayers offered by Native Americans during their worship.

Around Sturgis there are working ranches and people who are still making their living from the land. Sturgis provides them with goods and services. So while Sturgis is best known for one event that happens for two weeks out of the year, during the other 50 weeks it is a home, center of commerce, and health-care provider for people throughout Meade County and the region.

GUIDANCE **Sturgis Chamber of Commerce** (www.sturgis-sd.org), 2040 Junction Ave.

Sturgis Motorcycle Rally Official Site (605-720-0800; www.sturgismotorcycle rally.com), 1147 Sherman St.

GETTING THERE Sturgis is easily accessible off I-90, or from US 14A going east from Deadwood. Sturgis is 28 miles from Rapid City.

GETTING AROUND There is no public transportation in Sturgis.

MEDICAL EMERGENCIES **Sturgis Regional Hospital** (605-720-2400), 949 Harmon St.

✳ To See

CULTURAL SITES **Bear Butte State Park** (605-347-5240; www.sdgfp.info/ Parks/Regions/NorthernHills/BearButte2.htm), on SD 79, northeast of Sturgis. Open year-round for day use, $3 entry fee. The Bear Butte Education Center is open 8–6 from early May through September. This is the place to learn the geology of Bear Butte as well as its significance to Native Americans. For thousands of years Plains Indians have considered Bear Butte one of their most sacred sites and have come here to fast and pray. Encroachment by development has caused concerns for Indians and recently they sued to stop the building of a rifle range near the butte. People are still allowed to climb to the top of Bear Butte and the 1.75-mile limestone surface trail gains approximately 1,000 feet in elevation and offers a view of four states from the mountain's peak. Please be very aware of altars and offerings left behind on the butte by Native Americans and do not disturb them.

MUSEUMS ☂ **Fort Meade Museum** (605-347-9822; www.fortmeademuseum .org), at Ft. Meade, east of Sturgis on SD 34. Open 8–6 May 15 through September 5. The museum has exhibits about Fort Meade and its past as a cavalry post,

BEAR BUTTE IS A VOLCANIC MOUND RISING ABOVE THE SOUTH DAKOTA PLAINS OUTSIDE STURGIS. NATIVE AMERICANS COME TO BEAR BUTTE FOR RELIGIOUS CEREMONIES.
South Dakota Tourism

including home of the Seventh Cavalry. Here you can learn more about Western history and the army's role in it. $3 for adults, free for ages under 12.

⚘ Sturgis Motorcycle Museum (605-347-2001; www.sturgismuseum .com), 999 Main St. Open 7 days a week, hours vary by season. This museum opened in 2001 and has grown tremendously since. It is what the name says, a museum with motorcycles and exhibits about motorcycles from the 1900s to present. While widely popular during the rally, it's fun any time of year. $5 for adults, free for ages under 12.

FORT MEADE IS NOW A VA HOSPITAL BUT WAS ONCE A TRAINING GROUND FOR THE U.S. CAVALRY.

✳ To Do

FISHING ᵴ **Bear Butte Lake** (www.sdparks.info), 6 miles northeast of Sturgis off SD 79. This lake features a wheelchair-accessible fishing dock where you will find bullheads, crappies, and northern pike.

HIKING See the listing for Bear Butte State Park under *Cultural Sites*.

SWIMMING ∂ **Sturgis Community Center** (605-347-6513), 1401 Lazelle St. Open 5 AM–9 PM Monday through Friday, 8–6 Saturday, abd 12–6 Sunday. Open to visitors, the community center has a 72-foot water slide, pool, sauna, and hot tub. Also available are a weight room, gym, and indoor running and walking track. Day passes are available for free for ages 5 years and under, $2.50 for students ages 6 to 18, $4 for adults, and $3 for seniors ages 62 and over.

✳ Lodging

There are several chain motels along the I-90 exits for Sturgis, including the **Best Western** (605-347-3604) and **Days Inn** (605-347-3027).

CAMPING **Bear Butte State Park** (605-773-3391; www.sdparks.info), 6 miles northeast of Sturgis off SD 79. There are 16 nonelectrical camping sites on Bear Butte Lake. $8 a night.

✳ Where to Eat

EATING OUT **Bob's Family Restaurant** (605-720-2930), 1039 Main St. If you like good old American diner fare, Bob's is your place. Nothing fancy,

nothing expensive, and you won't leave hungry. $5–$15.

Boulder Canyon Bar and Grill (605-561-0562), 2695 Lazelle St. Open 10–midnight. This restaurant features steak, burgers, and pasta dishes for lunch or dinner. Alcohol is limited to beer and wine only. Entrées $6–$19.

Olde World Café and Bookery (605-720-1950), 923 Junction Ave. Open 7–5 Monday through Saturday. This café serves all the coffee drinks as well as breakfast sandwiches, quiche, salads, and paninis for lunch. They also offer new and used books in pleasant surroundings with comfortable furniture for lounging awhile.

✳ Special Events

AUGUST THE special event in Sturgis is the **Sturgis Motorcycle Rally and Races**. Dating back to 1938 the rally draws an average of 500,000 bikers to South Dakota each year along with hundreds of vendors selling everything from souvenirs to food and tattoos.

The number one activity of the rally is cruising the beautiful Black Hills and seeing the sights. Part of that is seeing and being seen by other bikers and visiting with friends old and new. The Jackpine Gypsies, who started the rally, hold races; there are also a number of concert venues at campgrounds and bars; and Harley Davidson takes over the Rapid City Civic Center to introduce their new models. And then there are those who come to Sturgis to tie the knot. Weddings go on constantly during the rally.

The rally is, on paper, one week but bikers start arriving a week before and generally there are lots of people around the week after. The riders come from all walks of life; for some, riding a motorcycle is a statement about who they are, for others it's a hobby, and then there are those who rent a bike and grow out their beard just for the rally. It takes all kinds to make up 500,000 and generally everyone gets along, there are no major hassles, and the only downers are afternoon thunderstorms and a few serious traffic accidents.

If you are considering going to the rally, it takes a great deal of planning as all accommodations go up in price and many rent a year in advance. Lots of homeowners in the hills pack up, move out, and rent their homes to bikers, and many campgrounds open just for the rally; the listings in this guide do not include those that are only open during the rally. The best advice is to get on the official rally Web site and do your homework. If you know the ins and outs of the rally, it can be a lot of fun, if not you will simply be lost in a sea of engine roaring humanity.

Final bit of advice? If you want a quiet family vacation, check the rally dates and don't come to the Black Hills then. It's fun to see the motorcyclists everywhere but it gets really tiresome waiting in traffic and not being able to find a seat at a restaurant. Every year people somehow get caught unaware by the rally and it spoils what would have otherwise been a great vacation.

THE BIGGEST TOURIST EVENT OF THE YEAR, THE BLACK HILLS RALLY AND RACES DRAW AS MANY AS 500,000 MOTORCYCLISTS.
South Dakota Tourism

AUGUST Black Hills Steam & Gas Threshing Bee, includes a parade of 100 years of tractors, threshing machines, and cars. Demonstrations of threshing, hay binding, lumber milling, rock crushing, blacksmithing, a tractor rodeo on Friday evening, and a barn dance on Saturday evening. It is held on Hereford Road, near the Sturgis Airport.

SPEARFISH

Spearfish is one of the few communities in the Black Hills that is not dependent on tourism for its survival. Named for the, then, Spear Fish River, Spearfish was founded in 1876. Although it was gold that brought people to Spearfish, they stayed to farm and create a center of commerce for the wilder areas of the hills.

At the northern end of Spearfish Canyon, Spearfish has the advantage of having room to grow—Spearfish is known for never having lost population, even at the end of the Gold Rush or during the Depression. Some say, because of the irrigated land and diversified economy, that Spearfish didn't even have a Depression.

In 1883, the Spearfish Normal School was established—now known as Black Hills State University. In 1896 Spearfish became the site of the Federal Fish Hatchery. The D.C. Booth Fish Hatchery, as it is known today, is still in operation and open to visitors. The Matthew's Opera House was built in 1906 and became the center of entertainment for the town. The opera house is still standing and began major renovations in 1989 but still stages productions.

The first real tourist attraction came to Spearfish when Josef Meier arrived from Germany and started the Black Hills Passion Play in 1938. The production depicts the last seven days of the life of Christ and has been seen by over 10 million people. Professional actors and local townspeople perform the show three nights a week during June, July, and August

Spearfish is not necessarily a tourist town but is a friendly place to visit with a lot to recommend it. Spread out a little and enjoy.

GUIDANCE **Spearfish Information**: www.spearfish.sd.us.

GETTING THERE *By car:* Spearfish is conveniently located on I-90, and at the north end of US 14A, or Spearfish Canyon. Spearfish is 46 miles from Rapid City.

GETTING AROUND There is public transportation in Spearfish.

MEDICAL EMERGENCIES **Spearfish Regional Hospital** (605-644-4000), 1440 North Main St.

✳ To See

HISTORIC SITES ✿ **D.C. Booth Fish Hatchery** (605-642-7730; www.R6.FWS .gov/DCBooth), 423 Hatchery Circle. The grounds are open year-round from dawn to dusk. Tours are available mid-May through mid-September. Located next to the Spearfish Creek, this hatchery is still raising trout for release in South Dakota lakes and streams. Exhibits include a history of hatchery and fisheries, the Booth House, which is furnished with circa 1905 items, a really cool underground viewing area where monster trout can be seen swimming, and the fishponds. Bring along some quarters to feed the fish from the machines on site. Admission is free.

✿ **Thoen Stone Monument**, located on Street Joseph St., west of the Passion Play. The Thoen Stone received its name from the brothers that found it buried east of Spearfish. The stone was carved in 1834 by a group of prospectors shortly before they were killed by Indians. There is some controversy as to its authenticity but if it's true, killing those prospectors kept word of gold in the hills from slipping out and saved the Indians for a good 40 years. It's a fascinating piece of Western history.

MUSEUMS ✝ **High Plains Western Heritage Center** (605-642-9378; www .westernheritagecenter.com), 825 Heritage Dr. Open daily 9–5. The center features 17,000 square feet of displays about the history of the high plains, including the Native Americans, the cattle and sheep industry, mining, and ranching. There are some neat displays like old stagecoaches and chuckwagons and a fully furnished one-room schoolhouse. $7 for adults, $3 for children.

SCENIC DRIVES **Spearfish Canyon**, accessible going south from Spearfish on US 14A. See more information under Lead, *Scenic Drives*. There are interpretive stops throughout the canyon so you can learn more about the geology and history.

✳ To Do

BICYCLING **Big Hills Trail** (www.fs.fed.us/r2/blackhills/recreation/trails/ brochures/big_hillx.html), located 7 miles south of Spearfish on Tinton Road. There are six loops ranging from 0.5 mile to 5.5 miles and of varying difficulty. The trails are used by bikers, hikers, horseback riders, and cross-country skiers. In the winter the trails are groomed for cross-country skiers.

FISHING There are ample trout in **Spearfish Canyon Creek**. Stop at any of the pullouts and find a promising spot. Fishing licenses are required and are available at the **Spearfish Canyon Lodge** and the **Cheyenne Crossing Store**.

GOLF **Spearfish Canyon Country Club** (605-717-GOLF; www.spearfishcanyon countryclub.com), 120 Spearfish Canyon Dr. This is a semiprivate club with an 18-hole championship course winding through the Black Hills. Visitors may play the course except on Wednesday or during tournaments. Green fees $42–$54.

HIKING (See **Big Hills Trail** under *Bicycling* and **Spearfish Canyon** hikes under Lead, *Hiking*).

WILDLIFE REFUGES **Spirit of the Hills Wildlife Sanctuary** (1-877-761-7754; www.wildlifesanctuary.net), 500 North Tinton Rd. Open Tuesday through Sunday, tour times 10:00 and 2:00. This sanctuary provides homes for over 200 animals including lions and bears—many were rescued from breeding operations and fur farms. The sanctuary is dedicated to providing a "life of solace" for the animals, free of abuse or exploitation. Come visit and contribute to a good cause but call ahead as they may be too busy tending to very needy animals to have visitors. $12 for adults, $7 for children.

✳ Lodging

There are a number of chain motels located along the I-90 exits for Spearfish, including **Rodeway Inn** (800-606-2350), **Best Western** (605-642-7795), and **Holiday Inn** (1-800-999-3541).

BED & BREAKFAST INNS **The Wander Inn** (605-722-5040; www.wanderinnbythecreek.com), 333 S. Third St. A beautiful garden located right on Spearfish Creek invites you into this bed-and-breakfast. Two of the upstairs rooms have private baths and balconies overlooking the garden. Room rates range from $85–$125 a night.

CAMPING **City of Spearfish Campground** (605-642-1340; www.spearfishparksandrec.com/camp ground), located next to D.C. Booth Fish Hatchery at 625 Fifth St. Open May 1 through October 1. Located along Spearfish Creek this campground has 57 sites with full hookup and 150 sites without hookup. Fees range from $17–$26 for sites both with and without electricity.

✳ Where to Eat

EATING OUT **Bay Leaf Café** (605-642-5462), 126 W. Hudson St. Open 11–9. Housed in a historic building from 1892, the Bay Leaf Café specializes in fresh, local ingredients with a cross-cultural twist. They have American favorites like Black Hills trout and gourmet burgers, but also a little taste of the Mediterranean with Greek salads and a combo plate with hummus

and tabbouleh. Also check out Berry's Best for desserts and sweet treats like handmade chocolates, pies, and gorgeous wedding cakes. Entrées $13–$20.

Roma's (605-722-0715), 701 N. Fifth St. Open 11–2 and 4–9. Located in the historic Lown Building built over a hundred years ago, this Italian restaurant is upscale but has a casual environment where you will be comfortable enjoying pastas and specialties like white truffle chicken and pheasant ravioli. They also have a great wine list. Entrées from $7–$20.

Sanford's Grub and Pub (605-642-3204), 545 W. Jackson Blvd. Open daily 11 AM–10 PM. This is the original Sanford's and has great burgers, salads, steaks, pasta, and more in a great atmosphere of antiques and old signs. They also have an amazing selection of draft beers and a complete bar. Entrées range from $7–$21.

Spearfish Chophouse and Whiskey Bar (605-642-1134; spearfishchop house.com), 523 Spearfish Canyon Rd. Open 11 AM–10 PM. As the name suggests, this place specializes in steaks and has dozens of kinds of whiskeys, but the menu also includes sandwiches, seafood, and pasta. Entrées range from $10–$26.

Common Grounds Gourmet Coffee Shop and Deli (605-642-9066), 111 E. Hudson. This attractive coffee shop has all the specialty drinks, as well as bagels, sandwiches, wraps, and salads, with a nice seating area to relax and enjoy your food. $3–$6.

Stadium Sports Bar and Grill (605-642-9521; www.stadiumsportsgrill.net), 744 Main St. A sports bar with lots of TVs and pool tables, the menu features beef tips, burgers, and salads. They have nightly specials and a happy hour so stop in for a beer and watch a game with your friends. Entrées range from $7–$15.

✳ Entertainment

THEATER **Black Hills Passion Play** (1-800-457-0160; www.theblackhills passionplay.com), located just south of Spearfish on US 14A. Performances on Sunday, Tuesday, and Thursday at 8 PM. The Black Hills Passion Play has been going since 1938 and tells the story of Christ. The play has attracted millions of visitors to their 6,000-seat, outdoor amphitheater. It is best to call and reserve tickets. Tickets are $20–$25.

Spearfish Arts Center and Matthews Opera House (605-642-7973; www.spearfishartscenter.org), 614 Main St. Art gallery hours are 10–5 Tuesday through Saturday. Opened in 1906 and paid for by a local Wyoming rancher, the opera house began as a live venue and has finally returned to one. Over the years it has been a movie theater, a basketball court, and a dance hall. In the mid-1980s a group got together to restore the opera house and it is now the center of the arts community in Spearfish. The opera house productions begin at 7:30, ticket prices range from $11–$15. Call or check the Web site for up-to-date gallery events and shows.

✳ Selective Shopping

Downtown Spearfish has a number of fun shops, so wander down Main Street.

Book Trader (605-722-6952), 608 Main St. Open 9:30–5:30 Monday through Friday, 9:30–5 Saturday. Featuring local history and travel books this shop sells used books with some new.

Termesphere Gallery (605-642-4805; www.termesphere.com), 1920 Christensen Dr. Dick Termes is a nationally known artist who creates his artwork on spheres, using six-point perspective. These canvases hang from the ceiling and turn to show different viewpoints as they rotate before you. It's one of those things you really must see to appreciate. It is so distinctively different that it's worth the effort to visit his studio.

✳ Special Events

JULY **Festival in the Park** (605-642-7973; www.spearfishartscenter.org/), Spearfish City Park. Free. This festival is one of the best arts and crafts shows in the upper Midwest and draws the very best artists. There are 200 booths and live entertainment.

✳ Nearby

The geographic center of the total landmass of the United States is about 20 miles north of **Belle Fourche**, off US 85. It is located on the open prairie; the official designation is 44 degrees 58 inches north and longitude 103 degrees 46 feet west. It was moved here when Alaska and Hawaii were admitted into the United States in 1959.

Badlands Area

BADLANDS NATIONAL PARK

WALL

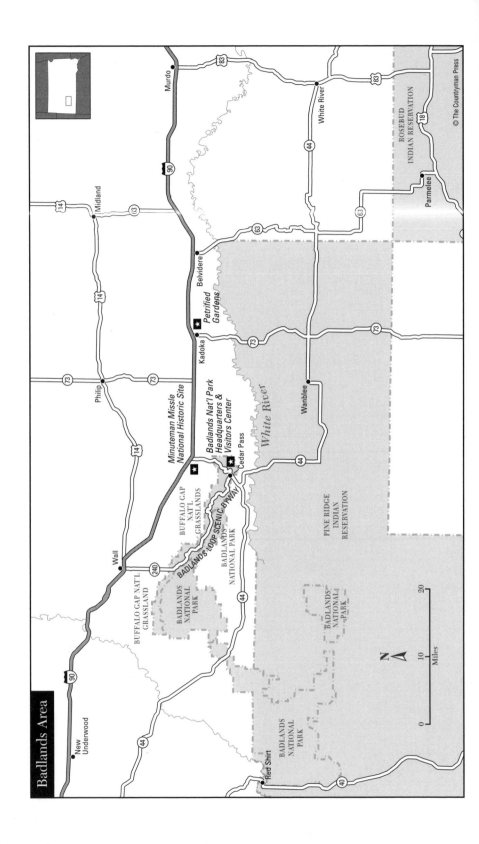

Badlands Area

© The Countryman Press

THE BADLANDS

The Badlands creep up on you. You begin to notice the flat, seemingly end-less expanse of the prairie give way to a gully here, a small multicolored mound there. And it just keeps getting more pronounced and more dramatic until you have entered a land that seems totally alien, filled with majestic spires, canyons, pinnacles, buttes, and deep gorges. This is the magic that nature has created, and continues to sculpt day in and day out.

As weather patterns shifted 65 million years ago, the floor of a former sea was compressed into a band of rock now known as Pierre Shale. Forests grew and fell to decay, volcanic ash was deposited, and rivers ran through the area leaving layers of sediment. With each layer, animal bodies and bones were trapped, leaving behind fossilized remains.

Wind, rain, and rivers that are now long gone, in collaboration with freezing cold and searing heat, began their work eating away at the soft deposits and created the

THE SPIRES OF THE BADLANDS RISE MAJESTICALLY OVER THE SURROUNDING PRAIRIE.

THE PRAIRIE HOMESTEAD HAS HISTORIC BUILDINGS FROM THE EARLY HOMESTEADING OF
SOUTH DAKOTA, INCLUDING A "SODDIE."

moonscape that is now the Badlands. The erosion continues every day, sculpting
new and different formations and exposing fossils and rocks long ago buried.

The Badlands are frighteningly alive. Not just with the endless cycle of erosion
but with mammals, reptiles, and birds that have adapted to the harsh environment.
Look for hawks and eagles soaring overhead in search of a meal of mice, shrew, or
rabbits. Watch a fox or coyote skulking about a prairie dog village looking for a
quick lunch. Or see pronghorn sheep delicately climbing the formations.

The Badlands are most dramatic at the beginning and end of the day when the
sun is low and spotlights the colored bands of deposits. Orange, rust, gold, browns,
and tans clearly delineate the earth that was laid down and has since been eaten
away.

Drive the entire loop through the Badlands National Park and stop to read the
interpretative signs. Take a closer look with a short walk on a well-marked path, or
take a longer hike with plenty of water. Visit for a day or stay for awhile and try to
comprehend the majesty of it all. The Badlands will likely entrance you and will
definitely create a lasting impression.

BADLANDS NATIONAL PARK

Badlands National Park was established in 1939 to preserve 244,000 acres of mixed-grass prairie. It is an ever-changing landscape, eroding as much as 1 inch per year. With deposits 37–28 million years old, this area contains the world's richest Oligocene-epoch fossil beds. Very early ancestors of the pig, horse, rabbit, and rhinoceros can be found here. Ongoing digs, like the "Pig Dig," bring together scientists and students every summer.

There is a 32-mile loop that takes you through the North Unit and offers many overlooks and interpretive signs. Most people who visit the park drive the loop, stop a few times for pictures, and move on. To really experience the park, it can take days of hiking and exploring but, at a minimum, an overnight stay and a sunrise or sunset make the experience far richer. Watching how the sun changes the colors of the Badlands as morning comes or as night falls is truly a magical experience.

The park is open year-round, $15 per car. If the weather is really bad, snow or heavy rain, it can be a tricky, if not impossible, drive. But don't let a little fog dissuade you—those spires peeking out of a fog bank can be really spooky and beautiful.

GUIDANCE **Badlands National Park** (605-433-5361; www.nps.gov/archive/badl/exp/home.htm).

GETTING THERE *By car:* take I-90 to exit 131 (Cactus Flats) or 110 (Wall). You will travel 7–10 miles to the park entrance.

GETTING AROUND There is no public transportation at Badlands National Park. Cars, motorcycles, and RVs drive the loop as well as very intrepid bicyclists.

MEDICAL EMERGENCIES Call 911.

SCENIC DRIVES **The Badlands Loop Road** is 32 miles long and paved. The speed limit is 45 miles per hour and there are numerous pull offs for picture taking and short hikes.

✳ To Do

BICYCLING Bicycles are allowed only on paved roads.

HIKING The entire park is open to hikers but common sense is required. The weather in the Badlands is extreme, so care must be taken to dress appropriately and to take adequate water. When it rains the ground can become extremely slick and streams can suddenly appear making paths impassable. Always stay at least 100 yards away from wildlife and assume they are dangerous. All plants, animals, rocks, and fossils in the Badlands National Park must remain undisturbed. Should you encounter a fossil that appears particularly interesting, report it to a ranger.

Castle Trail 5 miles. Castle Trail stretches from the Fossil Exhibit Trail to the Door and Window parking area. The trail is fairly level and offers an opportunity to see wildlife as well as Badland formations. Allow five hours.

Cliff Shelf Nature Trail 0.5 mile and located 0.5 mile north of the visitor center. The trail climbs approximately 200 feet in elevation, which makes it moderately easy, through a juniper forest with great views of the White River Valley. Allow a half hour.

Door Trail 0.75 mile. Starting at the northern end of the large Door and Window parking area, 2 miles northeast of the Ben Reifel Visitors Center, the Door Trail penetrates into wildly eroded badlands through a break called "The Door" in the Badlands Wall. This trail is easy but if you continue beyond the maintained trail, beware of drop0offs. Allow 20 minutes.

A BEAUTIFUL SUNRISE OVER THE PRAIRIE NEAR PIERRE.

&. **Fossil Exhibit Trail** 0.25 mile. Located 5 miles northwest of the Ben Reifel Visitor Center, the trail is a very easy walk and displays examples of Badlands fossils. During summer months, park naturalists give presentations about the fossil history of the park. Allow 20 minutes.

Notch Trail 1.5 miles. The trail begins at the north end of the Door and Window parking area and is considered moderate or strenuous. This trail offers great views but is not for those afraid of heights and is very treacherous during or after heavy rain. Allow one to one and a half hours.

Saddle Pass Trail 0.3 mile. The trailhead and parking area are located 2 miles west of the Ben Reifel Visitors Center. This a short but very steep trail. Allow a half hour to one hour.

Window 0.25 mile. This trail begins at the center of the Door and Window parking area and leads you to a window in the Badlands wall. Allow 20 minutes.

VISITOR CENTERS **Ben Reifel** located at Cedar Pass just inside the park entrance. The center is open year-round 7–7 in the summer, 9–4 in the winter. The visitors center houses a museum and exhibits as well as the park headquarters. In the 97-seat auditorium there is a movie about the park and restrooms and water is available. The Badlands Natural History Association sells books, postcards, posters, and other educational materials at the visitors center.

White River Visitor Center located in the south unit of the park on SD 27. Open during the summer 10–4. There are two units of the Badlands, one run by the National Park Service and one by the Oglala Sioux Tribe. The National Park unit is more developed, although rustic by the standards of some parks, and the tribe unit is completely undeveloped. This center is run by the Oglala Sioux Parks and Recreation Authority and has park information as well as tribal information. There are restrooms and water.

✳ Lodging

CAMPING If you are a hiker and want to go a little farther afield in the Badlands backcountry, camping is permitted anywhere in the park that is 0.5 mile from a road or trail. No fires are allowed and you must pack in everything you need and bring it out with you. No fees are charged and it is recommended that you tell the rangers where you are going and sign a trailhead log just to be on the safe side.

Cedar Pass Campground, located just inside the park entrance. Right in the park and adjacent to the restaurant and gift shop, this campground has 96 sites and is open year-round with water and toilets available, April through September. Open fires are not permit-

ted. First come, first served, $10 a night with a 14-day limit.

Sage Creek Primitive Campground, located 35 miles from the park entrance. For folks that really want to experience the Badlands without the distractions of the modern world, this campground is open year-round and has pit toilets and tables. There is dirt road access, which may be restricted depending on weather and is not recommended for large vehicles like RVs. There is no water available and no open fires are allowed. No fees are charged.

Badlands/White River KOA (605-433-5337; www.koa.com/where/sd/

JACKALOPES!

You are now in western South Dakota, so keep your eyes peeled for the dreaded jackalope! Jackalopes are a species of antlered rabbit and are extremely shy so they are sometimes rumored to be extinct. They are found throughout the western United States and are known to be extremely fierce when attacked.

Jackalopes can mimic the human voice and have been heard singing along with cowboys around their campfires. They also use their vocal abilities to avoid capture by yelling out things like "There he is over there," to throw off pursuers. The best way to capture a jackalope is to lure it with whiskey, as they are very fond of it and become very docile when drunk.

BEWARE THE WILY SOUTH DAKOTA JACKALOPE!

Jackalope milk is highly sought after for its medicinal qualities but difficult to get as it is very dangerous to milk a jackalope. The best time to try to milk a jackalope is when it is sleeping, as they tend to sleep belly up.

Check any tourist shop while in West River and you will find postcards and, very likely, head mounts of jackalopes. Buy a postcard or two and send them to your soon-to-be-astonished friends back home.

41111/index.htm), 20720 SD 44, Interior, SD. Just 4 miles from the park, this campground is next to the White River and has large shade trees. There is a pool for cooling off, mini golf, and camping cabins, as well as tent and RV sites. $22–$42 per night.

CABINS/MOTELS Cedar Pass Lodge (605-433-5460; www.cedarpasslodge.com). Open mid-May to October. Opened in 1928 this lodge predates the park and was a dance hall with music by the likes of Lawrence Welk. Each cabin has heat and air-conditioning and a bath but no phones or TV. The cabins may be rustic but they are right in the park so you will experience the Badlands sunrise to sunset. They are also located next to the only restaurant in the park. Cabins $75–$90 a night, cottages $105 a night.

Badlands Inn (605-433-5401; www.cedarpasslodge.com), Open mid-May to October. Located 1.5 miles from the Ben Reifel Visitors Center. Slightly more upscale and still in the park, these 18 motel rooms include TV and phone, as well as heat and air-conditioning. $80 per night.

✳ Where to Eat

EATING OUT Cedar Pass Lodge Restaurant (605-433-5460; www.cedarpasslodge.com). Open 7 AM–8:30 PM, seven days a week, serving breakfast, lunch, and dinner. This is the only restaurant option in the park but has good diner fare with great Indian tacos and fried chicken. If there is a tour bus in the parking lot when you arrive, come back later as there won't be any seats left.

SELECTIVE SHOPPING Cedar Pass Lodge Gift Store (www.cedarpasslodge.com). Open 7 AM–9 PM in the summer, 8–4 in the winter. This is the only store in the park, and worth a stop for its nice selection of Native American crafts. Besides souvenirs, gifts, clothing, and snack foods they also have essential Badlands items such as the all important bug spray for when you encounter a swarm of "no-see-ums."

WALL

Why go to Wall? Wall Drug, of course. If you've been traveling any roads in South Dakota you have seen the WALL DRUG, FREE ICE WATER signs and know the exact mileage to Wall Drug. What is Wall Drug? Nothing less than 76,000 square feet of Americana. In business since 1931, Wall Drug survived the Depression by offering travelers free ice water and is now one of America's best-known roadside attractions.

But there are museums and sights in or near Wall, including the Wounded Knee Museum and the Minuteman Missile National Historic Site. Wall is a good place to set up a home base for exploring the Badlands, the Buffalo Gap National Grassland, and, of course, Wall Drug.

GUIDANCE **Wall Badlands Chamber of Commerce** (1-888-852-9255; www .wall-badlands.com).
Buffalo Gap National Grassland (www.fs.fed.us/r2/nebraska/units/frrd/ bgng.html).

GETTING THERE *By car:* Wall is on I-90, about 50 miles east of Rapid City.

MEDICAL EMERGENCIES Call 911.

✳ To See

HISTORIC SITES **Minuteman Missile National Historic Site** (605-433-5552; www.nps.gov/mimi), exit 131 off I-90. The park visitors center is open 8–4:30 Monday through Friday, all year-round. Tours take about two hours and are extremely limited so you need to call for reservations. Beginning in 1962, 1,000 Minuteman Intercontinental Ballistic Missiles were deployed in silos throughout the Midwest to act as a deterrent against a nuclear war with Russia. The missiles had a range of up to 6,000 miles, a distance they could reach in half an hour. Two Air Force officers lived in underground command centers and were responsible for the launching of 10 missiles should the order come. At the end of the Cold War, through treaties with Russia, many of the missiles were decommissioned, although the U.S. still has 450 that are operational. The launch sites were taken apart and the missiles silos filled with concrete but one was turned into a National Historic Site for the purpose of teaching Americans about the Cold War and American history. This site is interesting, and perhaps chilling, for those of us who remember duck-and-cover drills and instructional for the younger crowd who don't remember when Russia was not our friend. Free.

Prairie Homestead (605-433-5400; www.prairiehomestead.com), off I-90, exit 131. Go 2 miles south on SD 240. Open sunup to sundown. With a sod dugout and other buildings from the early 1900s, this site reflects the living conditions of early settlers. And what was a "soddie"? Due to the lack of trees in the prairies, early settlers cut chunks of sod and used them for building blocks to create a house. Perhaps not the cleanest place to live, the sod did act as an insulator and helped folks survive frigid winters. It's an interesting history lesson for the family on how harsh conditions were for the folks that settled South Dakota and the plains. They also have the only white prairie-dog village and a very nice gift shop with lots of good books on western history. $5 for adults, $4 for children.

MUSEUMS **Wounded Knee Museum** (605-279-2573; www.woundedknee museum.org), 207 10th Ave., Wall. Open 8:30–5:30 seasonally until October 10. On December 29, 1890, 300 Lakota men, women, and children were gunned down by the Seventh Cavalry not far from Wall, putting an end to the Indian uprisings in the West. It is a complex story of the Lakota people and how their lives were forever altered by the arrival of white settlers and this museum tells the story in great detail. You can spend several hours reading all the exhibits and looking at all the photographs and documents or you can skim the abridged version provided with each panel. Not for little kids, but older ones could learn a lot from this chapter in American history. $5 for adults, free for children ages 12 and under.

✳ To Do

BIKING/HIKING You can hike or bike anywhere in the **Buffalo Gap National Grasslands**. There is one developed trail near Wall. To access this trail, from I-90 take exit 116, go south, cross two auto gates, then park. Wooden 4x4 posts mark this 5.5-mile loop trail. There is an extension of this trail to make it a 15-mile loop. The Badlands Wall formation is always in view off this trail.

WOUNDED KNEE WAS THE SITE OF AN INDIAN MASSACRE THAT MARKED THE END OF THE INDIAN UPRISINGS IN THE WEST.

South Dakota Tourism

GOLF Wall Community Golf Course (605-279-4653), 1802 Golf Course Rd. This is a nine-hole golf course that is suitable for beginners and experienced players. There is a clubhouse available. Green fees $21–$24.

HUNTING The Buffalo Gap National Grassland has hunting for deer, turkey, game birds, and varmint hunting for prairie dogs and coyotes. South Dakota regulations apply—visit the Game, Fish, and Parks Web site for details (www.sdgfp .info/Index.htm); licenses are available at **Wall Building Center**, 109 South Boulevard.

ROCKHOUNDING The Buffalo Gap National Grassland is rockhounding heaven. There are numerous types of minerals, including Fairburn Agates, Banded Jasper, Rose Quartz, Prairie Agate, Chalcedony, Bubble Gum Agate, Puddingstone Conglomerate, Water Agate, Black Agate, and Moss Agate, and fossils galore. There are restrictions and the main ones is that you cannot collect for commercial use, and a permit is required for vertebrate paleontological specimens on federal land. In other words if you find a dinosaur, don't disturb it and go tell a ranger. Be very certain you are not on private property when collecting.

✳ Green Spaces

PARKS National Grasslands Visitors Center (605-279-2125; www.fs.fed.us/ r2/nebraska/units/frrd/bgng.html), 708 Main St., Wall. The 600,000-acre Buffalo Gap National Grassland is dotted throughout southwestern South Dakota. The visitors center provides information about the grasslands, activities available there, and is staffed by Forest Service people who can provide you with guidance.

✳ Lodging

There are a number of small motels and chain motels in Wall along I-90. They fill up toward the end of the day with travelers coming off the interstate, so it is wise to book early. Some options include **Best Western** (800-528-1234) and **Days Inn** (605-279-2000).

BED & BREAKFAST INNS Dakota Memories B&B (605-279-2948; www.dakotamemorieswallsd.com), 608 Glenn St. Open May 1 through October 31. This is the only bed-and-breakfast in Wall and a nice one. The upstairs is where the owners live and the downstairs has two rooms available, as well as a living room and dining room. It is very nicely decorated with antiques and handmade quilts and both rooms have flat-screen TVs. $110.

CAMPING (see other camping options under **Badlands National Park**).

French Creek Campground is the only campground in the Buffalo Gap National Grasslands. It is located 10 miles east of the town of Fairburn. Pit toilets and tables are available. You can do primitive camping anywhere in the grasslands but must bring in anything you will need, including water, and carry it out.

✳ Where to Eat

Honestly, Wall is not for the gourmet. Wall Drug has cafeteria-style food, there is a Dairy Queen, and then a few other small restaurants. Eat to survive in Wall and save dining out for when you get to the Black Hills.

EATING OUT Cactus Café (605-279-2561), Main St. across from Wall

Drug. Opens at 6 AM and serves breakfast, lunch, and dinner. There are burgers, steaks, Mexican food, sandwiches, and pasta in a small, casual space. You can also order from the same menu at the bar next door. Entrées $8–$18.

Elkton House (605-279-2152), 203 S. Blvd. Open 5:30–10:00 PM. The menu looks considerably better than the food tastes but they have burgers, sandwiches, salads, steak, and chicken strips. Entrées $8–$16.

✳ Selective Shopping

Wall Drug (605-279-2175; www.walldrug.com), 510 Main St. Open 6:30 AM–6 PM in the winter, 6:30 AM–10 PM in the summer. To put it simply, if you can't find it at Wall Drug, you probably don't need it. Wall Drug started as a small town drug store in 1931 and it has mushroomed into 76,000 square feet of free attractions, shopping, and a restaurant that holds 520. There is the ultratacky, right next to classy. There is tourist junk and honest to goodness collectibles. You can find cowboy apparel, books, Native American arts and crafts, pottery, South Dakota–made products, T-shirts, sculpture, rocks and minerals, toys, and the all-important Jackalope, just to name a few. Plan on spending several hours wandering and gawking, or longer if you are a serious shopper. Two tips: 1) This is a great place to buy Black Hills Gold at excellent prices, and 2) don't miss the fresh-made doughnuts.

✳ Nearby

Murdo is home to the **Pioneer Auto Show and Prairie Town**. They may call it an auto show, but there is much more to 42 buildings that go on forever with every conceivable antique as well as a really nice mineral collection. The

WALL DRUG HAS SOMETHING FOR EVERYONE FROM TOURIST ITEMS TO FINE ARTS.

whole thing started in 1954 with a gas station and a few cars and has continued to grow. It now includes 275 cars, not to mention motorcycles and tractors. There is also a decent café, ice cream, and a really nice gift shop for the car enthusiast, with books, signs, T-shirts, and collectibles from every car maker old and new. $9 entrance fee.

Just west of **Murdo** is the **1880 Town,** which has 30 historic buildings outfitted as they would have been in the 1880s. Since parts of it were filmed, nearby there are also set pieces from *Dances with Wolves.* You'll also find memorabilia of Casey Tibbs, a world-champion rodeo star. $9 for adults, $5–$6 for children.

PIONEER AUTO NOT ONLY HAS CARS ON DISPLAY BUT ANTIQUE FARM EQUIPMENT AND MOTORCYCLES.

VISITING THE PINE RIDGE INDIAN RESERVATION

South Dakota is home to nine Indian Reservations, including the nation's second largest, Pine Ridge, which adjoins Badlands National Park. Pine Ridge Reservation was originally part of the Great Sioux Reservation, which included all of South Dakota west of the Missouri River. Today Pine Ridge is 2.7 million acres and has about 40,000 people living on the reservation. Pine Ridge is very rural with few job opportunities and an unemployment rate of 85 percent, with 97 percent of the population living below the poverty level. Shannon County, where much of Pine Ridge is located, is the poorest county in the United States. Most income for the reservation comes from ranching, the tribe, Oglala Lakota College, Indian Health Services, the Bureau of Indian Affairs, and the Prairie Winds Casino.

There are other serious issues facing the residents of Pine Ridge including a 70 percent drop-out rate, a life expectancy of 45 years old, an infant mortality rate 300 percent higher than the national average, and a diabetes rate 800 percent higher than the national average, just to name a few. Fortunately, the Lakota people are proud and determined to overcome the problems of reservation life. Unfortunately, funding is always an obstacle to their success.

Pine Ridge is open to visitors and features two sights that are of particular interest to those wanting to understand and appreciate the history and culture of the Lakota people. It is wise to carefully check directions before driving on the reservation as not all roads are paved and it is pretty easy to get lost.

The Heritage Center of the Red Cloud Indian School (605-867-5491; www.redcloudschool.org/museum), located on the campus of the Red Cloud Indian School, 100 Mission Dr., Pine Ridge. Open 8–6 in the summer, 8–5 in the winter. The Heritage Center's collection includes over two thousand paintings, drawings, and sculptures representing a large number of different Native American tribal traditions. Free, donations accepted.

Wounded Knee Massacre Site, located off Bureau of Indian Affairs Highway 27, east of Wounded Knee. Open year-round. This site is not highly accessible and marked by only a stone monument. There is a small cemetery where the massacre victims and others have been buried, as well as some historical information. If you want a better understanding of the Wounded Knee Massacre, visit the Wounded Knee Museum in Wall.

Missouri River

PIERRE AND FORT PIERRE

CHAMBERLAIN–OACOMA

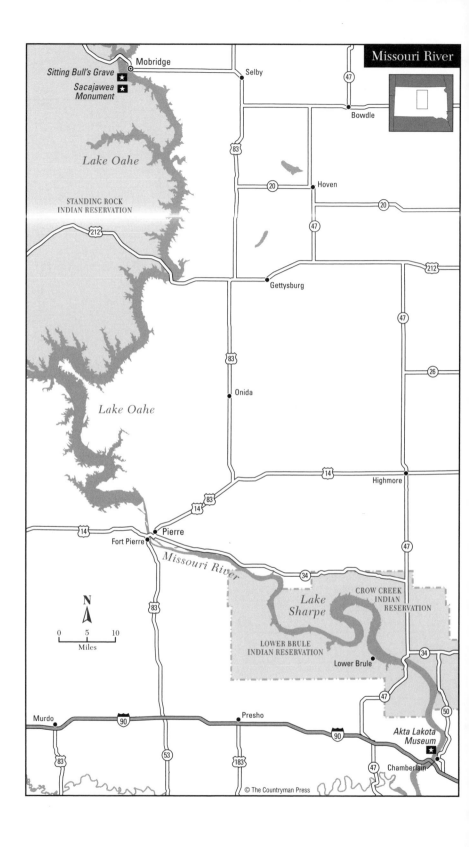

Missouri River

Mobridge
Sitting Bull's Grave ★
Sacajawea ★
Monument

Selby

47

Bowdle

83

Lake Oahe

20

Hoven

20

STANDING ROCK
INDIAN RESERVATION

47

212

212

Gettysburg

47

83

26

Onida

Lake Oahe

14

Highmore

14

83

Pierre

Fort Pierre

Missouri River

14

47

34

N
0 5 10
Miles

83

Lake
Sharpe

CROW CREEK
INDIAN
RESERVATION

LOWER BRULE
INDIAN RESERVATION

Lower Brule

34

47

50

Murdo

90

Presho

90

Akta Lakota
Museum
★

53

183

47 Chamberlain

83

© The Countryman Press

MISSOURI RIVER

The Missouri River, America's second longest, is formed by the joining of the Gallatin, Madison, and Jefferson Rivers, near Three Forks, Montana. The Missouri River flows south-southeast and joins the Mississippi at St. Louis, Missouri.

Before being modified by man, the Missouri River was known for its shifting channels and periodic floods. Called the Big Muddy, the Missouri provided a travel way for man and wildlife, including the major "highway" for the Lewis and Clark Expedition.

Today the river has been tamed by dams and is divided into three parts—the lower one-third, below Sioux City, Iowa, is channelized; one-third is impacted by six large dams; and one-third consists of remnant "free-flowing" stretches of water. Only 1 percent of the river's entire length remains truly uncontrolled by humans.

In South Dakota, the Missouri River enters the state in the north-central region near Pollock and flows generally south. Near Pickstown the river turns southeast, forming a common boundary with the state of Nebraska, until it leaves South Dakota at the southeast corner, near Jefferson. As it flows through South Dakota, the Missouri River is fed by seven major tributary rivers and streams—the Grand, Moreau, Cheyenne, Bad, White, James, and Big Sioux Rivers. There are four major dams on the Missouri in South Dakota—Oahe, Big Bend, Ft. Randall, and Gavins Point. The dams serve multiple purposes, creating hydroelectric power, flood control, navigation, municipal water, irrigation, fish and wildlife habitat, and recreation.

PIERRE AND FORT PIERRE

Pierre is close to the geographic center of South Dakota and is the capital city. Pierre was founded in 1880 to provide support for gold prospectors headed to the Black Hills when the railroad came. Pierre was soon established as a hub for goods and people moving throughout the region.

South Dakota became a state in 1889 and the next question was, where should the capital be? Some thought Pierre's location made it a logical choice, while others wanted it closer to the population centers of the eastern part of the state. It took two costly elections to decide the issue and in the first Huron challenged Pierre, in the second Mitchell. In the end the legislature voted to build a permanent state capitol building in Pierre, putting an end to the controversy.

Today Pierre is a relatively small town of 14,000 on the hills above the river, and home of the state government. There are many historic homes, large deciduous trees, and the Missouri River. Pierre is also a recreation center because of its location on the Missouri River and the plains. People come to Pierre to conduct government business and to fish, boat, hunt, and enjoy all that the river and its reservoirs have to offer.

Fort Pierre is located across the river from Pierre and is where the Verendyne brothers left their marker claiming South Dakota for France in 1743. Fort Pierre's central location on the Missouri made it a trailhead for the Fort Pierre Deadwood Trail, where thousands of people traveled to the Black Hills in search of gold.

GUIDANCE Pierre Chamber of Commerce (605-224-7361; www.pierre.org), 800 West Dakota Ave.

City of Fort Pierre (www.fortpierre.com).

GETTING THERE *By car:* Pierre is located on US 14 going east to west and US 83 going north to south.

Fort Pierre is directly west of Pierre on US 83. Pierre is 171 miles from Rapid City and 226 miles from Sioux Falls.

GETTING AROUND
River Cities Transit (605-945-2360) provides taxis and bus service in the area but plan on driving yourself.

St. Mary's Healthcare Center (605-224-3100; www.st-marys.com), 801 E. Sioux Ave., Pierre.

✳ To See

CULTURAL SITES ⬆ South Dakota Cultural Heritage Center (605-773-3458; www.sdhistory.org), 900 Governors Dr., Pierre. Open Memorial Day through Labor Day, Monday through Saturday 9–6:30, Sunday and holidays 1–4:30; winter hours, 9–4:30. A part of the South Dakota State Historical Society, this 63,000-square-foot, earth-covered building features permanent and rotating exhibits of the state's Sioux Indians and early European settlers. There is also a gift shop, the Heritage Store, with 400 book titles, items made in South Dakota, and Native American arts and crafts. $4 for adults, free for ages 17 and under.

🐚 Oahe Dam Visitor Center (605-224-5862; www.corpslakes.usace.army.mil/visitors/projects.cfm?Id=G612960), 7 miles north of Pierre on SD 1804. Open Memorial Day through Labor Day. Stretching 245 feet high and 456 feet across, the Oahe Dam created the fourth largest reservoir in the United States. Begun in 1948 and dedicated in 1962, Oahe is one of the six dams that were built to tame the wild Missouri River. It generates electricity using seven turbines that provide power for five states. The visitors center provides a complete history of Lake Oahe, the Missouri River, and the construction of the Oahe Dam and power plant. Tours are available. Free.

HISTORIC SITES 🐚 The State Capitol (www.sd.gov), 500 East Capitol Ave., Pierre. Open 8 AM–10 PM year-round. Built in 1910, the capitol interior is truly spectacular with great murals of prairie history, marble staircases, stained glass, and tile work including a terrazzo floor that was laid by 66 workers from Italy. The interior of the dome, towering 96 feet above the floor, with its stained glass and wooden beams, is itself worth the visit. On the capitol grounds are a number of memorials and monuments, a 5-acre lake, and 48 acres of cultured grass. A self-guided tour brochure is available at the tour office located at the north entrance of the capitol.

The Fighting Stallion Memorial This dramatic statue is a bronze replica of a sculpture created by Korczak Ziolkowski, who is responsible for the carving of Crazy Horse Mountain near Custer. The two stallions entwined in combat are a memorial that honors

THE CAPITOL ROTUNDA SOARS ABOVE THE MARBLE FLOOR BELOW.

THIS BRONZE SCULPTURE MARKS A MEMORIAL FOR GOVERNOR GEORGE MICHELSON AND SEVEN OTHERS WHO WERE KILLED IN A TRAGIC PLANE CRASH.

Governor George Mickelson and seven other South Dakotans who died in a 1993 plane crash. Information about each is displayed on the base of the statue.

The World War II Memorial On a peninsula built into Capitol Lake this memorial honors all who served in World War II. The memorial consists of six dramatic life-size bronze figures representing each of the military branches.

The Korean War Memorial has a wall bearing the name of South Dakotans who died in that war and a life-size statue of a soldier for that war.

The Vietnam Memorial was dedicated in 2006 and has the names of South Dakota soldiers who died there.

The Flaming Fountain is fueled by an artesian well that has such a high-gas content it can be lit. It burns continuously as a memorial to all veterans.

There is also a memorial that honors fallen state firefighters and police officers.

Lewis and Clark Historic Trail (www.lewisandclarktrail.com and www.nps.gov/lecl). The Lewis and Clark Trail traces the route of the explorers 3,700 miles through 11 states (see further information about Lewis and Clark in the section on Southeast South Dakota, page 162). The expedition traveled the Missouri River through present-day Pierre in September 1804. There are several stops on the trail in Pierre and information can be found in brochures distributed by the **Pierre Convention and Visitors Bureau**.

REPRESENTING EACH BRANCH OF THE MILITARY SERVICES THIS MEMORIAL HONORS WWII VETERANS.

You can also visit the **Lewis and Clark Family Center** to enjoy interactive displays. The center is located at the **Farm Island Recreation Area**, 1301 Farm Island Road, Pierre (605-773-2885).

🏛 **Historic Pierre and Fort Pierre Driving Tour** (www.historicpierre.com/historicsites.pdf), maps available at the **Pierre Area Chamber of Commerce,** 800 West Dakota Ave., Pierre. This self-guided tour takes you to 35 sites in the Pierre and Fort Pierre area including museums, parks, lakes, and historic markers. Many items on the tour are included in this book but

pick up a map as it provides other history and information about Pierre and Fort
Pierre that may be of interest.

⚲ Historic Pierre Homes Driving Tour (800-962-2034; www.historicpierre
.com), maps are available at the **Pierre Area Chamber of Commerce**, 800 West
Dakota Ave., Pierre. This driving tour takes you past homes dating from the 1800s
through the mid-20th century. A number of the homes are on the National Register of Historic Places. Allow an hour to complete the tour.

The Verendrye Monument, Verendrye Dr., Ft. Pierre. In 1743, on a windy bluff
overlooking Fort Pierre, Louis Verendrye and his brother planted a lead plate
claiming the land for Louis XV, King of France, the first proof of whites in South
Dakota. The plate was unearthed accidentally in 1913 by school children and is on
display in the **Cultural Heritage Center**, in Pierre. The monument marks the
spot the plate was found, includes a replica, and offers a great view of the Missouri
River and Fort Pierre.

✳ To Do

BICYCLING **La Framboise Island Nature Area** is a sandbar island in the Missouri located on the southwest side of Pierre. It offers 7–10 miles of bike trails.
Lewis and Clark Bicentennial Trail, 26 miles running from Farm Island just
south of Pierre to Oahe Downstream
Recreation Area.

BOATING AND FISHING This area
is boating and fishing heaven with
access to the **Missouri River, Lake
Oahe,** and **Lake Sharpe**. Fishing is
accessible from the many miles off-
shore or by boat. Fish species include
walleye, northern pike, bass, Chinook
salmon, trout, and catfish. From April
through October Missouri River fishing conditions are available by calling
toll-free 1-800-445-FISH (3474).

There are three-dozen boat ramps
along the shores of **Lake Oahe** and
Lake Sharpe. Check the state's Web
site for boat ramp conditions at www
.sdgfp.info/Wildlife/Boating/Ramp
Conditions.htm.

Fishing licenses are required and are
available at numerous outlets in Pierre
including:

Wal-Mart 1730 N. Garfield, **Kmart**
1516 N. Harrison, and **Runnings** 1600
N. Harrison.

Some consider Lake Oahe to have
the best freshwater scuba diving and

THE INTERIOR OF THE SOUTH DAKOTA
CAPITOL IS DECORATED WITH BEAUTIFUL
MURALS, MARBLE, AND STAINED GLASS
WINDOWS.

THE MISSOURI RIVER IS THE SECOND LONGEST RIVER IN AMERICA AND JOINS THE MIS-
SISSIPPI IN ST. LOUIS.

spear fishing available. Sailing, Jet-Skiing, and water skiing are also popular activities on the lakes.

FAMILY FRIENDLY 🌲 **South Dakota Discovery Center and Aquarium**
(605-224-8295; www.sd-discovery.com), 805 West Sioux Ave, Pierre. Summer
hours, 10–5 Monday through Saturday, 1–5 Sunday. Featuring interactive science
exhibits, this discovery center can keep the family amused for quite awhile playing
and learning. Suitable for all ages, there is also an aquarium where you can learn
about the species of fish native to the Missouri River. $4 for adults, $3 for children.

Capital City Queen River Boat Tours (605-224-7361; www.pierre.org/cap
queen.shtm), located at the end of Poplar Avenue on the La Framboise Island
Causeway. Sunday and Tuesday at 7 PM, weather permitting. This two-hour tour
goes up the Missouri River and visits historic landmarks in the Pierre area. Included is the mouth of the Bad River, where Lewis and Clark held counsel with
the Teton Sioux. $20 for adults, $9 for children.

GOLF **Dakota Dunes Golf Course** (605-223-2525; www.golfdunes.com), 111
Fort Chauteau Rd., Ft. Pierre. Established in 1887 this public 18-hole course is
one of the oldest in the country. It has won numerous mentions as best-in-the-
state. $24 for 18 holes.

Hillsview Golf Course (605-224-6191; www.hillsviewgolfcourse.com), 4201 E.
SD 34, Pierre. An 18-hole golf course where the wind can really come into play.
There are also water hazards on eight holes. $24 for 18 holes.

Oahe Trails Golf Course (605-224-9340; www.oahetrails.com), 101 Lake Place,
Pierre. This is a nine-hole course that uses water and bunkers to make it exciting.
$25 for nine holes with a cart.

Willow Creek Golf Course (605-223-3154), SD 1434, Ft. Pierre. This nine-hole public course provides a challenge for any skill level. $14 for nine holes.

HIKING **Farm Island Recreation Area**, 4 miles east of Pierre on SD 34, has several trails for hiking, including the following:

Nature Exploration Trail, 3 miles long, begins at the south end of the causeway. You can imagine what it was like when Lewis and Clark were here over two hundred years ago while you observe the wildlife and many birds.

Lewis and Clark Trail 14.5 miles long from Farm Island to Oahe Downstream. Trailheads are at **Farm Island Recreation Area, LaFramboise Island Nature Area,** and **Oahe Downstream Recreation Area**.

La Framboise Island Nature Area, located on the southwest side of Pierre, connects to the Lewis and Clark Trail. There is also the La Framboise Island Nature Trail, which is 7 miles long and begins at the end of the causeway. It is not uncommon to see bald eagles and deer on the island.

Oahe Downstream Recreation Area, 5 miles north of Pierre on SD 1806, connects to the Lewis and Clark Trail. There is also the Cottonwood Path Trail, which is 1.5 miles, and the trailhead is northwest of the marina. In the winter bald eagles nest in the trees just below the dam.

HUNTING More than 15 million ducks and 750,000 geese pass through South Dakota from October to January and a main corridor for their migration is the Missouri River. The **Fort Pierre National Grasslands** has grouse and pheasant hunting mid-October through January. August through December there are hunting seasons for turkey, deer, and antelope. **The Cheyenne Ridge Outfitters and Lodge** (877-850-5144) offers guided hunting trips. November through January, the **Triple U Ranch** (605-567-3624), located 35 miles northwest of Pierre, is a buffalo ranch that offers guided trophy-buffalo hunts and meat hunts. Varmint

THE MISSOURI RIVER WINDS THROUGH SOUTH DAKOTA NORTH TO SOUTH AND PROVIDES GREAT RECREATIONAL OPPORTUNITIES.

hunting for prairie dogs is allowed on the **Fort Pierre National Grasslands** June through February and coyotes may be hunted year-round throughout the state. All hunting in South Dakota requires licenses and they are available at various retailers in Pierre (see *Boating and Fishing*) or by going to the state Web site at www .sdgfp.info.

SWIMMING Water, water everywhere . . . where do you want to spend the day swimming?

Pierre Aquatic Center (605-224-1683), 900 E. Church St. Open year-round, 4 AM–10:30 PM Monday through Friday, 6–5 Saturday, and 1–5 Sunday. This city-run aquatic center features water slides, pools, and spray toys. A good bargain for a water park, admission is only $5 for adults, $3 for students (14–18), $2 for children.

Farm Island Recreation Area (605-773-2885; www.sdgfp.info/parks/Regions/ OaheSharpe/FarmIsland.htm), 4 miles east of Pierre on SD 34, has a swimming beach. $5 park entrance fee.

Oahe Downstream Recreation Area (605-223-7722; www.sdgfp.info/parks/ Regions/OaheSharpe/OaheDownstream.htm), 5 miles north of Ft. Pierre on SD 1806, on the south side of Oahe Dam, has a swimming beach. $5 park entrance fee.

Pierre Municipal Pool (605-773-7445; ci.pierre.sd.us/parks/outdoorpool.shtm). Open 1–5 PM and 7–9 PM June through August. $1.50 for adults, $1 for children.

West Bend Recreation Area (605-223-7722; www.sdgfp.info/Parks/Regions/ OaheSharpe/WestBend.htm), located on the Missouri River 35 miles southeast of Pierre on SD 34, has a swimming beach.

Fort Pierre Fisher Lilly Park (605-223-7696; www.fortpierre.com/Parks.aspx). Open Sunday through Friday 12–5 and 6–8, Saturday 12:30–5. This is a city pool, open to visitors. 75¢ for adults, 50¢ for children.

THE OAHE DAM PROVIDES ELECTRICITY TO FIVE MIDWESTERN STATES.

SOUTH DAKOTA RODEOS

Since there have been cowboys there have been rodeos. Any time a group of cowboys got together they ended up showing off their riding and roping skills in friendly competitions. And long before the tradition of rodeos evolved, the local town folks would show up to watch.

Rodeos have been going on in South Dakota for at least 200 years. As early as 1918 a rodeo in Belle Fourche drew in 16,000 spectators. Today there are dozens of rodeos in South Dakota celebrating the cowboy heritage that built the ranching industry of the state. Just about every community has an arena and some kind of rodeo throughout the year. Rodeos are sanctioned by a number of organizations, the largest being the PRCA, or Professional Rodeo Cowboy Association. They're the "big daddy" of rodeo and crown the world champions in various events every year in Las Vegas. In South Dakota you will also find the South Dakota Rodeo Association (SDRA), National Intercollegiate Rodeo Association (NIRA), National High School Rodeo Association, and Great Plains Indian Association (GPIA) events. Some folks rodeo part-time, others are true professionals competing for 30 million dollars worth of prize money every year.

There are a number of rodeo events and all are timed and some are judged. You can expect to see some or any of the following if you go to a rodeo:

Barrel racing is a competition for women in which they ride as fast as they can around a line of barrels.

In steer wrestling a rider chases a steer, then jumps off his horse, grabs it by the horns, and throws it to the ground.

Calf roping requires the cowboy to rope a calf by the neck and then jump off the horse to tie three of its feet together. In this event the horse and rider work together because the horse keeps the rope tight while the cowboy ties the calf.

In team roping two cowboys ride together after a steer. The lead rider lassos the steer's horns while the second rider lassos the back legs. The two riders then pull the steer down with the two ropes.

Bronc riding is done with or without a saddle, known as bareback riding. The object is to stay on a bucking horse for a certain amount of time.

Probably the most well-known event of modern day rodeos is bull riding in which a cowboy tries to stay on a very agitated bull for eight seconds. It is a very dangerous sport and that's where the rodeo clowns, or bull fighters, come in to distract the bull after a rider falls off, so the cowboy can run to safety.

There are ample opportunities to enjoy rodeo, while visiting South Dakota, especially in the summer. Check with the community you are visiting or the events calendar at www.travelsd.com.

UNIQUE ADVENTURES **Korkow Ranch Rodeo School** (605-224-5607, www .korkowrodeos.com/school.html), Korkow's Anchor K Ranch, Pierre. No joke, you can go to rodeo school and learn bareback riding, saddle-bronc riding, bull riding, and bull fighting from rodeo champions. The three-day classes run around $280 per event. A waiver of liability is required, but then you probably figured that. For all manner of unique adventures stop into **Steamboat's Inc.** (1-800-239-9380) at 511 W. Dakota St. They'll rent you a boat or Jet Ski, teach you how to scuba dive, or drop you off at the Oahe Marina and send you downriver in a kayak or canoe after a bit of instruction. During the winter they process game for the local and visiting hunters.

✳ Green Spaces

PARKS The city of **Pierre** has 11 parks with various facilities; please see information under specific categories such as *Camping, Swimming,* and *Hiking.* Further information can be found at www.ci.pierre.sd.us/parks/parkmaps.shtm

WILDLIFE REFUGES **Fort Pierre National Grassland** (www.fs.fed.us/r2/ nebraska/units/fp/ftpierre.html), located south of Fort Pierre on US 83, is available for primitive camping, hunting, fishing in the small lakes and ponds, hiking, and biking. It is also a good spot for birding and viewing blinds are available in April and May with reservations. Within the grasslands is the **Richland Wildlife Area,** which includes Richland Reservoir and over 500 acres of treeless mixed-grass prairie that is not grazed by livestock.

WINTER SPORTS ✳ All the trails in the Pierre area are used for snowshoeing and cross-country skiing in the winter. Ice fishing for walleye, northern pike, and yellow perch takes place at **Griffin Park** and **Farm Island** as well as **Oahe Downstream**. There are two ice rinks at the **Fort Pierre Community Expo Center**, open mid-October through March. Hours and fees vary so call the Expo Center at 605-223-2178.

✳ Lodging

There are many motels in Pierre, if for no other reason than to provide a place for people doing business in the capital to stay (including legislators). One of the most popular is the **Best Western Ramkota Hotel** (605-224-6877) because it is an event center with an indoor pool.

BED & BREAKFAST INNS **Norbeck House Inn** (605-224-7474; thenorbeckhouseinn.com), 106 E. Wynoka St., Pierre. Built in 1904, this inn was once the home of the first South Dakota born governor, Peter Norbeck, well known in the Black Hills for the Peter Norbeck Scenic Highway. Completely restored, the inn includes the original maple wood floors and visitors are welcome to relax in the library, parlor, or formal dining room. There are five elegantly restored period rooms, some with private baths and sitting areas. Amenities include high-speed Internet, cable TV, and bathrobes, and massages are available with advanced appointments. $115–$180.

CAMPING **Cow Creek Recreation Area** (605-223-7722; www.sdgfp.info/ Parks/Regions/OaheSharpe/CowCreek.

htm), located on the Lake Oahe Reservoir 15 miles northwest of Pierre on SD 1804. Open year-round. There are showers and water. $10 nonelectrical, $14 electrical per site.

Farm Island Recreation Area, see listing under *Swimming*. Open year-round with 90 campsites in two campgrounds, all with electric. There are showers, water, and a dump station. $16 per site.

Fort Pierre Fisher Lilly Park (605-223-7696; www.fortpierre.com/Parks .aspx), SD 83. This is a city-owned campground with 12 RV pads with water and electricity. $10 a night, first come, first serve availability.

Griffin Park Campground (www.ci.pierre.sd.us/parks/camp grounds.shtm), Parkwood Dr. This is a city-owned campground and has 16 sites available first come, first serve. There are restrooms and a dump station. Open year-round, $15.

Oahe Downstream Recreation Area, see listing under *Swimming*. Open April through December. There are 205 sites in three campgrounds, all with electric, water, showers, and dump station. With direct access to Lake Sharpe, this is a great spot for all recreational activities and the place to see bald eagles. $16 per site. There are also five camping cabins, which sleep four for $35.

Okobojo Point Recreation Area (605-223-7722; www.sdgfp.info/Parks/ Regions/OaheSharpe/OkobojoPoint .htm), located on the Missouri River 17 miles northwest of Pierre on SD 1804. Open year-round. There are 17 sites with water and showers. $10 per site.

West Bend Recreation Area, see listing under *Swimming*. Open year-round. There are 126 shaded campsites, some right on the lake, with showers, water, and a dump station.

$10 nonelectrical, $14 electrical site. There are also four camping cabins available for $35.

✳ Where to Eat

DINING OUT **La Minestra** (605-224-8090; www.laminestra.com), 106 East Dakota, Pierre. Open 11–2 and 5–9 Monday through Thursday, 11–2 and 5–10 Friday, 5–10 Saturdays. Located in a historic downtown building that was once a funeral parlor, La Minestra offers fine Italian dining in a comfortable atmosphere. The building is completely restored, revealing the original pressed metal ceilings and walls. Sit adjacent to the open kitchen and watch the chefs at work, or take a quieter table in the dimly lit main dining area. The food is good enough to have been featured in *Bon Appetit* magazine and specialties include eggplant parmesan and veal stroganoff. There is a nice selection of wine and beer available as well. Entrées $9–$21.

EATING OUT **Pier 347** (605-224-5450), 347 S. Pierre St. The place to meet in Pierre, Pier 347 is hopping every morning as everyone fills up their travel mug with coffee specialties before reporting to the office. For breakfast try a toasted bagel with a variety of smears to choose from, an omelet, or breakfast sandwich. For lunch sit at the bar or one of the tables scattered about the long, narrow room and have one of their soup and sandwich combos. $0.99–$8.

Mad Mary's Steakhouse and Saloon (605-224-6469), 110 E. Dakota. Open 5 PM for dinner. This casual dining restaurant and lounge has subdued lighting with vinyl booths and locals sitting at the bar. The menu offers the standard burgers, chicken, steaks, and seafood. Entrées $8–$23.

McClellands Restaurant (605-223-9162), 902 Walleye Dr. (on the road to

INDIAN CASINOS

Like elsewhere in the country, gambling is legal on Indian reservations in South Dakota. South Dakota Indian casinos aren't as lavish as in areas closer to major metropolitan areas, such as Minneapolis, and are often a bit out of the way.

Most Indian casinos have Blackjack, slots, poker, roulette; others only have bingo or some combination of games. Some have overnight accommodations and restaurants, others do not. Visit the Web site for any casino you plan to visit for directions and listings of facilities, as well as this Web site www3.travelsd.com/vsd/#first.

The following are the Indian casinos in South Dakota:

Golden Buffalo, Lower Brule (1-605-473-5577)

Grand River Casino, Mobridge (1-800-475-3321)

Lode Star Casino, Ft. Thompson (1-605-245-6000)

Prairie Wind Casino, Pine Ridge (1-800-705-9463)

Rosebud Casino, Mission (1-800-786-ROSE)

Royal River Casino, Flandreau (1800-833-8666)

Oahe Dam). Open 7 AM–10 PM Monday through Saturday, 9–10 Sunday with brunch from 9–2. Near the Oahe Dam and the campgrounds, this casual dining restaurant is great for a break from fishing and boating. They offer hearty breakfasts from $5.99, a lunch buffet for $8.95, and dinners of burgers, steaks, and seafood from $11–$22.

✷ Selective Shopping

Pierre has a decent-size mall as well as most discount stores. The old downtown of Pierre, along Pierre Street, is attempting to revitalize itself with a major reconstruction of the sewers and streets scheduled for the summer of 2009. Meanwhile it's worth a walk, if for no other reason than Pierre Street is a couple of blocks from the river. Stop in at the only coffee bar in town at **Pier 347** or **Prairie Pages** for gifts and books.

Prairie Pages (605-945-1100), 321 Pierre St. Open 9–6 Monday through Friday, 9–5 Saturday. A very nicely decorated book and gift store, Prairie

Pages offers the latest fiction and non-fiction, as well as local history books and a wide assortment of cards and gifts. If they don't have a book you are looking for, they'll be happy to order it.

✷ Special Events

JUNE Casey Tibbs Match of Champions (www.matchofchampions .com), Ft. Pierre. Bronco riding event.

Oahe Days (www.oahedays.com), Steamboat Park Pierre. This citywide event runs three days and features a juried art show, parade, raft race, and concerts.

JULY Fourth of July Rodeo takes place July third and fourth. There is a parade on the fourth of July and fireworks.

NOVEMBER–DECEMBER Christmas at the Capitol (206-773-3301; www.state.sd.us), Capitol building and grounds. Features 100 decorated trees, entertainment in the Rotunda, and exhibits at the Cultural Heritage Center.

CHAMBERLAIN–OACOMA

Chamberlain and Oacoma are two small towns that sit on a bend in the Missouri River and are crossed by I-90. Both towns have had their ups and downs from the 1880s to today but have been kept alive by their great locations on the river, the interstate, and the railroad. River traffic, cars, and trains all pass through Chamberlain and Oacoma and inevitably have stopped here for supplies, something to eat, and a place to sleep. Good people and great hunting and fishing make these two small towns worth a visit.

GUIDANCE **Chamberlain–Oacoma Chamber of Commerce** (605-234-4416; www.chamberlainsd.org), 115 W. Lawler.

GETTING THERE *By car:* Chamberlain and Oacoma are on I-90 when you cross the Missouri River. Chamberlain is 209 miles from Rapid City and 141 miles from Sioux Falls.

MEDICAL EMERGENCIES **Sanford Mid Dakota Medical Center** (605-234-5511), 300 S. Byron Blvd., Chamberlain.

✳ To See

CULTURAL SITES ⚲ **Akta Lakota Museum and Cultural Center** (1-800-798-3452; www.aktalakota.org), at St. Joseph's Indian School, I-90 exit 263. Open 8–6 Monday through Saturday, 9–6 Sunday May through September, with limited winter hours. Begun in 1927 by a Catholic priest, St. Joseph's Indian School now has 200 students attending elementary through high school. The students live in group homes with house parents; the elementary students attend school at St. Joseph's, the high school students attend Chamberlain High School. *Akta*

PART OF THE ST. JOSEPH'S INDIAN SCHOOL, THE AKTA LAKOTA MUSEUM CELEBRATES PLAINS INDIAN TRIBES.
South Dakota Tourism

Lakota means "to honor the people" and that is the mission of this museum: to honor and preserve the Lakota traditions. Included is a 36-foot diorama entitled "Lakota Buffalo Days" by artist Tom Phillips, which gives a view of life on the prairie and Missouri River. Much of the art and artifacts on display were donated by former students and there is also a Collectors Gallery that shows work by local artists. Don't miss the gift shop with a wide selection of Native American arts, crafts, and gifts, including star quilts, dream catchers, and pottery. Free, donations accepted.

HISTORIC SITES ✿ **Lewis and Clark Information Center** (605-734-4562; www.chamberlainsd.org), I-90, exit 264. Open 8–6 summers. At this state rest stop you can learn more about the history of the Lewis and Clark Expedition in the area. There is a replica of the keelboat the expedition used to navigate the Missouri, a campsite re-creation, along with interpretive information. Free.

The Chamberlain–Oacoma Bridge, I-90 Chamberlain. This bridge crossing the Missouri River is on the National Register of Historic Places and was dedicated in 1925. It is comprised of four 336-foot, iron spans that were fabricated in Leavenworth, Kansas.

South Dakota Tourism

POWWOWS ARE HELD THROUGHOUT THE STATE AND PROVIDE AN OPPORTUNITY FOR NATIVE AMERICAN PEOPLE TO MEET AND COMPETE IN DANCING AND DRUMMING.

POWWOWS

Powwows are a traditional Native American gathering in which the people join together to visit, dance, sing, and renew friendships. Powwows can vary in length from a couple of hours to several days, depending on the occasion.

Traditionally when different tribes would gather together they would share their songs. Indian singers are a very important part of the Powwow. Not only do they provide music for the dancers, they are also a reminder of the cultural heritage the song represents. Singers are usually accompanied by drummers, who often gather around one large drum together.

Each session of the Powwow begins with a grand entry in which all

MUSEUMS ❧ **South Dakota Hall of Fame** (800-697-3130; www.sdhalloffame .com), 1480 S. Main. Open10–5 Monday–Friday, 10–4 Saturday, 1–4 Sunday. The Hall of Fame's mission is to recognize pioneers and leaders who have contributed to the development of South Dakota. There are presently over 500 inductees including Native Americans, artists, politicians, and business people. Probably the best-known inductees to non-South Dakotans are Tom Brokaw, who grew up in Webster, and Mary Hart from Sioux Falls. Free, donations accepted.

SCENIC DRIVES **Native American Scenic Byway** (byways.org/explore/byways/2596). This 357-mile byway travels along the Missouri River from near Chamberlain, South Dakota, to Bismarck, North Dakota, and travels through four Indian Reservations. You can drive all of it or portions, depending on what you are interested in seeing. The route follows a number of different highways so a map is recommended. In Pierre, you can find a visitors information center located near the waterfront and receive information about the byway.

of the participants enter the arena displaying their costumes. The first to enter are the men's dancers, followed by the women, each dancing their particular style. Following the dancers are the flag bearers and then the Powwow royalty.

There are many styles of dancing at Powwows and each has an elaborately decorated costume for it. Jingle dancers wear special multicolored dresses and shawls, also called prayer dresses, which are decorated with snuff cans that make a jingling sound when the dancers move. Fancy dancers are known by their elaborate clothing covered with beadwork, as well as a feather bustle that forms a circular spray on the dancers back. Their dancing style has a basic step in beat to a drum and a more complicated contest step that involves fancy footwork and twirls. The Traditional Dance is sometimes characterized as that of a prairie chicken. The dancers wear headdresses often made of porcupine quills that bounce with their movement and beaded arm and kneebands. All dancing is done to the accompaniment of drummers and singers.

Attending a Powwow can offer you a deeper understanding of Native American culture and many Powwows are open to visitors. But keep in mind Powwows are not done to entertain the public but as a traditional way of maintaining Native American cultural heritage. If you go, you are a guest and are expected to behave accordingly. A few words to the wise—Powwows are alcohol and drug free, do not take photographs or videos without asking permission, pay close attention to the announcements, and stand or remove your hat when asked to show proper respect.

✷ To Do

BIKING/HIKING Lewis & Clark Discovery Trail 3–4 miles. Begins at Barger Centennial Park, crosses American Creek Marina, past St. Joseph's Indian School, and to Roam Free Park north of Chamberlain. The trail has a very gentle grade on hard and gravel surfaces and is suitable for all types of walkers and most bicyclists.

BOATING AND FISHING Chamberlain–Oacoma offers many opportunities for boating and fishing along the **Missouri River**. There are boat ramps at **Cedar Shore** (see listing under *Camping*) and **American Creek** (309 E. Glenn Ave.). For fishermen there are walleye, northern pike, large and smallmouth bass, and flathead catfish. For further information go to www.chamberlainsd.org.

GOLF Chamberlain Country Club (605-734-4451), Exit 260, 4 miles west of Chamberlain. Green fees $20–$22. This nine-hole course is open to the public and has a full restaurant and bar.

HUNTING Chamberlain–Oacoma is a prime pheasant hunting area, beginning in October. Licenses are available at **Cedar Shore Resort** (see listing under *Camping*), **True Value** at 122 Main Street, and **Midwest Supply**, 206 W. Clemmer, among other outlets.

SWIMMING American Creek Campground (605-234-5151), 701 N. Main. Has a day use beach available on the river.

Chamberlain City Pool (605-234-4413), 600 S. Main. Open 1–5 Monday through Friday end of May to the end of August. $2 for adults, $1.50 for children.

✷ Green Spaces

PARKS Barger Park, N. Courtland St. Located along the biking and hiking trail, this park has a great view of the river.

Roam Free Park, north of town on Main. Located on the bluffs above the river, the park is intended to teach about the ecology of the area.

✷ Lodging

There are a number of small motels in Chamberlain, as well as a few chains along the interstate, including **Holiday Inn Express** (605-734-5593), and **Oasis Inn** (1-800-635-3559).

CAMPING Al's Oasis (1-800-675-6959; www.alsoasis.com), I-90, exit 260. Right on the interstate for easy access, this campground includes a pool, Laundromat, play area, restrooms, and showers. $17–$27 per night.

Cedar Shore Resort (605-734-5273; www.cedarshore.com), I-90, exit 260.

Open April 1 through September 1. On the banks of the Missouri River, there are 39 RV sites, tent sites, restrooms and showers, coin laundry, a convenience store, ice and firewood, playground, a sport court, dump station, and potable water. $15–$30 per night.

RESORTS Cedar Shore Resort, see listing under *Camping*. Open year-round. Folks come to Cedar Shores to enjoy all the river has to offer. This is a full-service resort with conference facilities, a hotel, campground, restaurant, lounge, spa, and marina located right on the river. The hotel has 99 rooms ranging from $69 (winter rate for two people) to $200 for the large family suite. Call for reservations and further information.

☀ Where to Eat

EATING OUT **Bridges Restaurant**, Cedar Shore Resort, see listing under *Camping*. Open 7AM–9 PM daily, Sunday brunch from 9:30–1. Bridges offers the standard South Dakota menu of burgers, steak, and walleye. They serve three meals a day to folks attending conferences or vacationing with their families and have complete menus. There is a buffet on Sundays with a breakfast station featuring eggs, potatoes, and caramel rolls, a salad bar and a variety of entrées. The adjacent lounge has a complete bar with video lottery. Dinner entrées from $10–$20.

Al's Oasis, see listing under *Camping*. Open 6 AM–10 PM, Sunday buffet 11–2. Al's offers three meals a day as well as a Sunday buffet. Famous for their 5-cent coffee and prime rib, the menu includes burgers made from beef or buffalo, a salad bar, a "Whipper Snapper" menu, and homemade pie. There is a lounge as well that offers beer, wine, and a limited menu of sandwiches and appetizers. Entrées $10–$25.

☀ Selective Shopping

Al's Oasis, see listing under *Camping*. Rather like Wall Drug, if Al's Oasis doesn't have it, you probably don't need it. With a gas station, fishing supplies, clothing, supermarket, gift shop, saloon, cabins, and campground, what else do you need in your travels?

☀ Special Events

JULY **River City Racin'** (605-234-2628; www.rivercityracin.org). Light hydroplane racing on the Missouri River. Also a concert, street dance, and car and bike show.

SEPTEMBER **Gathering of the Wakanyeja Pow Wow** (605-734-3300), St. Joseph's Indian School, Chamberlain.

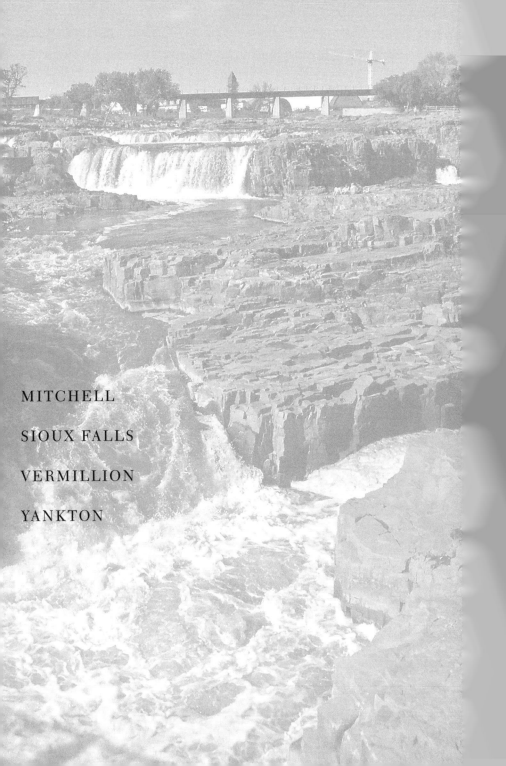

Southeast

MITCHELL

SIOUX FALLS

VERMILLION

YANKTON

SOUTHEAST

Southeast South Dakota is an interesting combination of the rural heart of the state and home of its biggest, most metropolitan city, Sioux Falls. Just a little ways off I-90, you find yourself in the middle of farm country spotted with tiny towns that are only there to support the agricultural community. This is flat prairie land, where you can see for miles. It is also home to three major rivers and 175 natural and man-made lakes, creating a recreation heaven.

Along I-90, I-29, or the lower portion of the Missouri are larger cities that house the medical facilities, colleges, and centers of commerce that the smaller towns rely on. And then there is Sioux Falls, the commercial and transportation hub for all of eastern South Dakota and some of western Minnesota.

Unlike the Black Hills, southeast South Dakota is not reliant on the tourist trade but instead on what made the state in the first place, agriculture. That's not to say there are not things to do and see; it's just that there isn't a water park or mini golf course every time you turn around. Every town has a story and something unique to offer of its own history and contribution to South Dakota. This is working land, with hard working people. This is where you will find what South Dakota is really all about and the people that keep it going.

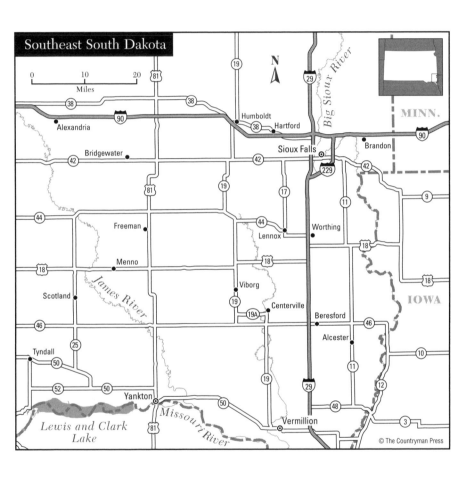

Southeast South Dakota

MITCHELL

Mitchell is best known for having the World's Only Corn Palace, which is pretty distinctive. What exactly is a Corn Palace? Well, in 1892 the folks in Mitchell decided they needed something to celebrate the end of the harvest and to bring people together. Little did they know it would turn into a major tourist attraction but they are happy to oblige anyone who wants to come and visit. Today's Corn Palace was built in 1921 and is actually the third. It serves as an event center for the community, hosting plays, basketball games, and even high school graduation. Everyone who grew up in Mitchell has some story to tell about their moment in the sun at the Corn Palace, whether it was a play they were in or their first prom. Every year local artists design the murals that decorate the outside of the Corn Palace with a specific theme, such as "America's Destinations," in mind. These murals require thousands of bushels of corn, grain, grasses, wild oats, brome grass, blue grass, rye, straw, and wheat each year.

Mitchell is otherwise a small South Dakota prairie town with tree-lined streets and enough businesses to serve as a commercial center for the surrounding farmers whether they need a new tractor or a bag of groceries. Mitchell is home to 15,000 folks who prefer a place where the kids can actually walk or ride their bikes anywhere and people know one another.

GUIDANCE Corn Palace Convention and Visitors Bureau (605-996-6223; www.cornpalace.com), 601 N. Main St. There is a **Visitors Center** located at I-90 exit 332. Open daily 8–6 May through September.

GETTING THERE *By car:* Mitchell is located directly on I-90, 66 miles west of Sioux Falls.

MEDICAL EMERGENCIES Avera Queen of Peace Hospital (605-995-2000), 525 N. Foster St.

✳ To See

CULTURAL SITES ⚲ Prehistoric Indian Village (605-996-5473; www.mitchell indianvillage.org), 3200 Indian Village Rd. Open 9–4 April through October. This ongoing archaeological dig (as funds permit) and museum attempt to solve the mystery of Native Americans that inhabited 70 lodges on the site more than 1,000 years ago. Sifting through what remains, archaeologists are learning more about how the Native Americans lived and what their homes may have looked like. In the museum you will find a model of how the village might have looked, as well as a full-scale reproduction of an earth lodge originally built of timber posts that support mud daub walls, with roofs covered by turf. Other clues to the Native American's lifestyle are being found in what amounts to the local landfill, where scientists have uncovered bones, shells, seeds, and corncobs, telling us something about their diet, as well as pottery shards and bone and shell tools. When archaeologists are on site you can watch them work inside a dome covering the site, which also makes this a year-round attraction. An extensive gift shop sells books as well as Native American arts and crafts. You may wander around on your own or join a guided tour. $6 for adults, $4 for children.

HISTORIC SITES 🌾 **Carnegie Resource Center** (605-996-3209; www.mitchell carnegie.org), 119 W. Third Ave. Open 1–5 Monday through Saturday. Built in 1902 this quartzite building was once the city library and is now home of the Mitchell Area Historical Society. The center houses a permanent collection of Corn Palace memorabilia as well as changing exhibits of Mitchell history. Don't miss the dome painted by famed Dakota Sioux artist, Oscar Howe, in 1940. Titled "Sun and Rain Clouds over Hills," the mural was inspired by the Depression and is a prayer for rain and fertility. The dome murals are in the style of traditional Sioux skin paintings, which appear very flat with a sharp outline. The murals really began Howe's career and afterward he was sent to study with a famous Norwegian muralist in Oklahoma. When he returned to Mitchell, Howe designed the Corn Palace murals from 1949–1971 and became an artist-in-residence and instructor at the University of South Dakota. His work is collected by museums throughout the world and Mitchell is understandably proud of the connection. Free.

🌾 **The Corn Palace** (1-866-273-CORN), 604 N. Main St. Open 8–9 Memorial Day through Labor Day. You can't go to Mitchell and not go to the Corn Palace—after all, it is the only one in the world and 500,000 folks a year come to see it. To create the murals that cover the Corn Palace they use 13 different colors or shades of corn: red, brown, black, blue, white, orange, calico, yellow, and green. Murals with different themes are created every year and ear-by-ear the corn is nailed to the building. It's a little weird, especially the seemingly out of place minarets, but certainly something you won't see anywhere else and the murals are pretty impressive. Free admission.

MUSEUMS 🌾 🌲 **Dakota Discovery Museum** (605-996-2122; www.dakota discovery.com), 1300 McGovern Ave., Dakota Wesleyan University Campus. Open 9–6 May through September, 10–4 October through April. Featuring displays of Plains Indian culture and pioneer life, this museum also has the work of a number of local artists, including Oscar Howe, Harvey Dunn, James Earle Fraser, and Gutzon Borglum, who carved Mount Rushmore. On the second floor there is the Charles Hargens Studio and Gallery. Hargens's Western illustrations graced the covers of Zane Grey Western novels as well as covers of the *Saturday Evening Post* and *Boy's Life*. Set up like Hargens's studio, visitors can see, not only his work, but how he worked. In Discovery Land kids and parents get to work together on activities, like visiting a teepee and making arts and crafts. $5 for adults, $2 for students.

◈ The George and Eleanor McGovern Library and Center for Leadership and Public Service (605-995-2937; www.dwu.edu), 1201 McGovern Ave., on the campus of Dakota Wesleyan University. Open 8–5 weekdays.

In 1972 George McGovern ran for president and became one of South Dakota's most famous citizens. An ordained Methodist minister, McGovern began his life in politics when he ran for the House of Representatives in 1956. He served two terms in the House then won a seat in the Senate where he served three terms. Even though he represented a very conservative state, McGovern was about as liberal as they come, including being an outspoken opponent of the Vietnam War. After Bobby Kennedy's assassination in 1968 McGovern was drafted to run for the Democratic nomination for president but he was soundly beaten by Richard Nixon, even failing to win South Dakota. He returned to the Senate and made another unsuccessful run for the presidency in 1984. McGovern may have failed in those endeavors but no one questions his public service and he is remembered for his work to end world hunger and reform the Democratic Party. As a graduate of Dakota Wesleyan, this is the official repository of artifacts from George McGovern's life and an interesting look at his place in American history. Free.

✳ To Do

BIKING/HIKING If you need to stretch your legs while in Mitchell, there are several trails in the city.

Dry Run Creek Park Trail This asphalt trail runs from Minnesota Street to Burr Street for 1.1 miles. Running through a city park, the trail is tree lined and goes past tennis courts, a disc-golf course, picnic shelters, and a skateboard park.

Northridge Park Trail A 0.5₂-mile concrete trail, which extends from Northridge Park to 15th Avenue to 11th Avenue to Capital Street. Mostly going through a Mitchell neighborhood, this trail also passes by Mitchell High School.

Dakota Wesleyan University Trail A 0.5-mile concrete trail that encircles beautiful Dakota Wesleyan University campus and goes right past the McGovern Library.

There is a one-mile trail at **Lake Mitchell**, starting at the campground that follows the shore of the lake.

BOATING AND FISHING There are many opportunities for boating and fishing in the Mitchell area. Licenses are available at **Cabela's,** 601 Cabela Drive and **Hagen's,** 3150 West Havens, among others.

Lake Mitchell is right in town so it is plenty convenient. At 670 acres, Lake Mitchell can be fished from the dock and shore, or launch your boat from two boat ramps. The catch includes largemouth bass, bluegill, bullhead, crappie, muskie, northern pike, and walleye. With several parks around the lake this is a great place to bring a picnic and spend the day with the family.

James River 307 total miles. The James River south of Mitchell has some of the best flathead and channel catfishing anywhere. The best bet is to find a spot with good access from the shore and you'll keep busy pulling in catfish from 3–10 pounds. Other species found in the river include smallmouth bass, bullhead, catfish, crappie, northern pike, perch, sauger, and walleye.

GOLF Mitchell is lucky enough to have two first-rate golf courses to choose from. Try them both, if you have the time.

Lakeview Municipal Golf Course (605-995-8460; www.cityofmitchell.org/golf), 3300 N. Ohlman St. Ranked number seven in South Dakota this 18-hole course is perfect for all skill levels. There is a new, full-size driving range. Green fees are $34.

Wild Oak Golf Club (605-996-2084; www.wildoakgolfclub.com), 2500 First Ave. Flat with a creek that comes into play on five holes this 18-hole golf course dates back to the 1920s. There is also a pro shop and driving range. Green fees range from $22–$25.

HUNTING Pheasant hunting is big in the Mitchell area. The season opens in October and requires a state license. See license information under *Boating and Fishing.*

SWIMMING **Mitchell Outdoor Aquatic Center** (605-995-8458; www.mitchell parksandrecreation), 1201 E. Hanson. Open 1–8:30 daily during the summer. For a small town this aquatic center is really impressive with a 50-meter lap pool and a 100-foot slide. There's also a zero depth pool for the little ones with water toys like bubbling geysers and critters that spray. $6 for adults, $4 for youth.

UNIQUE ADVENTURES **Starlite Drive In** (605-996-4511), 4601 Main St. Open during the summer, seven nights a week. How many kids have been to a drive-in movie theater? Well, Mitchell still has one and it has double features, a mini golf course, a playground, and, of course, a snack bar. Don't miss the opportunity to share some of the past with your kids before it's gone. $7.50 for adults, free for kids.

✳ Lodging

Mitchell has a number of chains and a few locally owned motels along the interstate, including **Comfort Inn** (605-990-2400), **Days Inn** (1-800-329-7466), and **Hampton Inn** (1-866-252-2900).

BED & BREAKFAST INNS **Flavia's Place** (605-995-1562), 515 E. Third Ave. The only bed-and-breakfast in town not catering to hunters, Flavia's Place is a comfortable getaway right in Mitchell. This private home, built in 1880 in the Italian-Bracket style, survived both a fire and being turned into apartments. In 1996 Lelia Guilbert purchased the house and has put her heart and soul into restoration and decorating. The two upstairs apartments have been converted into four guest rooms, one with a private bath. Each room is decorated according to the seasons. Christmas is Lelia's favorite holiday and the winter room reflects that with its spruce green walls and year-round Christmas decorations. The summer room is the bed-and-breakfast's "honeymoon" suite with a small sitting area and private bath complete with a claw-footed tub for leisurely soaking. Lelia, an artist and square-dance caller, has converted the basement into her studio and the garage for square dancing. Stay the night and maybe you can do a little dancing as well. Rooms $60–$75.

CAMPING **Lake Mitchell Campground** (605-995-8457), SD 37 N. Open April 15 through October 15. This city-owned campground on the north side of town has over 70 sites with abundant shade and is adjacent to Lake Mitchell. Recreational opportunities abound as the lake is great for swimming or fishing and there are canoes available to rent at the campground. A good value, this campground will give the family plenty to do. Basic site is $14 a night with additional fees for electricity, sewer, or water hookup. There are water, showers, and a dump station available.

✳ Where to Eat

DINING OUT **The Brig** (605-996-7444; www.brigsteakhouse.com), 2700 N. Main St. Opens at 5 PM nightly. Overlooking Lake Mitchell, the Brig has been a Mitchell tradition since 1947. With a very complete menu of everything from steaks and prime rib to pasta and seafood, you can enjoy fine dining in a relaxed atmosphere. If you're not up for a full meal, there is a smaller lounge menu, which features the two-pound Big Daddy Burger—if you eat it all, they'll buy you a drink, but who would have room for one? Entrées $9–$38.

Chef Louie's (605-996-7565), 601 E. Havens. Open 4:30 Monday through Saturday. You won't have any trouble finding Chef Louie's since there's a monster fiberglass steer by the side of the road with a sign on its prime rib pointing in the right direction. Open since the 1940s, this upscale restaurant has a full menu with steaks, seafood, and pasta, as well as an extensive wine list. But like the sign says, it's all about the beef and Chef Louie's is best known for their steaks and prime rib. Entrées $8–$54 (the most expensive is the steak and lobster).

EATING OUT **Café Teresa** (605-990-2233), 312 N. Main St. Open 7–6. A homey place with brick walls and comfy furniture, Café Teresa serves a breakfast of Belgian waffles, scrambled eggs, or lighter fare like a scone or muffin. They have a full selection of specialty coffees and teas to sip while you eat. For lunch try their homemade soup and sandwiches, with sides of coleslaw and potato salad available. On Thursday night they start hand-tossing the pizza. Try the chicken pesto and enjoy a glass of wine from their wide selection. Entrees $6–$8.

Depot Pub and Grill (605-996-9417; www.mitchelldepot.com), 210 Main St. This 1909 train depot was converted into a family-friendly bar and grill in 1990. Now registered as a historic site, they serve a variety of burgers and sandwiches as well as a great selection of buffalo, including steaks and barbecued ribs. If you're not a carnivore, try the meatless spaghetti, or Fettuccini Alfredo. The kids will be satisfied with their own menu including a ground buffalo steak or chicken strips. Entrées $6–$26.

Jitters (605-996-3447), 512 N. Main St. Open Monday through Saturday 7–5, Sunday 9–1. As the name suggests this is a coffee shop with all the specialty drinks, but they also serve breakfast all day including eggs, hash browns, and their secret-recipe pancakes. Family run, Jitters isn't fancy but more like coming home for a visit. The menu reflects the atmosphere and when you sit down to a plate of chicken and noodles, or roast beef with all the fixings, they taste just like Mom used to make. Everything is homemade so the menu varies depending on the owner's inspiration and also includes satisfying bagel sandwiches and wraps. Breakfast is $3.50 and lunch specials are $5.50.

Steak 'N' More (605-990-6673), 1801 N. Main St. Opens at 5 PM. This newer entry in the Mitchell restaurant scene is more for families than the higher-priced Chef Louie's and the Brig but that doesn't mean they skimp on quality. Quiet with a choice of booths or tables, as the name suggests they specialize in steaks, including a rib eye that will cut with a fork. For something a little different try the pork chops that come wrapped in bacon, either plain or barbecued, or a chop doused with Jack Daniels, cinnamon, and apples. In the bar they offer a large variety of drink specials. Entrées $9–$17.

✳ Selective Shopping

Cabela's (605-996-0337; www.cabelas .com), 601 Cabela Dr. Open 8-9 Monday through Saturday, 9–6 Sunday. You may have even seen their catalog and if you like outdoor activities you have to stop at Cabela's. This 80,000-square-foot flagship store features an unbelievable assortment of hunting, fishing, hiking, and camping supplies. With a highly trained staff, you will find what you need to enhance any outdoor adventure. Even if you don't need new gear, stop in for the museum quality animal displays and huge aquariums, which provide some free education and entertainment. The deli restaurant departs from the ordinary with selections such as a wild boar or ostrich sandwich, but you can play it safe and go for the tamer tuna salad.

Corn Palace Gift Shop (866-273-2676), 604 Main St. Open 8–9 daily,

CARNEGIE LIBRARIES

Andrew Carnegie was an Irish immigrant who made his fortune in American steel. In 1901 he sold his steels interests for $480 million or the equivalent of $10 billion today. Carnegie saw many needs in early 20th century America and he set up his Carnegie Corporation of New York to try to meet some of those needs, thus inaugurating the modern era of philanthropy. John D. Rockefeller followed Carnegie's lead two years later by beginning his own charitable foundation and today there are no less than 65,000 grant-making organizations in the United States.

One of Carnegie's passions was for libraries. He believed that libraries "outrank any other one thing that a community can do to help its people." He endowed 2,509 libraries throughout the English-speaking world between 1881 and 1917, including 1,681 in the United States, 25 of which were in South Dakota.

The Carnegie Corporation required each town submitting a grant application to commit to providing funds to support the library. Each town chose its own design but each library included an entry staircase that symbolized a person's elevation of learning and, outside, a lamppost that symbolized enlightenment.

While some of the libraries have been turned into museums, cultural centers, or may have been torn down, nearly half still serve their communities as public libraries. While in South Dakota check out the unique design of different community Carnegie library buildings and reflect on how much one man is able to accomplish.

mid-May through August. Featuring products grown or made in South Dakota, this is the place for corncob jelly and buffalo jerky. The emphasis is all things corn, so look through the assortment of must-haves like a corn platter or a corn lollipop. No collector is forgotten, so pick up a Corn Palace commemorative spoon, Christmas ornament, or the ever popular "Kiss Me, I'm Corny" T-shirt.

Finishing Touches by Bonnie (605-996-7839; www.finishingtouchesby bonnie.com), 115 E. Third Ave. Featuring a variety of home décor items, large and small, Bonnie's can help you complete any look from Western to Tuscany. But what this shop is really known for is their beautiful silk floral arrangements, which come premade or can be special ordered to fit your individual needs. The store is beautiful enough to visit even if you don't buy anything and it's a great spot to pick up a wedding or anniversary gift.

Moody's Western Wear (605-995-5879), 305 N. Main St. What do you mean you haven't bought your Western wear yet? Get on over to Moody's! With Wrangler, Ely, and Roper clothing, boots by Justin and Tony Lama, and hats of felt or straw, you can deck out the entire family and fit right in at the next rodeo. Should your horse needs a little something new they also have saddles, bridles, and other tack.

Prairie Breeze Gallery (605-996-5402; www.prairiebreezegallery.com), 215 N. Main St. Open 10–8 May through October, 10–5:30 November through April. South Dakota artists are drawn to the beauty of the natural world around them and this gallery shows work by some of the best. Representing dozens of artists, the gallery includes one of a kind paintings, jewelry, pottery, folk art, and photography. They also have latch-hook rugs created by members of the nearby Hutterite colony, a religious sect that fled perse-

THE CORN PALACE IN MITCHELL ATTRACTS THOUSANDS OF TOURISTS EVERY YEAR TO VIEW THE MURALS MADE OF CORN AND OTHER SOUTH DAKOTA GRAINS.

cution in Europe and settled to farm in South Dakota in the 1870s.

✳ Special Events

JULY **Corn Palace Stampede Rodeo** (www.cornpalacestampede .com/index.html), Horsemen Sports Arena located just North of Lake Mitchell on SD 37. PRCA rodeo and other events such as a golf tournament and chili cook-off. Held the third week of July, general admission is $12 for adults, $5 for children.

AUGUST **Corn Palace Festival** (www.cornpalacefestival.com), Corn Palace, 604 Main St. There are concerts by various artists as well as a carnival. Ticket prices vary by concert.

VOLUNTEERS ATTACH CORN TO ONE OF THE CORN PALACE'S MURALS.

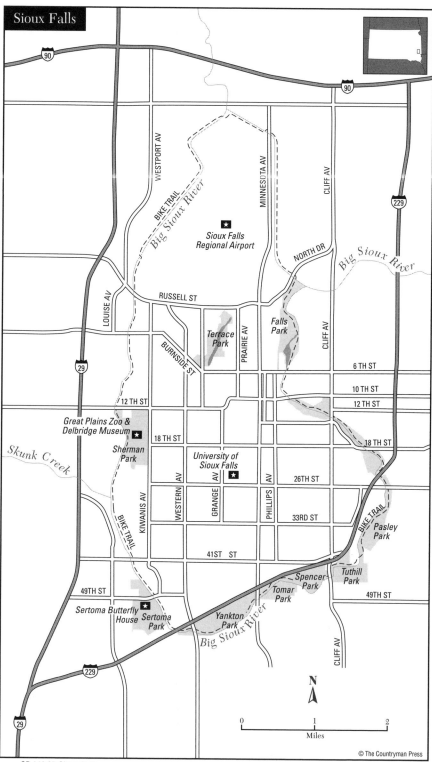

Sioux Falls

© The Countryman Press

SIOUX FALLS

What first drew humans to Sioux Falls, and eventually gave the town its name, are the falls of the Big Sioux River that cascade through town. Created 14,000 years ago by glacial ice, the falls run over ancient quartzite that was once the bottom of a shallow sea.

The falls drew prehistoric people, Lakota and Dakota Native Americans, French trappers who used the landmark as a rendezvous point and, eventually, land speculators who thought the waterpower of the falls made for a great town site.

The development of Sioux Falls has had its ups and downs over the years. First bought up by speculators in 1856 it was pretty much abandoned over fears of Indian wars until Fort Dakota was built there in 1865. Sioux Falls was incorporated in 1876 and started to grow with the arrival of the railroads in the 1880s. Then Sioux Falls took a step backwards with a general economic depression and a plague of grasshoppers that wiped out crops. Nothing much happened in Sioux Falls from 1890–1900.

FALLS PARK IN DOWNTOWN SIOUX FALLS HAS THE FALLS THAT GAVE THE CITY ITS NAME.

But given its location on the falls, adjacent to Minnesota, and so close to Iowa, Sioux Falls was bound to prosper and in 1909 they got a meatpacking plant that still provides jobs today. An airbase came, then in the 1960s the interstate highways intersected in Sioux Falls and the town was firmly established as a transportation hub and center of commerce for the region.

Today there are 210,000 people living in the Sioux Falls metropolitan area, by far the largest metropolitan area in the state. The economic base is diverse and includes banking, tourism, manufacturing, transportation, and education. Like any metropolitan city there is a lot to see and do in Sioux Falls but, unlike many cities, Sioux Falls maintains its rural roots and small town character. Folks are friendly and crime is low, as is the cost of living. People don't move to Sioux Falls just for the jobs but for a way of life. Visitors can enjoy the same.

GUIDANCE Sioux Falls Convention and Visitors Bureau (1-800-333-2072; www.siouxfallscvb.com), Commerce Building, Eighth St. and Phillips Ave.

Visitors Information Center, located at Falls Park, 309 E. Falls Park Dr. The visitors center is in the same building as the five-story-viewing tower that overlooks the falls. They also have a gift shop with a variety of Sioux Falls souvenirs.

GETTING THERE *By car:* Sioux Falls is located a few miles south of I-90 on I-29.

By air: Sioux Falls Regional Airport is serviced by Northwest, Delta, United Express, and Allegiant Airlines.

GETTING AROUND Sioux Falls Transit offers bus service throughout the Sioux Falls area (605-367-7183; www.siouxfalls.org/Transit.aspx).

THIS STATUE, MONARCH OF THE PLAINS, CELEBRATES THE BISON THAT ONCE COVERED THE SOUTH DAKOTA PLAINS.

The Sioux Falls Trolley (605-367-7183), runs 10 AM–8 PM Monday through Saturday, mid-April through mid-October. The trolley provides service downtown for free. The trolley route includes Main and Phillips Avenue, as well as stops at Falls Park and the Washington Pavilion every 30 minutes.

MEDICAL EMERGENCIES Avera Heart Hospital (605-977-7000; www.southdakotaheart.com), 4500 W. 69th St.

Avera McKennan Hospital & University Health Center (605-322-8000; www.averamckennan.org), 800 E. 21st St.

Sanford USD Medical Center (605-333-1000; www.sanfordhealth.org), 1305 W. 18th St.

South Dakota Tourism

HOUSING A SCIENCE MUSEUM, ART GALLERY, AND PERFORMANCE SPACE, THE WASHINGTON PAVILION DRAWS MANY VISITORS.

✳ To See

CULTURAL SITES 🎨 **Visual Arts Center at the Washington Pavilion of Art and Sciences** (605-367-6000; www.washingtonpavilion.org), 11th and Main Ave. Open 10–5 Monday through Thursday, 10–8 Friday, 10–5 Saturday, 12–5 Sunday. Six galleries feature changing art exhibits of local, regional, and touring art exhibits. One of the more recent exhibits was a huge wall installation of burned baguettes baked on site, which sounds really strange but was very visually amusing and had quite a distinctive odor. The center's second floor gallery shows an impressive permanent collection of over 300 works by regional and national artists, including Oscar Howe and Henry Moore. Take a little time to visit the Children's Studio where the kids can do hands-on art activities. Free except for special exhibits.

🎨 **Sculpture Walk** (605-338-4009; www.sculpturewalksiouxfalls.com), located throughout downtown Sioux Falls. A great draw for downtown, which is worth visiting anyway, artists display their sculptures as public art for one year so you can enjoy 55 original pieces of art from realistic bronzes to kinetic and abstract pieces. There is enough sculpture that you can't walk a block on Phillips Avenue without encountering several, so you're sure to find something you will enjoy. You can vote for your favorite online or at boxes throughout downtown.

DOWNTOWN SIOUX FALLS HAS DOZENS OF SCULPTURES ON DISPLAY FOR THE PUBLIC TO ENJOY.

❧ **The Center for Western Studies** (605-274-4007; www.augie.edu/CWS), 2201 S. Summit Ave. Open 8–12 and 1–5 Monday through Friday, and 10–2 Saturday. On the campus of Augustana College this center is dedicated to preserving the heritage of the northern plains. They have 500 collections and rotating exhibits, including the Cropp Case, which displays bead and quillwork on clothing and items used daily by Plains Indians, and the Fantle Collection, which has Scandinavian furnishings that emigrants brought to the plains. The permanent collection of artwork by regional artists includes Oscar Howe and Robert Wood. In addition to having a research library, the center is the largest academic publisher in South Dakota. Free, donations accepted.

❧ **Eide/Dalrymple Gallery, Visual Arts Center** at Augustana College (605-274-4010; www.augie.edu). Open 10–5 Tuesday through Friday, 12–5 Saturday through Sunday. Part of the Augustana College Fine Arts Department, the gallery has nine shows per year of student and professional artist's works. The schedule varies but has included the work of Augustana professor Yang Yang and the primitive art of New Guinea. Stop in and see what's hanging. Free.

❧ **Horse Barn Arts Center** (605-977-2002; www.siouxempireartscouncil.com/HBAC.htm), North End of Falls Park, 309 E. Falls Park Dr. Open 10–5 in the summer, 12–4 in the winter. Built sometime in the 1800s this former barn was acquired by the city in the 1930s and used to store machinery. The Sioux Falls Arts Council began converting the barn in 1998 with the addition of a heating system and new roof, and in 1999 it opened its doors to serve as galleries, and classrooms, and to sponsor public events. The Loft Gallery shows a different exhibit of local and regional art each month, while on the main level the Portfolio Gallery offers space to local artists on a rotating basis for exhibition of their art. There is also a gift shop. Free.

FOR FAMILIES **Great Plains Zoo and Delbridge Museum of Natural History** (650-367-7003; www.greatplainszoo.org), 805 South Kiwanis Ave. Open 9–6 April through September, 10–4 October through March. Covering 45 acres, this zoo is small enough to provide an intimate experience with the critters. There are over 500 animals, some residing in simulated natural habitats, including the Bear Canyon, Asian Cat Habitat, and the African Savannah. Take a half-hour train ride through the savannah and see the rhinos and tigers up close. For the kids there is also a children's petting area and a carousel with decorative zoo animals to ride.

Also part of the zoo is the Delbridge Museum, which has 145 mounted animals, including 36 vanishing species. The collection was started by a Sioux Falls businessman, Henry Brockhouse, who hunted all over the world between the 1940s and the 1960s and these are animals he bagged and had professionally mounted. Though Brockhouse shot them legally, it is ironic that 20 are now on the endangered species list. The zoo uses the exhibits as an educational tool to promote the protection of wild animals. Admission to both the zoo and museum is $7 for adults, $4 for children.

Kirby Science Discovery Center at the Washington Pavilion of Arts and Science (605-367-6000; www.washingtonpavilion.org), 11th and Main Ave. Open 10–5 Monday through Thursday, 10–8 Friday, 10–5 Saturday, 12–5 Sunday. You and the kids could spend a day here playing with the 80 hands-on exhibits and live science demonstrations, like the Stairway of Sound where you try to identify 21

THE SERTOMA BUTTERFLY GARDEN HAS DOZENS OF BUTTERFLY SPECIES FLYING FREE AMONG DELIGHTED VISITORS.

different sounds as you walk from the third to the fourth floor. In the gift store you'll find really awesome science kits, toys, and games for kids and adults alike. $7 for adults, $5 for children.

Sertoma Butterfly House (605-334-9466; www.sertomabutterflyhouse.com), 4320 Oxbow Ave. Open 10–4 Monday through Saturday, 1–4 Sunday during the winter; 10–6 Monday through Saturday, 1–5 Sunday during the summer. Bring your camera because the butterfly house has up to 800 vividly colored butterfly species to enjoy. The butterflies come to the Butterfly House as cocoons from tropical areas like Central America and hatch on site. If you get lucky you can watch one squeeze out of its cocoon in a glass display before it's released into this beautiful garden setting full of brightly colored flowers and tropical plants. As you walk around the humid interior, butterflies are on the flowers, in special feeding bowls of rotting fruit, and just fluttering around for your amusement. Amazingly, they are able to heat the butterfly house enough during the South Dakota winters to keep the butterflies alive, making this a year-round attraction. The spacious gift shop has all things butterfly, including souvenirs, but also educational materials about butterflies including books and science kits. $6 for adults, $4 for children.

THERE IS A LARGE HISTORIC DISTRICT IN SIOUX FALLS WITH MANY STATELY HOMES.

Wells Fargo Cinedome at the Washington Pavilion of Arts and Science (605-367-6000; www.washingtonpavilion.org), 11th and Main Ave. Open 11–4 Monday through Thursday, 11–8 Friday through Saturday, 1–4 Sunday. Another reason to spend the day at the Washington Pavilion is the cinedome. Its 60-foot screen and 24 speakers put you in the middle of the action whether diving into oceans, swimming with sharks, or climbing mountains. The films change seasonally and run 45 minutes to an hour. $7 for adults, $6 for children.

Catfish Bay—The Greatest Show on H_2O (605-339-0911; www.catfishbay .com), I-90 exit 399. Show at 7 PM Memorial Day through Labor Day. Right on the outskirts of Sioux Falls there is a small lake that is home to an all-volunteer water-skiing show. The skiers do stunts, pyramids, comedy, singing, and dancing, providing for an hour and a half of family entertainment. Skiing classes are offered and some of their performers are good enough to go pro and ski at places like Cypress Gardens and Sea World. $9 for adults, $7 for children.

HISTORIC SITES ✿ ♿ **Old Courthouse Museum** (605-367-4210; www.sioux landmuseums.com), Sixth Street and Main Ave. Open 8–5 Monday through Friday, 8–9 Thursday, 9–5 Saturday, 12–5 Sunday. Built in 1893, this stately quartzite courthouse with its soaring clock tower looms over downtown Sioux Falls. Now a museum of the region, it has three floors of history exhibits. You can also visit the former courtroom, the law library, and see the wall murals throughout the building. If you'd like a guided tour, call ahead and they will help you set one up. There is also a gift shop with regional history books. Free.

A FORMER COURTHOUSE, THIS MUSEUM HOUSES HISTORIC COLLECTIONS FROM THE SIOUX FALLS AREA.

✿ ♿ **Pettigrew Home and Museum** (605-367-7097; www.siouxland museums.com), Eighth St. and Duluth. Open 9–5 Monday through Saturday, 12–5 Sunday April 1 through September 30; 12–5 daily October 1 through March 31. Step back in time at this 1889 Queen Anne–style home built by R. F. Pettigrew, South Dakota's first senator. It is completely restored with silk wall coverings, intricate wood-working, and jeweled glass windows. Check out the interactive computer stations, pull-out drawers, and artifacts, which are there for you to explore. Tours are 30 minutes and led by trained guides. Free.

St. Joseph Cathedral (605-336-7390; www.cathedralofstjosephsiouxfalls), 521 Duluth Ave. It seems everywhere you go in Sioux Falls you see the twin steeples of this Catholic cathedral looming over the skyline. On the edge of the historic district, this stone 1918 Romanesque and French Renaissance cathedral is an active church and school, so visit accordingly.

MUSEUMS Sioux Empire Medical Museum (605-333-6397), 1305 W. 18th St. at Sanford Health. Open 1–4 weekdays. Chronicling the advances of medicine from the 1900s to the present this museum uses photographs and displays to show just how far medicine has come. Displays include a 1912 operating room and a 1940s iron lung, as well as period nurse's uniforms. The hours are very limited so plan your visit accordingly. Groups of 15 or more need to call ahead.

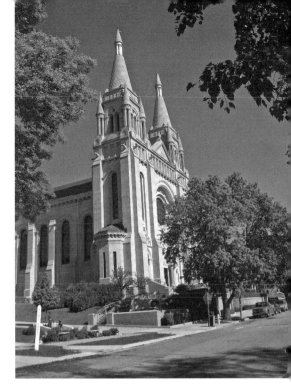

SPORTS Sioux Falls Canaries Professional Baseball (605-333-0179; www.canariesbaseball.com), 1001 N. West Ave. There is nothing like the excitement of minor league baseball and Sioux Falls has it. The Canaries play in the Birdcage from May through August and the fans love them. Check the Web site for home games. General admission is $6.

AN ACTIVE CATHOLIC CHURCH, THE SIOUX FALLS CATHEDRAL SOARS ABOVE THE CITY.

Sioux Falls Skyforce Basketball (605-332-0605; www.nba.com/dleague/sioux falls), 2101 W. 41st St. The Skyforce is a developmental team of the NBA, so check out some future stars. Go to the Web site for the season schedule. They play November through April and tickets range from $5 on up.

Sioux Falls Stampede Hockey (605-336-6060; www.sfstampede.com), 230 S. Phillips Ave. The Stampede is an amateur hockey team that has a huge fan base in Sioux Falls. They play October through April. Tickets are $8.50 and up.

Sioux Falls Storm Indoor Football (605-332-4225; www.siouxfallsstorm.com), 1910 S Minnesota. The Storm is affiliated with the United Indoor Football and plays March through June. All home games are played at the Sioux Falls Arena.

✳ To Do

BIKING/HIKING The Big Sioux River Recreation Trail, 19.2 miles, beginning at Falls Park, Phillips Ave., and Falls Park Dr. You will see folks bicycling all around Sioux Falls on this trail. The trail is paved and loops through the city, often along the river, ending at the Outdoor Campus, 49th Street, and Oxbow. It's a great way to see the parks in town and enjoy the river.

Big Sioux Recreation Area (605-582-7243; www.sdgfp.info/Parks/Regions/ Heartland/BigSioux.htm), located 4 miles S.W. of Brandon off I-90, exit 406, has three trails that pass through grasslands, trees, and provide good bird-watching or just some nice solitude.

Bike Trail is 2 miles on asphalt. The trailheads are by site 38E in the campground or by the park entrance.

Prairie Vista Trail is 2.8 miles and very hilly. The trailhead is located by the picnic shelter.

Valley of the Giants Trail is 1.25 miles and somewhat strenuous in some areas. The trailhead is located off the northeast parking loop.

Blue Diamond Multi-Use Trail, Newton Hills State Park (605-987-2263; www.sdgfp.info/Parks/Regions/Heartland/NewtonHills.htm), located 6 miles south of Canton off County Route 135. Newton Hill is heavily forested, which makes it a nice change in the middle of the prairie. There are 200 species of birds that visit the area each year and you may also see deer, turkeys, marmots, and rabbits. This trail is 6 miles long and considered very difficult due to the hilly terrain left by glacial deposits. The trailhead is at the horse camp.

BOATING AND FISHING There are lots of opportunities to fish and boat in the Sioux Falls area. Fish species include crappie, bullhead, pike, bass, and walleye. For more information go to www.travelsd.com/fishing/Southeast. Fishing licenses can be obtained at **Lewis Drug** on 10th, 41st, or 26th Street and **Scheels** 2101 W. 41st, among others.

Big Sioux River, Sioux Falls. The Big Sioux River runs 390 miles and the channel catfish is king. Fish from the bank or hit the water in a canoe. Smallmouth bass have been stocked in the river for diversity but don't be surprised to snag a walleye or northern pike.

Beaver Lake, near Humboldt, just northwest of Sioux Falls. Over 300 acres, this lake has a boat ramp as well as a dock for fishing. Expect to get bites from carp, bullhead, and perch.

FAMILY FRIENDLY **Wild Water West Waterpark** (605-361-9313; www.the adventurepark.com), 26767 466th Ave. Open daily 11–8 May 23 through September 1. On a hot, muggy summer day there is nothing like a water park. With numerous waterslides, including one off a 65-foot tower, this is one of the best. Relax on a lazy river, have a little interactive aqua play, or hit the beach for some sand volleyball. If you have a little one, there is even a baby pool. Showers and locker rooms are available as well as concessions to make for an enjoyable day. $6–$18 for a full day, $5–$10 for the evening.

Thunder Road Family Fun Park (605-334-4181; www.thunderroad.info), Eighth and Kiwanis Ave. Open 1–8, weather permitting. With go-karts, water wars, a climbing wall, batting cages, mini golf, and human foosball (where teams have to work together to score points), this place is plenty popular with kids and families. Prices vary by attraction.

The Adventurepark (605-361-9313; www.theadventurepark.com), 26767 466th Ave. Open daily 11–10 May 23 through September 1. For a little family fun, stop in for paintball, bumper boats, mini golf, go-karts, and batting cages. Come in the evening when it's a lot cooler and the prices are a lot lower. $24 for a day pass, $14 for an evening pass.

GOLF Sioux Falls, like all of South Dakota, plays a lot of golf. They have five great courses to choose from.

Bakker Crossing Golf Course (605-368-9700; www.bakkercrossing.com), 47172 Clubhouse Rd. Open February through November. This 18-hole championship course has very few trees and, this being the prairie, the wind can be a big factor in club selection. Green fees are $23 and up.

Elmwood Golf Course (605-367-7092; www.dakotagolf.com), 2604 W. Russell St. The terrain on this course is flat and easy to walk. The fairways are lined with elm trees, thus the name, and water comes into play on several holes. Green fees are $20.

Kuehn Park Golf Course (605-362-2811; www.dakotagolf.com), 2901 Kuehn Park Rd. This short 18-hole, par-30 course is great for beginners. There are many sand bunkers spread throughout the course providing an additional challenge. Green fees are $15 and up.

Prairie Green Golf Course (605-367-6076; www.dakotagolf.com), 600 E. 69th St. An 18-hole course set in the prairie, the small greens and water hazards on 15 of the holes make this course a little tricky. Green fees are $25.

Willow Run Golf Course (605-335-5900; www.willowrungolfcourse.com), 8000 E. SD 42. This hilly 18-hole championship course has a creek running through that comes into play numerous times. Green fees are $25.

HUNTING Sioux Falls is in a great area for pheasant hunting. Pheasant season is mid-October through mid-December. A state license is required so visit the following Web site for details: www.state.sd.us/gfp. See licensing retailers under *Boating and Fishing*.

SWIMMING Sioux Falls has eight nice city pools, two of which are aquatic centers with slides and water toys, and all are open to visitors. Pick one close by and have some family fun. They are open 1–9 during the summer.

Laurel Oak Park has a family aquatic center. 49th St. and Laurel Oak.

Terrace Park has a family aquatic center. Madison St. and Menlo Ave.

Drake Springs, 12th and Fairfax Ave.

Frank Olson Park, 18th St. and Judy Ave.

Kuehn Park, 41 St. and Kuehn Park Rd.

Mansor-Pioneer Park, Jessica Ave. and Pine St.

McKennan Park, 26th St. and Fourth Ave.

Spellerberg Park, 26th St. and Western Ave.

UNIQUE ADVENTURES ✿ **Wells Fargo Sound and Light Show**, Falls Park. 9:30 PM Memorial Day through Labor Day, weather permitting. This dramatic show begins with all the lights going off in the park leaving the audience in complete darkness before colored spots light up the falls. Through the use of lasers, images are projected on a wall adjacent to the falls, and the narrated show tells the history of Sioux Falls from its Native American heritage to the present. This is a great family-friendly introduction to Sioux Falls and really pretty to watch. Free.

✳ Green Spaces

NATURE PRESERVES **Beaver Creek Nature Area** (605-594-3824; www.sdgfp .info/Parks/Regions/Heartland/BeaverCreek.htm), 5 miles S.E. of Brandon off I-90, exit 406. Developed to create environmental awareness this park was named for the beavers that early settlers found along the winding creek. Explore the area on 1.5 miles of trails that wind through bottomland along the creek and prairie, keeping your eyes open for a variety of birds, animals, and trees to enjoy. Open year-round, no fees.

PARKS **Big Sioux Recreation Area** (605-582-7243; see listing under *Biking and Hiking*). Open year-round. With hiking, biking, fishing, canoeing, camping, and an archery range, everyone can find something to do at this recreation area. Check out the log house and storm cellar, which was where the original Ole Bergerson homestead stood. Built in 1868, Bergerson helped Ole Iverson, the area's first settler, build a dugout and the next year he built his own using hand hewn logs. This park is also popular for cross-country skiing in the winter. $5 per car.

Palisades State Park (605-594-3824; www.sdgfp.info/Parks/Regions/Heartland/ Palisades.htm), 10 miles north on I-90, Brandon, exit 406. Open year-round. Split Rock Creek, which flows through the park, is lined with Sioux quartzite formations varying from shelves several feet above the water to 50-foot vertical cliffs, making for some fantastic landscapes. Picnicking, fishing, and camping are available. Folks also come here to rock climb. $5 per car.

Sioux Falls loves its parks and has 70 of them with various facilities, go to www .siouxfallsparks.org for complete information. Here are some of the best:

Falls Park (605-367-7430), 309 E. Falls Park Dr. These are the falls that gave Sioux Falls its name. There are six viewing areas and the new Falls Park Visitors Information Center features a five-story observation tower and elevator. The falls are a must-see while in town and the park is beautiful, so bring a picnic and stay awhile.

Arrowhead Park (605-367-7060), E. 26th St. and River Bluff Rd. This park is a designated nature area. It is the location of a former granite quarry that is now a lake.

McKennan Park, 26th St. & Fourth Ave. Sioux Falls's oldest developed park is home of the Mediterranean Sunken Gardens, a restored 1926 band shell, a Statue of Liberty, and tournament play horseshoe pits.

Sertoma Park, 49th St. and Oxbow Ave. This park is home to the Butterfly House, the Outdoor Campus, and five educational play pods.

Sherman Park, 12 to 22nd Street, is Sioux Falls' largest at 205 acres. It houses the Great Plains Zoo and Delbridge Museum of Natural History, the U.S.S. *South Dakota* Battleship Memorial, the South Dakota Softball Hall of Fame, and the Indian Burial Mounds.

Terrace Park, Second St. and Grange Ave. Featuring Covell Lake, the Shoto-Teien Japanese Gardens, which were built from 1928 to 1936, and the family aquatic center. This park also has a band shell that is used for summer concerts.

Veterans Memorial Park, West Bailey St. The park, which was dedicated on September 9, 2006, includes an entryway with flags, plazas, walls, and an amphitheater. The infrastructure of the park allows for memorials to be built over time in various spaces.

Fawick Park, 10th St. and Second Ave. This park has the distinction of having one of three life-size replicas of Michelangelo's *David*. It was donated to the city by Thomas Fawick in 1971 and caused a great deal of controversy because of the statue's nudity. Fawick also donated a copy of Michelangelo's *Moses*, which can be found on the campus of Augustana College.

WINTER SPORTS ❈ **Great Bear Recreation Park** (605-367-4309; www.great bearpark.com), 2401 W. Rice St. Open seasonally. Who would have guessed there is skiing in the plains? Great Bear not only has skiing but snowboarding and tubing with 12 downhill trails, chair lifts, and a skiing school. Lift tickets are $21 for a full day.

❈ **Siouxland Trail** (www.sdgfp.info/Parks/Recreation/Snowmobiling/Maps/ ERSnowmo.pdf) is 68 miles of groomed trails for snowmobiling running from Sioux Falls north and northwest. The trail opens December 1.

❈ **Newton Hills State Park**, see listing under *Biking and Hiking*. Cross-country skiing is big in South Dakota and Newton Hills has extensive cross-country skiing trails with a warming shelter.

❊ Lodging

Sioux Falls has every major chain hotel and motel ranging from the inexpensive to upscale. Some of the choices include the **Sheraton** (605-339-7852), **Ramada Inn and Suites** (605-336-1020), **Best Western Ramkota** (605-336-0650), and **Holiday Inn City Centre** (605-339-2000), which is right near Falls Park. The visitors bureau has a complete listing at www.sioux fallscvb.com/hotels.cfm.

BED & BREAKFAST INNS The **Victorian** (605-376-4534; www.the victorianbedandbreakfast.com), 117 N. Duluth Ave. In the heart of the historic district, this Queen Ann–style home was built in 1888 and is on the historic register. The nicest bed-and-breakfast in Sioux Falls, there are three deluxe suites each with private baths, each named for members of the decorator's family. Reminiscent of her mother, the Gwendolyn June Chambers Room features photos of mothers and children as well as period outfits

for both. Have little girls? Then sign up for a Princess Dress Up Party where girls get to do hair and makeup and dress in a variety of Victorian dresses. They even offer an overnight option for the princesses. Rooms $70–$80.

IN A HISTORIC HOME DOWNTOWN, THE VICTORIAN B&B WELCOMES GUESTS FOR AN OVERNIGHT STAY.

CABINS/CAMPING Big Sioux Recreation Area see listing under *Parks*. Open May through September. 50 sites with water, showers, and a dump station. $12–$16 per night.

Palisades State Park see listing under *Parks*. Open year-round with 35 sites with showers and water. $12–$16 per night.

Lake Vermillion Recreation Area (605-296-3643; www.sdgfp.info/Parks/Regions/Heartland/LakeVermillion .htm), located 27 miles west of Sioux Falls, 5 miles S of I-90, exit 374. There are 66 sites, three cabins with water, showers, and a dump station. $12–$16 per night.

Newton Hills State Park (605-987-2263; www.sdgfp.info/Parks/Regions/Heartland/NewtonHills.htm), located 6 miles south of Canton off CR 135. Open year-round. There are 118 camping sites and seven cabins with water, showers, and a dump station. $12–$16 per night.

✳ Where to Eat

DINING OUT Carnaval Brazilian Grill (605-361-6328; www.carnaval braziliangrill.com), 2401 S. Carolyn Ave. Open 11–2 and 5–9 Tuesday through Saturday, Sunday brunch from 10–2. Take a trip to South America without leaving Sioux Falls! Carnaval is all about the meat and the service of the meat. With beef, lamb, pork, and sausage all roasted over an open flame in the traditional Brazilian fashion, your meat is brought to you on a skewer and served by a gaucho chef. The Mesa de Frios fills out your meal with a 55-item salad bar, including Brazilian-style potato salad, asparagus, hearts of palm, cheeses, and more. The full bar features Brazilian specialty drinks, including Mona Vie, a concoction of 19 fruit juices. Entrées $10–$27.

CJ Callaway's (605-334-8888; www .cjcallaways.com), 500 E. 69th St. The pub is open at 11:00 Monday through Saturday for lunch and dinner. The restaurant is open at 5 Friday and Saturday. The perfect stop for a romantic dinner, the low lighting and views of the landscaped golf course set the stage for fine food. Upscale choices include rack of lamb and beef medallions, but the signature dish is Maytag Beef Wellington, beef baked in a delicate pastry crust with the tangy addition of bleu cheese. For something lighter on the wallet and more casual, the pub menu in the bar has sandwiches as well as a simplified version of the main menu. Entrées $15–$25.

Foley's Fish, Chop, Steakhouse (605-362-8125; www.foleysrestaurant .com), 2507 S. Shirley Ave. Open at 4 PM every evening. This inviting wood paneled and elegantly appointed restaurant is the perfect spot for a romantic dinner for two or a family celebration. Many consider Foley's to have the best seafood in town and their all-time best seller is the Chilean sea bass brushed with herb garlic oil. There is also a nice selection of steaks, pork chops, and pastas, as well as dinner salads. If you prefer something lighter, try the lounge and their wood-smoked pizza. Entrées $16–$35.

Minervas (605-334-0386; www .Minervas.net); 301 S. Phillips. Open 11–2:30 and 5:30–10. Fine dining but never stuffy, Minervas is a very popular Midwest chain and has a diverse menu of pasta, salads, seafood, and steaks, all well done. For starters try the gooey crab artichoke bake, then select one of their steaks and pick your own additions such as the Michael Topping, which features horseradish, bleu cheese, and parmesan. Entrées $7–$29.

EATING OUT Café 334 (605-334-3050), 334 S. Phillips Ave. Open

10:30–9 Tuesday through Thursday and Friday, 9–3:30 and 5–10 Saturday, and Sunday brunch from 9–2. Eat in the wood-accented dining room or the large outdoor patio, either way you are bound to enjoy Café 334's seasonal menu. With both small and large plates, the upscale selections include mushroom-crusted Chilean sea bass and Portobello stuffed ravioli. For lunch try a deluxe grilled cheese with dill havarti, cheddar, tomato, scallions, and sunflower seeds. Entrées from $7–$28.

Food and Fermentations (605-332-4338; www.foodandfermentations .com), 431 N Phillips Ave. Open 11–8 Monday through Thursday, 11–9. Friday through Saturday. Located right at the entrance to Falls Park this is a great place to put a picnic together. Calling themselves a Culinary Center, Food and Fermentations sells an amazing assortment of gourmet food and wine. With gleaming wooden floors and a wood-beamed ceiling, the restaurant serves sandwiches and soups, as well as cheese and paté plates. Nothing mundane here, try the Sloppy Joe with the tang of Hoisin sauce, or the ham and strawberry sandwich. Don't forget to check out the cheese cave, which features dozens of gourmet cheeses from around the world. Entrees $6–$15.

Granite City Food & Brewery (605-362-0000; www.gcfb.com), 2620 S. Louise Ave. Open 11 AM–12 AM daily. They brew their own beer in a variety of styles including stouts, ales, and lagers, so try the beer sampler and find your favorite. With a huge menu to choose from—everything from sandwiches and salads to walleye and steaks—their signature selections include honey rosemary filet mignon and chicken florentine lasagna. If the weather cooperates, enjoy the 200-seat

outdoor patio and watch the world go by on the adjacent walking and biking trail along the river. Entrées $9–$25.

Inca's Mexican Restaurant (605-367-1992; www.incasiouxfalls.com), 3312 Holly Ave. Open 11–11 everyday. If you want authentic Mexican food of tacos, burritos, and enchiladas, you will enjoy a stop at Inca's. Start with a basket or two of their extra crispy chips and mild salsa, then hope you left some room for their entrées served on huge plates with sides of beans and rice. You will definitely leave full and for a very reasonable price. Entrees $9–$14.

Mama's Ladas (605-332-2772); 116 W. 11th St. Open 11:15–9 Monday through Thursday and Friday, and 11:15–10 Saturday. Mama's Ladas is a small place and does one thing and they do it well, enchiladas. You can have beef or chicken during the week and on the weekends they offer shrimp and spinach, or broccoli and cheese. There is only a beer and wine license but the locals swear by the homemade Sangria. Get there early because when the enchiladas are gone they're gone. $5–$12.

Phillips Avenue Diner (605-335-4977), 121 S. Phillips Ave. Built to look like a railroad dining car with shiny stainless steel inside and out, there are inside booths, stools at the counter, or a large outdoor patio. They serve a complete breakfast of eggs, omelets, pancakes, and sides, and for lunch or dinner try the burgers or some comfort food like meatloaf, pot roast, or mac and cheese. And don't pass up the soda fountain with handmade malts and shakes, sundaes, and floats. Entrées $7–$11.

Touch of Europe (605-336-3066; www.toejazz.com), 12th and Phillips. Open 5:30–9 Monday through Thursday, 5–12 Friday through Saturday.

The only jazz club in Sioux Falls also serves classical European cuisine. With entrées of borscht, dolmas, and weinerschnitzel this is not the kind of food you'll find just anywhere in South Dakota. Sit back and relax in this romantic setting filled with old-world charm and enjoy music provided by anything from a big band to a solo piano player. Entrées $14–$23.

Spezia (605-334-7491; www.spezia restaurant.com), 4801 S. Louise Ave. Open for lunch and dinner Monday through Sunday. Sunday brunch 9–1:30. A popular Italian-inspired casual-dining restaurant, Spezia is suitable for couples or the entire family. What makes Spezia special is the wood-burning oven for their thin-crust pizza. Try the chicken broccoli topped with alfredo sauce or the pesto spicy portobello. They also have a nice, extensive wine list served by the bottle or glass. Entrées $12–$30, Sunday brunch $13.95.

Sushi-Masa Japanese Restaurant (605-977-6968), 423 S. Phillips Ave. Open 11:30–2:30 Monday through Friday and 5–9:30 Monday through Saturday. Half a continent from an ocean, Sushi-Masa still manages to find the best fresh fish around and the chef knows how to make the most of it. The place is small, with quaint little alcoves for seating, and has over 200 menu items including teriyaki and tempura but the sushi is the reason for going. Get there early or you may face a long wait. Entrées $10–$30.

❋ Entertainment

South Dakota Symphony (605-335-7933; www.sdsymphony.org). The South Dakota Symphony has been performing and educating the public for 80 seasons. They perform September through May, with 10 full concerts. Check the Web site for the performance schedule.

Orpheum Theater (605-367-4616; www.orpheum.sfarena.com); 1201 N. West Ave. Built in 1913 the Orpheum was originally a vaudeville house. It is now home to the Community Theater and it also hosts plays, concerts, and musicals. The theater is known for its exceptional acoustics and hosts 100,000 visitors every year. Call for the performance schedule.

Husby Performing Arts Center at the Washington Pavilion of Arts and Science (605-367-6000), 11th and Main. The center has a great hall with 1,800 seats and a smaller hall that hosts Broadway shows, concerts, and dance tours. Call for the performance schedule.

❋ Selective Shopping

Sioux Falls is a commercial center, so if you want to go to the very large mall and every conceivable chain store, take the Empire Mall exit off I-29. Downtown Sioux Falls, along and off Phillips Avenue is very attractive with a large selection of specialty stores, restaurants, and the Sculpture Walk. Here are a few examples of the shops available:

Eastbank Art Gallery and Studio (605-977-2667; www.eastbankart gallery.com), 401 E. Eighth St. Open 12–5 Monday through Friday, 10–5 Saturday. This cooperative art gallery was established, is supported, and is maintained by 16 regional artists. They show their work at the gallery and take turns being on hand to talk about and sell the art. There are a number of painters, but also potters, photographers, and jewelers, displaying their work. Since it's member owned there is no mark-up, so you can buy very impressive art at great prices.

Great Outdoor Store (877-974-8844; www.greatoutdoorstoreonline.com), 235 S. Phillips Ave. Open 10–8 Monday through Friday, 10–5 Saturday, 12–4 Sunday. Whatever your outdoor sport, hiking, camping or climbing, this store has what you need whether it's shoes, clothing, or gear. You don't even have to be an outdoor enthusiast to like this place because they carry casual shoes, including sandals, commuter packs, coats, and clothes from brand names like Patagonia and North Face that will make you look great inside or out.

Rugs and Relic (605-331-5546), 401 Eighth St. Open 10:30–5:30 Monday through Saturday. Every rug in this store was hand selected by their resident rug expert, Steve Bormes, in his trips to Turkey and every rug comes with a story, which the staff will be happy to share. Also in stock are one-of-a-kind purses, pillows, luggage, and gift items.

Prairie Star Gallery-Timeless Indigenous Art (605-338-9300; www .prairiestar.com), 207 S. Phillips Ave. Open 10–6 Monday and Wednesday through Saturday. With fine art created by over 500 Native American artists, Prairie Star prides itself on authentic indigenous art. Featuring sculpture, paintings, bead and quillwork, drums, and handmade quilts in a hundred-year-old building of wood and brick, this shop is a fine place to immerse yourself in Native American culture and traditional art forms.

Sticks and Steel (605-335-7349; www .sticksandsteel.com), 401 E. Eighth St. Open 10–6 Monday through Saturday, 12–4 Sunday. If you are looking for arts and crafts that are handmade and high quality, Sticks and Steel is a great place to start. They represent artists from all over the United States and Canada with an eye for the unique and even whimsical. You can find jewelry, home décor, clothing, and signs and ornaments that are made on site of

steel. This is a great place to pick up a wedding or anniversary gift or a little something for yourself.

Zandbroz Variety (605-331-5137), 209 S. Phillips Ave. Located in a historic downtown building, this may be the coolest variety store ever—what the owners call their "personal antidote to Wal-Mart." Part bookstore, coffee bar, and gift shop, Zandbroz carries enough variety that you're bound to find something you can't live without. They have high quality product lines like Crabtree and Evelyn, Tao of Tea, and many items to make your life happier, like scented candles and aromatherapy. Plan on browsing awhile through the cards, educational and nostalgic games, tin toys, and high-end stationary and find that perfect gift for a friend, or to keep for yourself.

Prairie Meat and Market (605-275-0222; www.hutteriteprairiemarket .com), 3817 S. Western Ave. The Hutterites are a religious group that fled persecution in Russia and now farm in several states, including South Dakota, and this store carries many of the items they produce. The food products sold here are of the highest quality and contain no additives, sweeteners, colorings, or preservatives. South Dakotans have been buying food produced by the Hutterites for generations and many swear that there is no better meat available anywhere.

Strawbale Winery (605-543-5071; www.strawbalewinery.com), located just north of Sioux Falls on 257th St., off I-29, exit 86. Unique but also environmentally friendly, the winery is built of straw bales to re-create the environment of cellars or caves that have always been used to store wine while it naturally ages. Strawbale Winery produces grape wines as well as a large variety of fruit wines, including strawberry, black currant, chokecherry, and even jalapeno. They also make several kinds of mead, which is a fermented beverage made of honey. Stop in to the tasting room or take a tour to see how the wine is made.

✳ Special Events

JUNE **Artfalls** (605-332-8607; www.artfalls.com), Sioux Falls Park. There is a juried art show, entertainment, vendors, and food booths.

JULY **Jazzfest** (605-335-6101; www.jazzfestsiouxfalls.com), Yankton Trail Park, Minnesota St., and Big Sioux River. This two-day festival has 10 bands, food, and activities.

AUGUST **Sioux Empire Fair** (605-367-7178; www.siouxempirefair.com), 4000 W. 12th St. Carnival rides, 4-H, livestock, and nightly entertainment. **Lifelight Music Festival** (www.lifelight.com). 100 artists will perform over three days at this outdoor Christian music festival.

SEPTEMBER **Spirit of the West Festival** (605-334-9202; www.spiritofthewestfestival.com), 6200 N. Kiwanis. An annual event to promote the area's Western heritage. Performers, reenactors, trade show, food, and more.

Northern Plains Indian Art Market (605-856-8100; www.sinte.edu), Northern Plains Indian art show and traditional Powwow.

NOVEMBER–JANUARY **Winter Wonderland** (605-336-1620), Sioux Falls Park. The Park is lit up with thousands of lights over the holiday season. Throw in a little snow and you indeed have a winter wonderland.

✳ Nearby

Brandon is home to the **Wilde Prairie Winery,** which is open to visitors on Saturday and Sunday from 12–5. Stop in and try their dandelion wine, of which they are understandably proud. Contact them at 605-582-6471. Brandon is just west of Sioux Falls off I-90.

Canton holds the **Sioux River Folk Festival** every August at **Newton Hills State Park**. Come for the traditional music featuring folk, blues, and gospel.

Freeman is a community of German and Russian heritage and to celebrate they hold the annual **Schmeckfest** in March. Come for the great food, crafts, music, and a stage musical. In June, Freeman hosts **Quiltfest** with hundreds of handmade quilts on display, vendors, as well as another musical. Freeman is southeast of Sioux Falls on US 81, www.freemansd.com.

Try **Madison** in June for **Motongator Joe's Country Music Festival**. There are 15 different country acts, a flea market, chili cook-off, and a Daisy Duke look-alike contest. Madison is north of Sioux Falls on SD 34. Check out the Web site: www.motongator.com/sdak.

Tea, just south of Sioux Falls on I-29, holds **Teapot Day** every June where it is all things tea and everyone pulls out their personal collection of teapots. There is a carnival, tractor pull, entertainment, and the all-important crowning of Ma and Pa Tea. Go to www.teasd.com for more information.

VERMILLION

Vermillion is a town of 10,000 at the junction of the Vermillion and Missouri Rivers. The area had long been visited by Native Americans and was another stop on the Lewis and Clark expedition when they made their trek to the Spirit Mound.

The town itself was founded in 1859 and ensured its permanence when the University of South Dakota was opened there in 1862, which now includes a medical and law school. In 1881 three quarters of the town was washed away in a flood but merchants rebuilt their businesses on the bluffs above the river.

Today Vermillion is a mix of students, professors, and those involved in the agricultural field. The downtown is on the National Register of Historic Places and the town is committed to historic preservation, with an eye toward the future. The people of Vermillion are proud of their small town way of life and welcome visitors to see what makes it a great place to live.

GUIDANCE Vermillion Chamber of Commerce (1-800-809-2071; www.vermillionchamber.com).

GETTING THERE *By car:* Vermillion is located on SD 50 and SD 19, a few miles west of I-29. It is 56 miles south of Sioux Falls.

GETTING AROUND There is no public transportation in Vermillion.

MEDICAL EMERGENCIES San-ford Vermillion Medical Center (605-624-2611; www.sanfordvermillion.org), 20 S. Plum St.

ON THE UNIVERSITY OF SOUTH DAKOTA, OLD MAIN WAS BUILT IN 1883.

✳ To See

HISTORIC SITES ❧ **Austin Whittemore House** (605-624-8266), 15 Austin St. Open 9–12 and 1–3 Monday through Friday. Built in 1881 this home now houses the Clay County Historical Society. The house was built by Horace Austin and in 1969 was on the verge of being torn down when the historical society stepped in to save it. It is now restored and filled with Victorian furnishings and items of local historic interest, including many historical records and documents from the area. Visitors and researchers are welcome to visit the house or look through the historic records the society maintains. Free.

MUSEUMS **National Music Museum** (www.usd.edu/smm), 414 E. Clark St. on the University of SD campus. Open 9–5 Monday through Saturday, 2–5 Sunday. With an astonishing collection of American, European, and non-Western instruments from all time periods, including as early as the 1500s, this museum is on a national scale yet in a very small town. There are treasures like B. B King's "Lucille," band instruments from the Civil War, rooms full of pianos and harpsichords, and lots of things that you may not recognize as instruments except for the strings or horn attached. Take a self-guided tour with 50 stops using a CD player or just wander and read the interpretive signs. It is definitely time well spent and plenty educational. $7 for adults, $3 for students.

❧ **Oscar Howe Gallery** (605-677-5481; www.usd.edu/cfa/Art/UniversityGalleries/oscarhowegallery.cfm), Old Main building on the University of SD campus. Open 1–5 Monday through Saturday. Housing the largest collection of this celebrated Native American artist's works, there is no better place to learn about Howe's life

THE NATIONAL MUSIC MUSEUM IS LOCATED ON THE UNIVERSITY OF SOUTH DAKOTA AND INCLUDES MORE THAN 14,000 INSTRUMENTS.

INSTRUMENTS ON DISPLAY AT THE NATIONAL MUSIC MUSEUM COVER VIRTUALLY EVERY
CENTURY INCLUDING THE PRESENT DAY.

and artwork. Howe joined the faculty at USD in 1957 and worked there for 25
years. In the beginning of his time at USD he was an assistant curator of the W. H.
Over Museum, as well as teaching classes, but as his reputation grew Howe was
named Artist-in-Residence. As part of that obligation Howe donated paintings to
the university that eventually made up the gallery named for him. (There is more
information about Oscar Howe in the Mitchell section under *Historic Sites* in the
Southeast section.) Free.

🐚 **W. H. Over Museum of Natural and Cultural History** (605-677-5228; www
.usd.edu/whover), 1110 Ratingen St. Open 10–4 Monday through Saturday. This
museum is named for a fervent collector who, with only an eighth grade education,
became the assistant curator of the then University of South Dakota museum.
Over served there for 35 years and added tremendously to the knowledge of South
Dakota's natural history through his studies of trees, birds, flowers, geology, and
Native Americans. The museum has South Dakota's largest natural and cultural
history collection, including extensive Native American and pioneer exhibits. There
are many artifacts from the Sioux Indians as well as 500 stereographic cards of
Stanley J. Morrow's photographs, which document the settling of the West in the
period after the Civil War. Free.

✳ To Do

BIKING/HIKING **Spirit Mound Historic Prairie** (605-987-2263; www.sdgfp
.info/Parks/Regions/Heartland/SpiritMound.htm), located 5 miles north of Vermillion off SD 19. This 0.75-mile trail begins in the parking lot. Lewis and Clark
heard the story of little spirits with spears that inhabited the Spirit Mound and
hiked 9 miles to the mound to investigate. Though they found no such spirits, they
were impressed by the view and Clark wrote, "from the top of this mound we

LEWIS AND CLARK IN SOUTH DAKOTA

Because they navigated the Missouri River, Lewis and Clark spent the summer and fall of 1804 in South Dakota. Here they experienced many sights never before recorded by whites and had many friendly encounters with the Native American tribes that called the area home.

The Corp of Discovery entered South Dakota on August 22, 1804, in a place they called Elk Point, so named for the abundance of elk manure seen there. They conducted the first election west of the Mississippi when they voted to replace Sgt. Charles Floyd, who had died two days earlier, with Patrick Gass. Gass assumed the position of sergeant.

On August 25 the party was near what is now Vermillion. They visited the Spirit Mound after hearing Native Americans describe 18-inch devils armed with arrows that lived there. It took them four hours on foot to reach the mound where they saw numerous herds of bison, but no devils.

The expedition spent four days on Calumet Bluff near Yankton. They met with the Yankton Sioux and presented gifts of tobacco, corn, and flags. The Yankton prepared a feast for the visitors. The corps interpreter, Mr. Dorian,

LEWIS AND CLARK PASSED THROUGH SOUTH DAKOTA AS THEY MADE THEIR WAY UP THE MISSOURI RIVER. THERE ARE MANY PLACES IN SOUTH DAKOTA TO LEARN ABOUT THIS FAMOUS EXPEDITION.

South Dakota Tourism

stayed behind to negotiate peace with the Yankton's neighbors and arrange for the chiefs to visit Washington, D.C.

In September the Corps of Discovery saw their first prairie dogs in Gregory County. They were astonished by the "barking dogs" and the extensive tunnels they dug. They poured five barrels of water into one tunnel and didn't manage to fill it up.

On September 16 the expedition stopped at a place they called Camp Pleasant, which is near present day Chamberlain. Lewis spent a day hunting and described herds of buffalo, deer, elk, and antelope in every direction.

Traveling northward the corps encountered a "great bend" in the river. Lewis and Clark sent a man to measure the distance across the land to the other side of the loop and it measured a little more than a mile. By water the distance is 30 miles and is today called Big Bend.

The expedition reached present day Fort Pierre on September 24 and stayed at a small river they called the Teton, known today as the Bad River. A council with the Teton Sioux turned tense and Clark drew his sword while the Teton strung their bows. Black Buffalo, one of the Teton chiefs, calmed the situation or American history may have turned out very differently.

Near Gettysburg on October 4, the expedition passed an abandoned Arikara village. The village was circular, walled, and contained 17 lodges.

On October 8 the explorers discovered three Arikara villages near present day Mobridge. Clark described the fields around the village as covered with corn, tobacco, and beans. When they hold council with the tribe, the Indians were particularly impressed by York, Clark's servant, having never before seen a black man.

The court-martial of Private John Newman was held on October 13 near Pollock. He was charged with "mutinous expression" and found guilty by a jury of his peers. He received 75 lashes as punishment and was disbanded from the expedition. He was sent back to St. Louis in 1805.

In August 1806 the Lewis and Clark expedition passed through South Dakota on their return trip to St. Louis. They were tired and Lewis was suffering from a gunshot wound he got while hunting. While near present day Running Water they had a tense moment when gun shots rang out from what Clark assumed was an Indian war party. Clark gathered 15 men and ran in the direction of the shots only to find the Yankton Indians were shooting at a keg the expedition had thrown in the river. Clark invited the Indians to smoke, which they did. The explorers returned safely to St. Louis on September 23, 1806, having covered 8,000 miles in two years, four months, and ten days.

beheld a most butifull [his spelling] landscape; Numerous herds of buffalow [his spelling] were seen feeding in various directions. . . ." The trail takes you to the top of the Spirit Mound.

Union Grove State Park (605-987-2263; www.sdgfp.info/Parks/Regions/ Heartland/UnionGrove.htm), located 11 miles south of Beresford off I-29, this park is known for its lush grasses and trees, which attract a variety of birds and wildlife. With 150 acres to explore this park is very popular with hikers, bikers, and horseback riders. The trails are also used by cross-country skiers in the winter.

Brule Bottom Hiking Trail, 1.2 miles, is a slightly hilly trail that follows a dirt path. The trailhead is next to a comfort station at the campground.

Mosey Meadow Multi-Use Trail, 4.3 miles, trailhead in the horse camp. This moderately hilly trail is used by horses, bikers, and hikers.

GOLF Bluffs Golf Course (605-677-7058), 2021 E. Main St. This 18-hole municipal golf includes 10 acres of reflecting lakes and 8 acres of wetlands, making it great golfing and a chance to see some wildlife. Green fees $33–$39.

✴ Green Spaces

PARKS Spirit Mound Historic Prairie, see listing under *Biking and Hiking*. Encompassing over 300 acres of prairie that is being restored to its natural state, this park is home to a variety of prairie wildflowers and grasses including wild rose hips, evening primrose, sunflowers, silky aster, and whorled milkweed. Butterflies and wildlife are attracted to the renewed environment and it's a great spot for birding with dozens of species available.

Union Grove State Park, see listing under *Biking and Hiking*. Open year-round. This park is popular with horseback riders, hikers, and, in winter, cross-country skiers. There is lots of wildlife and it's a great place to view the fall colors because of the abundance of deciduous trees.

✴ Lodging

Vermillion has a number of chain motels including **Holiday Inn Express** (605-624-7600) and **Comfort Inn** (605-624-8333).

BED & BREAKFAST INNS Buffalo Run Resort at the Valiant Vineyard Winery (605-624-4500; www.buffalorunwinery.com), 1500 West Main St. Open year-round. Located at the Valiant Vineyard Winery, this is actually a bed-and-breakfast, as breakfast is included in the room rates. There are five rooms, most with private baths in this modern building. Each room has a different theme and furnishings to match, including the Frontier Room with lodgepole pine

furnishings, and the Queen Anne Room, which is decorated with period antiques. For a special treat book the Honeymoon Suite, which has a king-size bed and in-room Jacuzzi tub. While staying there check out the winery's tasting room and take a tour of the wine-making process. Rooms $95–$105.

CAMPING Union Grove State Park (605-987-2263; see listing under *Parks*. Open year-round with 25 sites, showers, and water available. $10–$14.

✴ Where to Eat

EATING OUT Coffee Shop Gallery (605-624-2945), 24 W. Main St. Open

7:30–6 Monday through Friday and 8–5 Saturday. As the name suggests this is a coffee shop with all the varieties and combos you crave. Throughout the long, narrow building there is artwork displayed on the brick walls, much of it for sale. A local hangout for students and faculty, there is a nice menu of homemade soups, sandwiches, and baked goods at very reasonable prices. Stop in, flip open your computer to access the free WiFi, and stay awhile. $3–$6.

Mona Lisi (605-624-6041), 7 Court St. Open 11–2 Monday through Friday, 4:30–9 Monday through Thursday, and 4:30–9:30 Friday and Saturday. A college town, Vermillion is not known for its fine dining so Mona Lisi must be a nice break from the fast-food when parents come to town for a visit and are going to pick up the tab. The menu features the traditional Italian favorites like lasagna and eggplant parmesan, all served in an attractive dining room with linen table cloths and napkins. Entrées $3–$15.

✳ Selective Shopping

Nook and Cranny (605-624-4611), 19 Main St. In the heart of historic downtown, this is a nicely laid out and decorated gift shop with cards, candles, and home, party, and children's gifts. It's a good place for students to do their Christmas shopping before heading home for the holidays and for you to find the perfect gift.

Valiant Vineyards Winery (605-624-4500; www.buffalorunwinery.com), 1500 West Main St. Open 10–5 daily in the summer; winter hours vary. The friendly staff at Valiant Vineyards will be glad to pour you a taste of their many wines while they fill you in on all the Vermillion gossip. There is also a 30-minute tour, which includes the winemaking facility, cask room, and bottling area and concludes with a wine tasting. Wine is available for purchase including whites, reds, blushes, and dessert wines—all are really tasty. Try the Jungfraulich, a sweet white wine or, if you prefer, the Vermillion Red.

✳ Nearby

Head east of Vermillion on SD 50 to a wide spot in the road that is the town of **Meckling** and stop at **Toby's Lounge**. Like many towns in South Dakota, Meckling has only a few homes and folks living there but they do have tradition in Toby's. The interior of Toby's is not much to look at, a beat up bar with a peeling vinyl front, a few video games, and a scattering of Formica topped tables, so don't be scared off, because for over 30 years the locals and visitors have come from miles around for Toby's roasted chicken. Pull up a bar stool, order a drink, and visit with the friendly local farmers who make Toby's home while your chicken is served.

YANKTON

Yankton has the distinction of being designated the first capitol of the Dakota Territory in 1861. When the capitol was "highjacked" to Bismarck the pressure was on to split the Dakotas north and south.

Yankton became a commercial hub for prospectors heading to the Black Hills in the 1870s and the population and businesses swelled. Yankton was also active in the steamboat industry with its ideal location on the Missouri River. But being on the river has its drawbacks: Yankton was subject to floods, particularly in the spring when melting ice and snow filled the river. The flood of 1881 devastated the town and wiped out much of the steamboat industry.

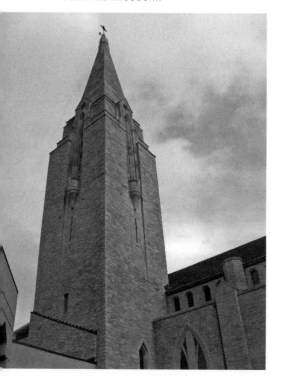

PART OF MOUNT MARTY COLLEGE, THIS CATHEDRAL SITS HIGH ON THE BLUFFS OVER THE MISSOURI.

When the Gavins Point Dam was built in 1957 the Missouri was at last tamed. The dam was one of six man-made structures that regulated the river and created hydroelectric power. An added benefit was the formation of Lewis and Clark Lake, which opened the door for recreation and tourism opportunities. Today the Lewis and Clark Recreational Area is the second most popular tourist attraction in South Dakota, the most popular being the Black Hills.

Yankton hosts tourists, but the community is also home to manufacturing, commercial enterprises, and Mount Marty College, a private Catholic school. With a population around 21,000 Yankton has a long history and a wide-open future.

GUIDANCE **Yankton Area Visitors Center** (605-665-3636; www.yankton sd.com), 803 E. Fourth St. Right on the highway into town, this visitors center offers maps, brochures, and individual attention.

GETTING THERE *By car:* Yankton is located on US 81 and SD 50. Yankton is 85 miles south west of Sioux Falls.

MEDICAL EMERGENCIES **Avera Sacred Heart Hospital** (605-668-8000; www.averasacredheart.com/ash), 501 Summit.

✳ To See

CULTURAL SITES 🎀 **G.A.R. Hall Art Gallery** (605-665-9754), 508 Douglas. Open 1–5 Monday through Friday, 1–3 Saturday. This Civil War era building has been restored, is home of the Yankton Area Arts, and holds monthly art exhibits. Free.

FAMILY FRIENDLY 🎀 **Gavins Point National Fish Hatchery and Aquarium** (605-665-3352; www.fws.gov/gavinspoint), 3 miles west of Yankton on SD 52. Open 10–4 daily April 1 through October 31. The hatchery's mission is to raise endangered fish species for release into the wild. In hopes of increasing their production in the wild, they raise 12–16 species of sport fish, including the endangered pallid sturgeon and the paddlefish, which is a species of concern. Started in 1961 the hatchery has produced over 5 billion fish that have been released in midwest waters. The aquariums on-site display 50 fish varieties in 13 large tanks and several smaller tanks with displays to help visitors learn about the fish and the work the hatchery does. Free.

HISTORIC SITES **Cramer Kenyon Heritage Home and Gardens** (605-665-7470), 509 Pine St. Open 1–5 Wednesday through Sunday, Memorial Day through Labor Day. Built in 1882 this restored house is the tallest Queen Anne home in South Dakota. Much of it is in the original condition, including the woodwork with

GAVINS POINT IS THE SMALLEST OF THE DAMS ON THE MISSOURI RIVER AND PROVIDES RECREATION ON ITS RESERVOIR, LEWIS AND CLARK LAKE.

its original finish and the gas and electric chandeliers. The home has its original décor including the art work hanging on the walls. $2 for adults, $2 for children.

Gavins Point Dam (402-667-2546; www.nwo.usace.army.mil/html/Lake_Proj/gavinspoint/dam.html), 4 miles west of Yankton on SD 52. Open 10–6 Friday through Sunday, Memorial Day through Labor Day. Located on the South Dakota–Nebraska border this is the smallest of the six dams on the upper Missouri and is used to generate hydroelectric power. The dam was built in 1957 and created Lewis and Clark Lake with all its recreational opportunities. Below the dam is the only non-channelized portion of the Missouri, which is designated as a Wild and Scenic River. Tours are available.

🐾 **Historic Yankton Tour** (1-800-888-1460), pick up a map at the visitors center. Yankton has some really beautiful historic homes, dating back to the 1870s on its tree-shaded streets. The tour provides information about the homes and where to find them.

🐾 **Bishop Marty Chapel**, 1005 W. Eighth St., on the campus of Mount Marty College. This chapel is named in honor of Martin Marty, a Benedictine missionary who first came to the Dakota Territory in 1876 and eventually became the first bishop of the territory. Father Marty invited a small group of Benedictine Sisters to establish a religious community in the territory. The sisters came from Switzerland and initially homesteaded in Zell, South Dakota, before taking over Father Marty's school and home in Yankton. Scared Heart Monastery is still alive and well in Yankton and the sisters are responsible for Mount Marty College and Sacred Heart Hospital. Built in 1954, the chapel is a distinctive landmark in Yankton with its soaring Gothic-style architecture high on a bluff overlooking the town. Stop in for a visit and wander around the campus. It is really quite beautiful and has great views of the Missouri.

THERE ARE NUMEROUS BIKE PATHS THROUGHOUT SOUTH DAKOTA FOR EXERCISE AND RECREATION.
South Dakota Tourism

MUSEUMS 🐾 **Dakota Territorial Museum** (605-665-3839), 610 Summit St. Summer hours 10–5 Monday through Friday, 12–4 Saturday and Sunday. Built in 1971, this museum holds a large collection of items from life in the Dakota Territory with both pioneer and Sioux Indian artifacts on display. Besides the indoor exhibits there are a number of outbuildings to explore on the premises, such as a Great Northern Railway depot, a retired Burlington Northern Railroad caboose, and a one-room schoolhouse. Free.

✳ **To Do**

BIKING/HIKING Yankton offers 8 miles of paved and lighted trails within the city and another 20 miles of trails around **Lake Yankton** and **Lewis and**

Clark Lake. Maps can be obtained from the **Yankton Visitors Center** or at www.yanktonsd.com/pdf_files/Yankton2_Trails_Map.pdf.

Some highlights include:

Chalk Bluffs Multi-Use Trail, 4.1 miles, at the west edge of the Lewis and Clark Recreation Area. The trail goes up and down the bluffs overlooking Lewis and Clark Lake and offers awesome views of the lake and town.

Arboretum Trail, 1.4 miles, located at 1891 Summit St. Following the perimeter of Yankton High School and the Summit Activities Center, this trail includes the arboretum, which has native trees, grasses, and flowers.

Auld-Brokaw Trail, 2.75 miles, parallels Marne Creek through Yankton. Built through the generosity of Tom Brokaw, a South Dakota native, this trail includes the Rotary Nature Area where signs identify native plantings.

Corps of Discovery Welcome Center Nature Trail, 1.5 miles, at the welcome center, 3 miles south of Yankton on SD 81. This interpretive trail has numbered guideposts, which identify local plants and animals.

Lewis and Clark Lake Trail, 6.9 miles, winds through the Pierson Ranch Recreation Area and the Lewis and Clark Recreation Area. The north side of the trail goes through forest, the south side follows the lake.

Highway 52 Trail, 3.14 miles parallels SD 52 from Yankton to the fish hatchery. This trail passes by a number of businesses near the lake.

LEWIS AND CLARK LAKE IS A BOATER'S PARADISE AND DRAWS VISITORS FROM THROUGHOUT THE COUNTRY.

South Dakota Tourism

SOUTH DAKOTA PROVIDES EXTRAORDINARY SETTINGS FOR CANOEING AND KAYAKING.

BOATING AND FISHING **Lewis and Clark Marina** (605-665-3111; www
.lewisandclarkmarina.com), located within Lewis and Clark Recreation Area. Lewis
and Clark Lake is 25 miles in length and 45 feet deep with 90 miles of shoreline.
Get everything you need to fish or sail at the marina, which includes 400 boat
slips, gas dock, boat rentals, and mechanical service.

Lewis and Clark Recreation Area has three boat ramps, an accessible fishing
dock, and a fish cleaning station. For fishing there are walleye, catfish, and large-
and smallmouth bass.

GOLF **Fox Run Golf Course** (605-668-5205), 803 E. Fourth St. This very well
maintained 18-hole golf course includes a number of water hazards. Green fees
are $30–$34.

Hillcrest Golf and Country Club (605-665-4621; www.hillcreStreet4t.com),
2206 Mulberry St. Open March through November. Open to nonmembers, this is
a highly rated 18-hole championship course with hilly terrain and a number of
water hazards. Green fees are $60.

HUNTING If you bird hunt, Yankton is for you. Not only do they have pheasant,
but there are turkeys and, being on the Missouri River Flyway, thousands of duck
and geese pass through every fall and winter. If you need a hunting license, try
Dakota Archery at 2305 E. SD 50, or **Erickson's** at 301 Broadway.

SWIMMING **Summit Activities Center** (605-668-5234), 1801 Summit St. Open
6–8. This city-owned recreation center has an indoor pool with a 134-foot water
slide as well as a weight room, basketball courts, and a walking track. They wel-

come visitors so you need not miss your workout while visiting Yankton. $5 for an individual day pass, $10 for a family day pass.

Lewis and Clark Recreation Area has three swimming beaches and a ski beach.

✳ Green Spaces

PARKS Lewis and Clark State Recreation Area (605-668-2985; www.lewis andclarkpark.com), SD 52, west of Yankton. Open year-round. This park hosts a million visitors a year for good reason, it includes 390 campsites, 6 miles of bike trails, 4.1 miles of multi-use trails, three beaches, boat ramps, a fishing dock, a motel, cabins, a marina, boat rentals, a restaurant, and a convenience store. See details under individual categories. $5 entry fee.

✳ Lodging

There are several chain and locally owned motels in Yankton, including **Best Western** (1-800-509-9923) and **Holiday Inn Express** (605-665-3177).

BED & BREAKFAST INNS Captain's Inn (605-665-2183; www .captainsinn.net), 517 Mulberry. Built in 1878 by Sanford B. Coulson, manager of the Missouri River Transportation Company, this elegant home includes a distinctive watchtower that Coulson used to keep an eye on his boats as they traveled the Missouri. In a historic neighborhood, this home features three Italian-marble fireplaces and black-walnut woodwork throughout. The home now has three suites, two with a Jacuzzi tub, and all with air-conditioning, a must in Yankton in the summer. Each room has a queen-size bed and is furnished with period antiques and reproductions. $70–$115.

CAMPING/CABINS Lewis and Clark State Recreation Area (605-668-2985; www.lewisandclarkpark .com), SD 52, west of Yankton. There are 374 sites, some directly on the lake, all with electric and showers, water for $16–$18 per site. If you don't want to sleep on the ground, there are also 15 camping cabins at $40 a night. Call for reservations at 1-800-710-CAMP.

RESORTS Lewis and Clark Resort (605-665-2680; www.lewisandclark park.com/resort.html), at Lewis and Clark Recreation Area. Open mid-April through mid-October. Two- and three-bedrooms cabins with kitchens and living rooms are available, as well as 24 motel rooms with easy access to the marina and the park. These units are

HOUSED IN AN ELEGANT HOME IN THE HISTORIC DISTRICT, THE CAPTAIN'S INN WAS BUILT IN 1878 AND HAS THREE SUITES AVAILABLE.

modern and comfortable enough to spend a night or a week enjoying all the outdoor activities the lake offers. Motel units $89–$115 per night, cabins $215–$255 per night.

✳ Where to Eat

DINING OUT **Quarry Steakhouse and Lounge** (605-665-4337; www .quarryrestaurant.com), 3 miles west on SD 52. Open at 5 PM Wednesday through Sunday. A restaurant now for 30 years, in its previous life this was the Western Portland Cement Company, a short-lived attempt at making cement from the chalk bluffs outside Yankton. In a timed honored South Dakota tradition, the Quarry specializes in prime rib and steaks but also has seafood and pasta if you want a change of pace. They also have a respectable wine selection and a full bar. $10–$25.

EATING OUT **JoDean's Steak House and Lounge** (605-665-9884; www.jodeans.com), 2809 Broadway Ave. Open at 11 daily. Looking suspiciously like a warehouse to match the massive parking lot, JoDean's manages to dull that impression with decorations of antiques hanging from the walls. You can order from the menu at JoDean's, but the real draw is the buffet. Every lunch and dinner they serve up buffets of beef, chicken, walleye, steamed vegetables, a salad bar, and dessert bar. On Friday and Saturday the buffet includes seafood and on Sunday it includes breakfast items like eggs and bacon. There is also a full bar. No one goes away hungry from JoDean's. $5–$20.

Minervas Grille and Bar (605-664-2244; www.minervas.net/restaurants .php), 1607 E. SD 50. A smaller version of the Minervas restaurants found in larger cities, they have the same menu in a more casual atmosphere. Pasta, dinner salads, steaks, and sandwiches provide plenty of choices for the entire family. $10–$20.

The River Rose Restaurant and Natural Bakery (605-260-7673), 214 W. Third St. Open 11–2 and 5–10. Housed in the limestone basement of one of the downtown buildings, this restaurant prides itself on making everything fresh and from scratch. It has wonderful home-baked goods like a cinnamon roll drowning in gooey icing, sandwiches, and a soup and salad bar for lunch with a wide variety of selections. They also offer a complete dinner menu including prime rib and seafood. $13–$20.

Waterfront Gourmet Grill (605-664-5333), 201 Capital. Open for lunch and dinner. The menu features burger, steaks, chicken, specialty sandwiches, and seafood. They also offer "pick your own pasta," where you combine pasta types, sauces, and vegetables or meats. They have a full bar and a pool room. Entrées $7–$20.

✳ Selective Shopping

Yankton has a very attractive historic downtown with nice shopping options. A few ideas include:

Books and Beans (605-260-8850), 104 W. Third St. Open 8–6 Monday through Saturday, 12–4 Sunday. This shop has all the coffee drinks and seating to enjoy the selection of new and used books.

Gifts and Giggles and Lulu's Dress Shop (605-665-6767), 217 W. Third St. Open 9:30–5 Monday through Saturday. Prepare to laugh while visiting this really cute gift shop. They have lots of humorous cards, T-shirts, and gifts. If you have a slightly bent sense of humor, you'll fit right in. There is a nice dress shop in the back that changes its fashions seasonally.

LilyCrest Cottage (605-664-8800; www.lilycrest.com), 211 W. Third St. Open seven days a week. For cottage décor this is the place with everything from pillows and candles to large pieces of furniture. They also have a nice selection of antique collectibles, jewelry, and decorating items. Custom framing also available.

Oneton Fine Art (605-664-0110), 110 W. Third St. Featuring local artist's works including paintings, pottery, and jewelry, this shop also has a nice selection of books and gifts. The back of the shop is a studio area where local artists offer classes in painting, drawing, and sculpture.

Outside of downtown you will find:

Fireborn Glass Blowing Studio and Gallery (605-665-5600; www.fireborn glass.com), 4210 W. Eighth St. Open Memorial Day through Labor Day. Located near the Lewis and Clark Marina, Fireborn Gallery has live glass-blowing demonstrations, which you really should experience some time. Watching someone manipulate molten glass with their bare hands, lungs, and a few scary looking tools is really astonishing and gives you an appreciation of glass art. Fireborn sells what they make and that includes glass beads, bowls, vases, and decorative items. They carry other artwork as well such as jewelry, pottery, and paper art.

Garrity's Prairie Gardens (605-665-2806; www.garritys.com), 5 miles east on Whiting Dr. and 2.5 miles north on 444th St. Open 9–5 Monday through Friday, 9–3 Saturday, June through December. Out in the country but worth finding, this is the place for fresh-picked fruits and vegetables. They also carry products made in South Dakota and a wide variety of jams, salsas, and soup mixes. If you want something fresh and good for you, this is the place to go.

TABOR CELEBRATES THEIR HERITAGE EVERY YEAR WITH CZECH DAYS.

South Dakota Tourism

✳ Special Events

JUNE Dalesburg Midsummer Festival (605-253-2575; www.dalesburg .org). This festival celebrates the areas Scandinavian heritage with a smorgasbord, entertainment, music, art and crafts, and raising of the midsummer pole.

AUGUST Riverboat Days (605-665-1657; www.riverboatdays.com). End of the summer celebration with arts and crafts, parades, an air show, concerts, and fireworks.

Lewis and Clark Festival (402-667-2546; www.lewisandclarkfestival.org). Every August reenactors set up camp along Lewis and Clark Lake to demonstrate frontier skills.

✳ Nearby

Since 1948 **Tabor** has held **Czech Days** to celebrate their heritage. The event is in June and features great Czech food, crafts, dancing, and a parade.

Glacial Lakes
and Prairies

HURON

BROOKINGS

WATERTOWN

ABERDEEN

GLACIAL LAKES AND PRAIRIES

The Glacial Lakes and Prairies region of South Dakota gets its name from the last glaciers in North America that moved across the land and then retreated, over and over again. All the hills and ridges in the area were created by sediment that dropped off from the glacier during its retreats. The many lakes were created by large chunks of ice left behind as the glacier melted away, or where the ground slumped in and was later filled with rain or snow. Some of these lakes, like Medicine Lake, contain one and half times more salt than the ocean from the minerals they have picked up from the soil.

This area has been inhabited since at least 1200 AD by tribes of hunters and gatherers. By the 17th century the Sioux came to the area and the Santees and Yanktonnais settled in northeast South Dakota. Whites entered the picture in the 1800s, first fur traders who contributed to the demise of the great herds of buffalo, and then missionaries, such as Pierre John De Smet, who came to convert the Sioux to Christianity.

Serious land settlement didn't happen until the Homestead Act of 1862, which encouraged farmers to claim 160 acres. Railroad companies laid tracks across eastern South Dakota to encourage settlers and the area experienced the Dakota Boom from 1880–1890 with the rest of the state.

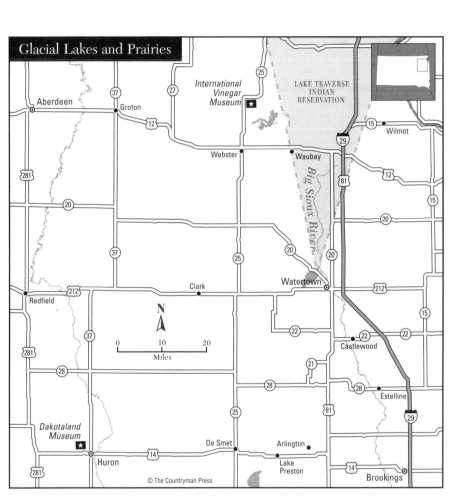

Glacial Lakes and Prairies

HURON

H uron was first explored as early as 1832 and named for the Indians near Lake Huron. Huron was one of the towns vying to become the state capitol but, in the end, lost out to Pierre. Huron is a small town, away from the interstate traffic and in the middle of farm country. It is flat, like the prairie surrounding it, with a main street and additional residential areas spreading out to house its 12,000 residents. Though it is a small town it serves the needs of some 50,000 area residents who come to Huron to shop, eat, and visit doctors. Huron's biggest claim to fame is hosting the annual South Dakota State Fair every August since 1905. People come from all over the state to attend the events and show their livestock. If you are a fan of fairs, this is the place to be in August.

GUIDANCE Huron Chamber and Visitors Bureau (800-487-6673; www .huronsd.com).

GETTING THERE *By car:* Huron is located at the intersection of SD 37 and US 14. Huron is 121 miles from Sioux Falls.

DOWNTOWN HURON HAS A NUMBER OF MURALS DEPICTING LOCAL HISTORY AND CULTURE.

AGRICULTURE BUILT SOUTH DAKOTA AND REMAINS THE LARGEST SOURCE OF STATE REVENUE. MANY OLD FARM BUILDINGS CAN BE SEEN ACROSS THE STATE.

MEDICAL EMERGENCIES **Huron Regional Medical Center** (605-353-6200), 172 Fourth St. S.E.

✳ To See

CULTURAL SITES **Murals on the Town**, located throughout the city on building walls. Painted by various artists and intended to brighten up downtown and draw visitors, these huge murals depict the history of Huron and the region with titles like, "The Land Rush," and "The Heart of Pheasant Territory."

MUSEUMS **Dakotaland Museum** (605-352-4626), Third St. Fair Grounds. Open daily 9:30–4 May 31 through Labor Day. Originally started as a display for the state fair in 1959, folks didn't want to take home the things they had donated for the display and a museum was born. With over 5,000 artifacts including maps, photographs, historical documents, a log cabin, and an exhibit of birds and mammals, this museum chronicles Huron and Beadle County history. Admission $1.50.

The Pyle House Museum (605-352-2528), 376 Idaho Ave. S.E. Open 1–3:30 daily. When Gladys Pyle passed away in 1987 she donated her home and everything in it to the town of Huron and they have been sorting through and archiving the contents since. Built in 1894 by her father John Pyle, this was home to the first-elected woman to become a U.S. Senator, Gladys Pyle. This Queen Anne home is largely in its original state and includes lead glass windows and oak woodwork. It is open to visitors.

✳ To Do

BOATING AND FISHING Just blocks from downtown, great fishing awaits at the **Third Street Dam** on the **James River**. Anglers can fish from shore or

THE CHINESE RING-NECKED PHEASANT

Hunting game birds is a South Dakota tradition and none is more sought after than the ring-necked pheasant, introduced to the United States from China as early as 1881, when they were brought to Oregon. No one is completely sure how they ended up in South Dakota but the fact is they love it here for one simple reason—habitat.

Pheasants need great habitat to survive, which includes somewhere to lay eggs and to keep them safe from predators such as owls and hawks. Pheasants in South Dakota have prospered because of the great cover created by fields of corn, wheat, oats, and hay. When the harvest is over the pheasant build their nests in the dead vegetation and every adult bird happily produces 7–10 eggs.

In 2007 there were 2 million pheasant harvested in South Dakota in a 79-day hunting season. There were over 181,000 hunters and they added a whopping $219 million to the state's economy. Small wonder South Dakota named the Chinese ring-necked pheasant the state bird.

launch a boat at the ramp. Species of fish include muskellunge, short-nose gar, gizzard shad, freshwater drum, and paddle fish.

Lake Byron, located 15 miles north of Huron on SD 37. Lake Byron has great walleye fishing and is also used for water skiing.

& **Ravine Lake Park**, 557 Fifth St. N.E. Located in town this lake is stocked with crappie, catfish, pike, walleye, and bullheads. You can fish from the shore or the dock and it is handicap accessible.

Fishing licenses are available at **Lewis Drug**, 1950 Dakota Avenue, or **Runnings**, 3061 Dakota Avenue, among other outlets.

GOLF **Broadland Creek Golf Course** (605-353-8525), SD 37 south of Huron. This 18-hole course is open to the public. Built on rolling terrain, it also features water hazards on nine of the holes. Green fees are $20–$22.

✳ Green Spaces

Maga Ta-Hohpi Waterfowl Production Area, 7 miles west of Huron on SD 14. The "potholes" created by glaciers that became lakes in South Dakota are essential to the production of ducks, geese, and other waterfowl. The government has acquired land from private owners and set it aside for this purpose and one of them is Maga Ta-Hohpi, which means "duck nest" in Yankton Sioux. This is a great place for birding and hiking and is completely undeveloped, making it a wonderful chance to get back in touch with nature.

HUNTING Huron is in the middle of pheasant hunting country. The season for pheasant hunting opens in mid-October. The daily limit is three pheasants and state hunting licenses are required. Licenses are available at **Wal-Mart**, 2791

Dakota Avenue. and **Kmart,** 1000 18th Street, as well as other retailers. Huron likes to call itself the **Pheasant Capital of the World** and has a 28-foot, 22-ton fiberglass pheasant on the edge of town to prove it. Stop by for a picture because they swear it's the world's largest.

SWIMMING **Ravine Lake** offers beach swimming right in Huron. **The Huron Municipal Pool** (605-352-9144) 25 Jersey Ave. N.E. Open 1–5 and 6–9 daily. $2 for ages 1–17, $3 for ages 18 and older. This city-run pool has water slides and diving boards and is open to visitors.

❋ Lodging

All of the motels in Huron are family owned or recognized chains, including **Best Western** (1-800-509-9023) and **Comfort Inn** (605-352-6655). The **Crossroads Hotel** (605-352-3204) is locally owned and houses the Event Center.

❋ Where to Eat

EATING OUT **Coffee Tree** (605-352-7611), 110 Third St. Open 7:30–5:30 Monday through Friday, 9–3 Saturday. This small café has all the coffee drinks as well as teas, smoothies, and paninis. They also carry gift items made in South Dakota like jams and honey. $5–$7.

Verto's Restaurant and Bar (605-352-3211), 100 Fourth St. S.W. Open for breakfast, lunch, and dinner. Sunday brunch 9–2. Located at the Crossroads Hotel, this place has a full menu with pastas, salads, and steaks as well as sandwiches. $7–$15.

❋ Special Events

AUGUST **South Dakota State Fair.** Ongoing since 1885, the South Dakota State Fair includes stock shows, arts and crafts, a midway, and entertainment.

HURON IS HOST TO THE SOUTH DAKOTA STATE FAIR EVERY AUGUST. THOUSANDS ATTEND EVERY YEAR TO VIEW THE LIVESTOCK AND ENJOY THE RIDES.

South Dakota Tourism

BROOKINGS

B rookings was platted in 1879 and became a village in 1881. Today there are 18,000 residents living in this quiet prairie town. Brookings is home to South Dakota State University, founded in 1881. It is the largest of the state universities with majors in agriculture, science, engineering, and pharmacy. SDSU provides Brookings with jobs and a variety of activities including arts and sports.

GUIDANCE **Brookings** (www.brookingssd.com).

GETTING THERE *By car:* Brookings is located 49 miles north of Sioux Falls on I-29.

MEDICAL EMERGENCIES **Brookings Hospital** (605-696-9000; www.brookingshospital.org), 300 22nd Ave.

✴ To See

MUSEUMS ❧ **State Agricultural Heritage Museum** (605-688-6226; www.agmuseum.com), located on the university campus at Medary Avenue and 11th Street, the museum is open to the public 10–5 Monday through Saturday, and 1–5 Sunday. Since the university has an agriculture department it stands to reason they would become a depository for artifacts from South Dakota's agricultural history. This museum is dedicated to preserving South Dakota's agricultural heritage and has displays including tractors, a replica farmhouse, and a homestead claim shack. Free.

❧ **South Dakota Art Museum** (605-688-5423; www.southdakotaartmuseum .com), located on the university campus at Medary Ave. at Harvey Dunn St. Open 10–5 Monday through Friday, 10–4 and Saturday, 12–4 Sunday. The museum has six galleries with changing exhibits and features the works of Harvey Dunn. Harvey Dunn was born in South Dakota and spent much of his life illustrating magazine and book covers. In his later years Dunn turned to painting more permanent works and in 1950 donated 42 of his prairie paintings to the university. Since then the collection has grown to 90 works and remains on display. Other artists on display in the museum including Paul Goble, an English artist who uses Indian traditions in his book illustrations, as well as 900 Native American art pieces from the 19th and 20th centuries. There is an area called Kids Sensation Station for children to create art and play. Free.

BIKING/HIKING The city of Brookings has a 6-mile trail that winds through their parks. A map can be found at www.cityofbrookings.org/departments/park_rec/parkmap.html

Lake Thompson Recreation Area (605-847-4893; www.sdgfp.info/Parks/Regions/GlacialLakes/LakeThompson.htm), located 6 miles S.W. of Lake Preston off SD 14. This park has one trail, the **Park Tour Trail**, which is 1.25 miles, a portion of which follows the lakeshore. The trailhead is located at any campground.

Oakwood Lakes State Park (605-627-5441; www.sdgfp.info/Parks/Regions/GlacialLakes/OakwoodLakes.htm), I-29, exit 140, 20247 Oakwood Dr. Bruce, SD 57220, has two trails of interest that follow the lake and historic sites, including the log cabin built by Samuel Mortimer in 1869.

Oakwood Lakes Prairie Trail 2.6 miles. The trailhead is southeast of the campground.

Tetonkaha Trail 0.75 miles. The trailhead is west of the entrance booth. This is an interpretative trail that tells about the glacial formation of the region.

BOATING AND FISHING There are a number of lakes in the Brookings area for boating and fishing. They include the following:

Lake Thompson is 18,000 acres and is considered the second best fishing in the state, after the Missouri River. Fish include walleye, pike, crappie, perch, and bass. There is a boat ramp at Lake Thompson Recreation Area (see listing under *Biking and Hiking*).

Oakwood Lake is 3,000 acres and is great for canoeing. Fish species include bullhead, pike, perch, walleye. (See listing under *Biking and Hiking*.) Licenses are available at **Ace Hardware**, 710 22nd Avenue South or **Wal-Mart**, 2233 Sixth Street.

FAMILY FRIENDLY **Dairy Barn at South Dakota State University** (605-688-5420). The first dairy courses were taught at SDSU in 1890 and today they are one of the leading cheese researchers in the world. Students learn the dairy business from the care of the cows to the production of butter, cheese, and milk. The SDSU Dairy Plant processes approximately 10,000 pounds of milk a week and produces 24 cheese varieties, butter, milk, and more than 90 flavors of ice cream and sherbet, and ice cream cookie sandwiches. Stop in and buy some really fresh cheese or milk and try some of the ice cream flavors they have concocted like Peanut Butter Cookie Dough and Chocolate Chip.

GOLF **Edgebrook Golf Course** (605-692-6995), 1415 22nd Ave. This is a regulation 18-hole course and water comes into play on five holes on the back nine. Green fees are $42.

HUNTING Brookings is in the middle of pheasant country. There are a number of farms that provide access to their fields for hunting. A listing is available at www.brookingssd.com/visitors_hunting.php. See license information under *Boating and Fishing*.

SWIMMING **Lake Thompson Recreation Area.** This park has a swimming beach, see listing under *Biking and Hiking*.

South Dakota Tourism

PART OF THE SOUTH DAKOTA STATE
UNIVERSITY, MCCORY GARDENS HAS
20 ACRES OF BOTANICAL GARDENS AND
45 ACRES OF ARBORETUM.

Oakwood Lakes State Park. This
park has a swimming beach, see listing
under *Biking and Hiking*.

Hillcrest Aquatic Center (605-692-
2387), 1505 Fifth St. Open 12–8:30
Monday through Friday, 1–8 Saturday
and Sunday. This city-owned center has
four pools including a leisure pool, and
multiple water features, such as a small
slide, water walls, and various spray
components. Daily admission is $3 all
ages.

✳ Green Spaces

✿ **McCrory Gardens** (www3.sdstate
.edu), located on the university campus,
the 45-acre site was designated the
South Dakota State Arboretum in 1988.
There are formal gardens, a prairie garden, a rock garden, and a children's
maze made of hedges totaling 1140 feet
in length, maintained at a height of 3–6
feet for the kids to get lost in. Free.

✳ Lodging

There are a number of chain and
smaller motels in Brookings, including
Holiday Inn Express (1-877-786-
9480) and **Fairfield Brookings** (605-
692-3500).

**CAMPING Lake Thompson Recre-
ation Area**, (see *Biking and Hiking*).
Open year-round. With great lake recreation this park is popular with campers.
There are 103 sites, four camping cabins
with lake views, showers, and dump station. $12–$16 per night.

Oakwood Lakes State Park, see listing under *Biking and Hiking*. Open
year-round. Because of the great lake
access and recreation available, this is a
popular spot for camping with 135
sites, most having electricity. There are
showers, water, and two dump stations.
$12–$16 per night.

✳ Where to Eat

EATING OUT Cottonwood Coffee
(605-692-7009; www.cottonwood
coffee.com), 509 Main Ave. Open 7 AM–
9 PM. Serving coffee, teas, and smoothies, as well as fresh-baked goodies,
sandwiches, and homemade soup.

Cubby's Sports Bar and Grille (605-
696-7978; www.cubbyssportsbarand
grill.com), 307 Main Ave. Open 11–2
AM everyday. While there is no doubt
this is a party spot for the college
crowd, Cubby's is nice enough to come
by for a beer or a meal. This is a huge
bar with sports memorabilia on the
walls, a pool table, big-screen TVs,
dozens of beers on tap, and a nice
menu. They have 15 varieties of gourmet burgers, specialty sandwiches like
the wild mushroom provolone chicken,
salads, and ciabattas including black-
ened salmon. $5–$17.

Nick's Hamburger Shop (605-692-
4324; www.nickshamburgers.com), 427
Main Ave. Open 11–7 Monday through

THE CHILDHOOD HOME OF LAURA INGALLS WILDER, DE SMET
CELEBRATES THE BELOVED AUTHOR EVERY SUMMER WITH A PAGEANT AND A PLAY.

LAURA INGALLS WILDER AND SOUTH DAKOTA

Laura Ingalls Wilder did not begin writing her famous Little House book series until 1932 when she was 65 years old and she completed the eight volume series in 1943. She had no idea of the fame that would come with the books. Many loved the stories, so much so that they have been translated into 40 languages.

Laura was born in Pepin, Wisconsin, in 1867 to Charles and Caroline Ingalls. Charles had a notorious need to roam and from Wisconsin the family moved to Independence, Kansas, north to Walnut Grove, Minnesota, and west to De Smet, South Dakota. Free land is what brought the Ingalls to South Dakota as they joined many others in the rush to homestead the newly opened territory. The land they chose had good water and was only a mile from town. In February 1880, Charles Ingalls filed a claim for 157.22 acres of land for the cost of the filing fee, $16. It is South Dakota that is commemorated in two of her books, *The Long Winter* and *The Little Town on the Prairie*.

In *The Long Winter* Laura tells of the winter of 1880–1881. The first blizzard hit on October 15 and by many accounts the weather did not clear until May. Many were caught unprepared and by Christmas much of De Smet was starving. In January heavy snow caused train service to be stopped, effectively cutting off the settlers from the rest of the world.

The Little Town on the Prairie tells of Laura's adolescence and her teaching career, which began at the age of 15. It also includes her romance with Almanzo Wilder, a homesteader 10 years her senior, who she would marry at age 18.

Laura and Almanzo moved from South Dakota and eventually settled in Mansfield, Missouri. Laura's parents remained in De Smet and both are buried there. Laura's sister Carrie moved to Keystone, South Dakota, where she married David Swanzey. She died in Keystone but is buried with the rest of the family in De Smet.

Laura Ingalls Wilder passed away at 90 at her home in Missouri, after becoming one of America's best-loved authors.

Friday, 11–4 Saturday. Nick's has been a tradition in Brookings since 1929 and this little shop has only 20 stools to accommodate its many patrons. The menu consists of one thing: burgers. You can choose your toppings, get a bag of chips, and a drink. Nothing fancy but every SDSU student has a story about eating Nick's hamburgers. The hamburgers sold for 5¢ through the Depression but are now up to $1.18.

The Ram Food and Spirits (605-692-2485; www.ramohares.com), 327 Main Ave. Opens 11 AM. Housed in a former bank, complete with the vault in the dining room, this restaurant has an attractive décor of wood and brick and offers private booths or tables. The Ram is best known for their stroganoff burgers topped with sour cream, Swiss cheese, and grilled onions and mushrooms. They also offer prime rib, steaks, and a variety of burgers and sandwiches. Downstairs is O'Hare's, an intimate bar. Entrées $7–$21.

✳ Entertainment

MUSIC ✿ **Thursday Music on Main** (605-692-1554), 425 Main Ave. 5–7 PM June through August. Bring your lawn chair and enjoy the free entertainment every Thursday night through the summer.

THEATER **Prairie Repertory Theater** (605-688-6045; www.www.prairie rep.org), Doner Auditorium, 970 Administration Ln. This group is the SDSU summer theater and presents plays and musicals first in Brookings and then in Brandon throughout the summer. Check the Web site for the schedule.

State University Theater (605-688-6045; www.learn.sdstate.edu/theatre), located at the University of South Dakota, these are student productions that take place throughout the academic year.

✳ Selective Shopping

Downtown Brookings has a number of antique stores, as well as other shops.

Cover to Cover (605-692-9512), 310 Main Ave. Open 9–8 Monday through Friday, 9–5 Saturday, and 12–5 Sunday. This is a full-service bookstore but has lots more including magazines, children's books, and gifts, educational toys for babies, office supplies, and gourmet coffee and food.

✳ Special Events

JULY **Brookings Summer Arts Festival** (www.bsaf.com). Held at Pioneer Park on West Highway. This festival has a juried art show, as well as food, historic, and children's booths.

✳ Nearby

De Smet (www.desmetsd.com) is 35 miles west of Brookings on US 14. Laura Ingalls Wilder's family had a homestead and store in De Smet and De Smet has pretty much made a living from her name. Home of the **Laura Ingalls Wilder Pageant** in July, the **Ingall's Homestead**, and the **Loftus Store**, among others. If you love the Little House books, you pretty much have to go to De Smet.

In June head to **Madison**, south of Brookings on SD 34, for the **Herman Luce Pioneer Days**. This event features pioneer arts and crafts like candlemaking, butter churning, quilting, and weaving.

Volga is just 10 miles west of Brookings on US 14 and is the home to **Schade Vineyard** (www.scadevine yard.com). They have a tasting room and gift shop that are open 1–6 Tuesday through Friday, and 10–5 Saturday. Come taste their chokecherry, plum, rhubarb, or raspberry wines.

WATERTOWN

Watertown is located at the intersection of two major highways; one goes east to Minneapolis, the other north to Fargo or south to Sioux Falls and Sioux City. The railroad also serves Watertown, making it a very convenient transportation hub for the upper Midwest. This is what has made Watertown grow into the fourth largest city in South Dakota with about 20,000 people. Most folks come to Watertown to conduct business or shop, but there is also great fishing and recreation at Lake Kampeska. The biggest draw to Watertown for visitors is the **Redlin Art Center**. If you are a Terry Redlin fan, it is a must-see.

GUIDANCE Watertown Convention and Visitors Bureau (1-800-658-4505; www.watertownsd.com), 1200 Michelson Dr.

GETTING THERE *By car:* Watertown is located on I-29, 93 miles north of Sioux Falls.

MEDICAL EMERGENCIES Prairie Lakes Healthcare System (605-882-7000; www.prairielakes.com), 401 Ninth Ave. N.W., Watertown.

✳ To See

CULTURAL SITES ❧ Redlin Art Center (605-882-3877; www.redlin art.com), 1200 Third St. S.E. Open 8–5 Monday through Friday, 10–4 Saturday, 12–4 Sunday. Terry Redlin is a South Dakota painter who grew up in Watertown and is much loved throughout the country for his atmospheric landscapes. This three-story brick and marble art center is a gift from Redlin to his hometown and shows 150 of his original works. There are also displays

ONE OF SOUTH DAKOTA'S BEST KNOWN CITIZENS, TERRY REDLIN'S WORK AND PERSONAL MEMORABILIA IS ON DISPLAY AT THE REDLIN CENTER IN WATERTOWN.

South Dakota Tourism

THE BRAMBLE PARK ZOO BEGAN AS A ROADSIDE ATTRACTION BUT HAS BECOME A CERTIFIED REHABILITATION CENTER AND ZOO.

of many of Redlin's personal items like his hunting rifles and a "Comforts of Home" cabin where you can step inside one of his paintings. The stores in the center sell prints of Redlin's paintings as well as numerous items with Redlin's pictures on them, including collector's plates, tree ornaments, cards, calendars, and home furnishings. Free.

FAMILY FRIENDLY Bramble Park Zoo (605-882-6269; www.brambleparkzoo .com), SD 20. Open 9–8 during the summer; 10–4 during the winter. This zoo was founded in 1912 as something of a roadside attraction and has undergone significant improvements in the ensuing years to meet all the requirements of a rehabilitation and breeding center. Though small they have 500 critters representing 130 varieties from around the world, including raptors, primates, snakes, penguins, peacocks, lemurs, wallabies, and a white Bengal tiger that has been on loan so long that it might as well be part of the collection. There is also a petting zoo with farm animals—bring your quarters because there are machines where you can buy food to feed the animals. This intimate zoo is a real treat to visit. $5 for ages 13 and older, $3 for ages 3–12.

BRAMBLE PARK ZOO IS A SMALL AND INTIMATE ZOO WHERE THE VISITOR CAN GET UP CLOSE TO THE ANIMALS.

HISTORIC SITES ✿ Mellette House (605-886-4730; www.mellette house.org), 421 Fifth Ave. N.W. Open

1–5 Tuesday through Sunday, May 1 through October 1. Built in 1885 out of local
brick, this is the restored home of the first governor of South Dakota, Arthur
Mellette. Inside you'll see a fabulous circular staircase, many of the original furnishings, and some of the original artwork donated by the last surviving Mellette
son. Free, donations accepted.

MUSEUMS ✤ **Codington County Heritage Museum** (605-886-7335; www
.cchsmuseum.org), 27 First Avenue S.E. Open 10–5 Monday through Saturday
during the summers; 1–5 Monday through Friday during the winters. Located in
the former Carnegie Library building, this museum is run by the Codington County Historical Society and preserves the county's history through thousands of artifacts and photographs. Researchers are welcome to go through their archives of
area history. Free.

✳ To Do

BIKING/HIKING **Fitness Trail** (www.watertownsd.us/ParkAndRecreation.aspx).
This is an 18-mile trail that runs through Watertown, including the shore of Lake
Kampeska. You can pick up the trail on Lake Drive, SD 20, or Golf Course Road.

Pelican Lake Recreation Area (605-882-5200; www.sdgfp.info/Parks/Regions/
GlacialLakes/PelicanLake.htm), located 9 miles S.W. of Watertown off US 212.
This park has two trails that are used by hikers, bikers, and horses. They travel
through prairie and lakeshore tree lines:

Observation Tower Trail 0.75 mile. The trailhead is located immediately west of
the warming shelter. This tower provides a great overlook of the lake and migrating birds.

Pelican Prairie Trail 5.2 miles. The trailhead is adjacent to the trail camp and
parking area.

BOATING AND FISHING Fishing and hunting licenses are available in Watertown at **Dunham's** in the Watertown Mall and **Wal-Mart** at 1201 29th Street,
among others.

Pelican Lake Recreation Area, see listing under *Biking and Hiking*. Fish
include walleye, pike, perch, and bullheads.

Lake Kampeska on the outskirts of town has walleye, perch, and crappie on miles
of shoreline. There is a boat ramp at Sandy Shore Recreation Area, see listing
under *Parks*.

FAMILY FRIENDLY **Thunder Road Family Fun Park** (605-882-6959), 825
Third St. S.W. Open 12–10. With go-karts, mini golf, water wars, and an arcade
this place is bound to keep the kids happy. Prices vary by attraction.

GOLF **Prairie Winds Golf Club** (605-886-3554; www.pwgolfclub.com), 555 S.
Lake Dr. This 18-hole semiprivate course has small greens and a general southern
wind blowing, which makes club selection a challenge. Green fees are $50.

Watertown Municipal Golf Course (605-882-6262), 351 S. Lake Dr. The front
nine of this course is flat while the back nine is on rolling fairways with trees.
There are two water hazards that come into play. Green fees are $34.

SWIMMING **Family Aquatic Center** (605-882-6267), U.S. Hwy 212 and Third St. S.W. Open 1–4 and 6–9. This very impressive city-owned center includes a main pool with zero depth entry, lap area, floatables, a basketball goal, 0.75-meter diving board, drop slide, water walk, frog slide, in-water playground, and four additional interactive play areas. Individual day passes are $4, family passes are $7.

Pelican Lake Recreation Area, see listing under *Biking and Hiking*. Pelican Lake has a swim beach.

Sandy Shore Recreation Area, see listing under *Parks*. On Lake Kampeska this park offers a long sandy beach.

Watertown Community Rec Center (605-882-6250), 200 Ninth St. N.E. Open 5:30 PM–10 PM Monday through Thursday, 5:30 PM–9 PM Friday, 8–1 Saturday, and 1–5 Sunday. This complete fitness center has an eight-lane pool, aerobics, racquetball, Nautilus, free weights, cardiovascular and exercise equipment, running track, gymnasium, whirlpool, and sauna. And it's open to visitors, so don't miss your workout just because you're on vacation. Day passes are $7 for adults and $10 for a family.

HUNTING Pheasant hunting is great south and west of Watertown and opening season is the third weekend in October. Goose and duck hunting is also popular in the area because of the ample lakes. See license information under *Boating and Fishing*.

✳ Green Spaces

PARKS **Pelican Lake Recreation Area**, see listing under *Biking and Hiking*. Open year-round. The real draw is the number of waterfowl that travel through the park during their migrations. In fact it was named for the large number of pelicans found there. Activities include swimming, boating, birding, and hiking. Entrance fee is $5.

Sandy Shore Recreation Area (605-882-5200; www.sdgfp.info/Parks/Regions/GlacialLakes/SandyShore.htm), located 5 miles west of Watertown off US 212. This is the smallest of the state parks. It's a nice spot to camp, fish, or swim, right on the shore of Lake Kampeska. Entrance fee is $5.

✳ Lodging

Watertown has a number of motels along the interstate, including **Country Inn and Suites** (605-886-8900), **Best Western Ramkota** (605-886-8011), and **Holiday Inn Express** (1-877-786-9480).

CAMPING **Pelican Lake Recreation Area**, see listing under *Biking and Hiking*. There are 46 sites with showers, water, and a dump station. $16 per night.

Sandy Shore Recreation, see listing under *Parks*. Open year-round. There are 20 campsites, some directly on the lakeshore with showers and water. $12–$16 per night.

Stokes-Thomas Lake City Park and Campground (605-882-6264), 90 S. Lake Dr. Open May through September. This is a city-owned campground with playground areas, a swimming beach, and an on-site manager. $17.50 per night.

✳ Where to Eat

EATING OUT **Second Street Station** (605-886-8304), 15 Second St. Open 4–10 Tuesday through Saturday. This popular restaurant has a diverse menu with a nice twist on the standards such as lobster ravioli, chicken or steak Oscar, as well as the all-important prime rib. They also have killer desserts like homemade bread pudding. Entrées $10–$27.

Lunkers (605-882-3422), 100 N. Lake Dr. Open at 5 PM daily. Located right on Lake Kampeska with large windows offering a nice view, Lunkers is best known for its walleye, which every South Dakotan swears is the best fish ever. They also have steaks, seafood, and a variety of pastas. Entrées $8–$29.

Past Time Café Grille and Bakery (605-882-5813), 16 West Kemp. Open 7–4 Monday through Saturday. This deli and coffee house features a nice selection of salads and sandwiches for lunch as well as baked goods to munch with your coffee. $5–$7.

Pond's Bakery (605-886-3322), 113 E. Kemp. Open 6–5:30 Monday through Friday. This is an old-fashioned bakery with breads, muffins, pastries, and cookies but also has lunch items like sandwiches.

✳ Selective Shopping

Watertown is a commercial center and has a small mall and many chain outlets. There is also an uptown retail area on Kemp Avenue.

✳ Special Events

JUNE **Uptown Festival of Arts and Crafts** held on Kemp Street featuring an arts and crafts show, vendors, and entertainment.

SEPTEMBER **Watertown Art Festival** held at Watertown Event Center, featuring a juried art show.

✳ Nearby

Clark is east of Watertown on US 212 and very proud of their potatoes. Come in August for **Clark Potato Day** (www.clarksd.com) and join in the mashed potato wrestling, cow pie bingo, potato sculptures, and a cooking contest.

South Dakota Tourism

CLARK AREA FARMERS GROW A LOT OF POTATOES AND THEY CELEBRATE THEIR FAVORITE CROP WITH CLARK POTATO DAYS.

Lake City is host to the **Fort Sisseton Historical Festival** each June. There is musical entertainment as well as cavalry, artillery, and infantry demonstrations. Lake City is on SD 10, north of Watertown.

Sisseton is in the northeastern part of the state on SD 10 and known for **Sica Hollow** where, along the Trail of the Spirits, you'll see gurgling reddish bogs, which Indians saw as the blood and flesh of their ancestors. Swamp gas and stumps glow in the dark, and small waterfalls are heard echoing as trapped air escapes. Native Americans named it *Sica*, which means "bad" or "evil."

ABERDEEN

Aberdeen is the third largest city in South Dakota and was founded in 1881 as a railroad town. Aberdeen is a regional center for the agricultural interests of northeastern South Dakota. With 25,000 residents, Aberdeen is nicknamed the Hub City for its railroad access, commercial offerings, and medical care. Aberdeen is also home of Northern State University and Presentation College, which offer sports and cultural events to the community.

GUIDANCE **Aberdeen Convention and Visitors Bureau** (800-645-3851; www.visitaberdeensd.com).

GETTING THERE *By car:* Aberdeen is located on US 12 and US 281, 197 miles from Sioux Falls and 160 miles from Pierre.
By plane: Aberdeen Regional Airport is serviced by Mesaba Airlines but flying there is pricey.

MEDICAL EMERGENCIES **Avera St. Luke's Hospital** (605-622-5000; www .averastlukes.org), 305 S. State St.

✳ To See

MUSEUMS **Dacotah Prairie Museum** (605-626-7117; www.dacotahprairie museum.com), 21 S. Main St. Open 9–5 Tuesday through Friday, 1–4 Saturday through Sunday. This museum has artifacts from the Native American and pioneer life of South Dakota with items like a piano harp from 1875 and a switchboard from 1880. There is also a wildlife gallery with 55 mounted animals from North America, Africa, and India, including an African elephant. Free, donations accepted.

✳ To Do

BIKING/HIKING Aberdeen has 20 miles of trails that run throughout the city. For a trail map go to: www.aberdeen.sd.us/parks/trail_d.html. Some highlights include the following:

Wylie Park has 3.35 miles of concrete trails that are great for walking, bikes, or inline skaters.

Moccasin Creek Trail is 1.8 miles and follows along the creek as it winds through the city. Pick up the trail between Melgaard Road and 10th Avenue.

Prairie Trail follows an old railroad corridor and is 1.72 miles long. Pick up the trail at Dakota Street and First Avenue.

Mina Lake Recreation Area (605-626-3488; www.sdgfp.info/Parks/Regions/GlacialLakes/MinaLake.htm), located 11 miles west of Aberdeen off US 12. This park has one interpretive trail, the **Shake Maza Trail**, 0.75 mile. Trailhead located at boat ramp loop.

Richmond Lake Recreation Area (605-626-3488; www.sdgfp.info/Parks/Regions/GlacialLakes/RichmondLake.htm), located 10 miles northwest of Aberdeen off US 28.

Cross Country Ski Trail 3 miles. Trailhead located at Forest Drive warming shelter. This trail is also used for hiking.

Forest Drive Trail 4 miles. Trailhead located at Forest Drive warming shelter.

Quaking Aspen Trail 0.25 mile. Trailhead located at the swimming beach. This is an interpretive trail that runs through the aspen trees.

BOATING AND FISHING Hunting and fishing licenses are available at **Kmart**, 1815 Sixth Avenue and **Kesslers**, 621 Sixth Avenue, as well as others.

Mina Lake Recreation Area (605-626-3488; www.sdgfp.info/Parks/Regions/GlacialLakes/MinaLake.htm), located 11 miles west of Aberdeen off US 12. Known as a great crappie lake, there are also walleye, pike, perch, and bass. Boat ramp available.

Richmond Lake Recreation Area (605-626-3488; www.sdgfp.info/Parks/Regions/GlacialLakes/RichmondLake.htm), located 10 miles northwest of Aberdeen off US 28. There is a boat ramp and fishing docks. Fish species include walleye, pike, bass, perch, crappie, bluegill, catfish, and bullheads.

Sand Lake National Wildlife Refuge (605- 885-6320; www.fws.gov/sandlake), located 27 miles northeast of Aberdeen on SD 10. There are five locations to fish at the refuge. Species of fish include walleye and pike.

FAMILY FRIENDLY **Wylie Park** (www.aberdeen.sd.us/parks) is located just north of Aberdeen on US 281 and is one of the nicest places in all of Aberdeen, and great for family fun. It covers over 200 acres and has camping, a swim beach, volleyball, horseshoes, picnic areas, and trails. A day spent at Wylie Park would be a day well spent in Aberdeen.

❧ **Storybook Land** Open 10–9 daily April 15 through October 15. At Wylie Park this wonderland for kids includes a castle and other nursery rhyme themes, *Wizard of Oz* activities and playground equipment. Ride the train, climb into the Three Little Pigs house and have your picture taken with Dorothy, the Tin Man, the Cowardly Lion, and the Scarecrow. There are also plays, concerts, and storytime during the summer. Free.

Wylie Thunder Road (605-225-8541; www.thunderroad.info), located at Wylie Park. Open Noon–10 Monday through Saturday, 1–10 Sunday May through September. Thunder Road offers bumper boats and go-karts within Wylie Park. $3–$6.

GOLF **Lee Park Golf Course** (605-626-7092), 1300 N. US 281. This is a city-owned 18-hole course with flat terrain and tree-lined fairways. Green fees are $22.

KIDS LOVE WILEY PARK'S THEMED PLAY AREA WITH MANY CHARACTERS FROM CHILDREN'S STORIES INCLUDING *THE WIZARD OF OZ.*

HUNTING Pheasant hunting is huge in the Aberdeen area and hunters come from around the world. There is even a Web site devoted to finding outfitters, lodging, and such at www.huntfishsd.com.

SWIMMING **Aberdeen Aquatic Center** (605-626-7015; www.aberdeen.sd.us/parks/aquatics.html), 1029 South Dakota St. Open during the summer. This is another great city-run center with lap pools, water slides, lazy river, and a sand playground. $6 for adults, $4 for children.

A PERFECT PLACE FOR A FAMILY OUTING, WILEY PARK HAS PLAYGROUNDS, GO-KARTS, PICNIC AREAS AND A FISHING POND.

Mina Lake Recreation Area, see listing under *Biking and Hiking*. There is a swim beach available.

Richmond Lake Recreation Area, see listing under *Biking and Hiking*. There is a swim beach available.

WINTER SPORTS ❈ **Richmond Lake Recreation Area** (see listing under *Biking and Hiking*) has cross-country ski trails.

❈ **The Dakota Midland Trail**, a 155-mile snowmobiling trail, is also accessible from Richmond Lake.

UNIQUE ADVENTURES By contacting the Convention and Visitors

PHEASANT HUNTING IS A SOUTH DAKOTA TRADITION AND DRAWS HUNTERS FROM ACROSS THE COUNTRY.

Bureau ahead of time it is possible to tour a Hutterite Colony. The Hutterites lead a self-sufficient, communal way of life and make their own electricity, craft furniture, and raise crops and livestock. The Hutterites, originally from Switzerland, Germany, and Northern Italy, moved around Europe escaping religious persecution before emigrating to the United States and Canada from Russia between 1874 and 1879.

WILDLIFE REFUGES **Sand Lake National Wildlife Refuge**, see listing under *Biking and Hiking*. Open April 1 through January 30. Established in 1935 as a refuge and breeding ground for migratory birds and other wildlife, as many as 246 different birds have been recorded in the refuge with thousands of geese stopping in at one time. Each year 75,000 people come here to reconnect with nature and observe the wildlife. There is a wildlife driving tour, an observation tower, and a visitors center.

✳ Lodging

There are a number of chain and privately owned motels in Aberdeen, including **Ramada** (605-225-3600) and **Americinn** (605-225-4565).

BED & BREAKFAST INNS **Foote Creek B&B** (877-922-1617; www.bb online.com/sd/footecreek), 12841 383rd Ave. Family-owned, this bed-and-breakfast has four rooms each with a private bath. The rooms are decorated with prairie themes such as the Prairie Rose room, which is painted a light pink and has roses as decoration. The home is located along

a creek and offers a front porch for sitting and enjoying the quiet of rural life. Breakfast includes brunch enchiladas (an egg, ham, and cheese casserole). $65 per night.

CAMPING **Mina Lake Recreation Area**, see listing under *Biking and Hiking*. Open year-round. There are 37 sites, with electric, showers, water, and a dump station. $12–$16 per night.

Richmond Lake Recreation Area, see listing under *Biking and Hiking*. Open year-round. Popular due to the lake access, there are 24 sites with electric, showers, water, and a dump station. $12–$16 per night.

Wylie Park (605-626-7015), US 281 north of Aberdeen. Open May through September. This city park has 96 campsites and seven camping cabins available. There are laundry facilities, electric, and a dump station as well as the park facilities. $14–$36 per night.

HOTELS Ward Plaza (605-725-4260; www.wardhotel.com), 104 S. Main St. In 1894 Alonzo Ward built his first hotel in downtown Aberdeen only to have it destroyed by fire. He rebuilt it in 1928 as a six-story fireproof building intended to be the most upscale hotel in the Midwest. Though the building fell on hard times, it has been completely restored and now has both luxury condominiums and hotel rooms. There are seven attractive guest rooms available at $75 per night.

✷ Where to Eat

DINING OUT Ward Plaza Pub, at the Ward Plaza hotel. This restaurant is in the historic Ward Hotel and has a complete menu with interesting entrées such as duck breast and linguini with mussels as well as steaks and chops. The menu also includes a prix fixe menu of salmon, steak, or chicken entrées with salad and dessert for $25 per person.

EATING OUT Canterbury Ltd. Deli and Catering (605-229-0226; canterburyltd.com), 412 S. Main St. Open 9–2:30 Monday through Friday, 5–8 Thursday, and 12–2 Saturday. Priding themselves on "from scratch cooking," some of the customer's favorites include chicken wild rice and mushroom soup and almond layer cake. They also have specialty sandwiches and pizza. On Thursdays they pull out an Italian menu including wild mushroom lasagna and manicotti. $6–$11.

Mavericks Steaks (1-800-953-8315; www.maverickssteak.com), 1702 Sixth Ave. S.E. Opens at 11 for lunch. Lunch buffet from 11–1:30. With South Dakota certified beef Mavericks does pride itself on steaks just like the name says. You can also order dinner salads, seafood, pasta, and barbecue. They also offer a lunch buffet with two soups, two entrées, potatoes, salad, and dessert. There is a full bar. $16–$28.

Minervas Restaurant and Bar (605-229-4040; www.wrrestaurants.com/rest_minAberdeen.php), 1400 Eighth Ave. N.W. Open 6:30 AM–10 PM Monday through Saturday, 7AM–9 PM Sunday. Sunday brunch 10–2. Minervas menu features steaks, chops, pasta, seafood, and salads. They are a Midwest chain with consistently good food. There is a full bar. $10–$20.

Red Rooster (605-225-6603), 202 Main St. Open 7–11 Monday through Friday, 8–12 Saturday. This funky place is a hangout for the younger crowd but is also popular with downtown workers. They have coffees, teas, smoothies, sandwiches, nachos, and salads. They also sell used books, fair-trade items, and gifts. $4–$8.

✷ Selective Shopping

Downtown Aberdeen is alive but not hopping since businesses have moved to the mall area. Since Aberdeen is a commercial center for the upper plains, there are many chain-retail outlets.

✷ Special Events

JUNE Arts in the Park (www.aberdeenareaartscouncil.com/aitpinfo.php). Held at Milgaard Park this event features 120 artists, booths, food, and entertainment.

JULY Great Aberdeen Pig Out (www.greatpigout.com). Features live entertainment, activities for kids, and a cook-off.

AUGUST Brown County Fair (www .thebrowncountyfair.com). A county fair with livestock shows, carnival, and food vendors.

✳ Nearby

Hoven is home to the **Cathedral of the Prairie**, a large cathedral completed in 1921. A great deal of the original work, and the 1980s restoration, was done by community volunteers. Check out their Web page for more information at www.stanthonys -hoven.com. Hoven is southeast of Aberdeen on SD 47.

Leola calls itself the Rhubarb Capitol of the World and hosts the **Leola Rhubarb Festival** every June. Leola is northeast of Aberdeen on SD 45.

Ipswich is east of Aberdeen on US 12 and has **Trail Days** in June with live music, bull riding, and a street dance.

Don't miss **Roslyn** in June for the **International Vinegar Festival**. There is a parade, cooking demonstrations, food, and a chance to visit the International Vinegar Museum! Roslyn is west of Aberdeen on SD 29.

INDEX

B